FRENCH BILINGUAL DICTIONARY

A Beginner's Guide in Words and Pictures

Third Edition

By Gladys C. Lipton

Coordinator of Foreign Language Workshops and Director of the National F.L.E.S. Institute Department of Modern Language and Linguistics University of Maryland, Baltimore, MD*

Dedicated to Bob Lipton and Judy, Michael, Lorrie, Jeremy, Nancy, Seth, and Rachel

All inquiries should be addressed to:
Barron's Educational Series, Inc.
250 Wireless Boulevard
Hauppauge, NY 11788
http://www.barronseduc.com

Library of Congress Catalog Card No. 98-70225

ISBN-13: 978-0-7641-0279-0
ISBN-10: 0-7641-0279-6

PRINTED IN THE UNITED STATES OF AMERICA
18 17 16 15 14 13

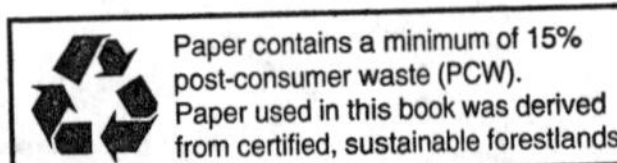

Table of Contents
Table des matières

Introduction

Learning another language can be fun for everybody! This beginner's bilingual *French-English/English-French* dictionary is a book that will be both pleasurable and functional. It will bring many hours of "thumbing-through" enjoyment to all who enjoy looking at pictures, who delight in trying to pronounce new sounds, who like the discovery of trying to pronounce new sounds, and who like the discovery of reading words and sentences in French and English. It can be very practical, too, for those who need a rapid course in bilingual language learning for a specific purpose, such as taking a trip to a French-, or English-speaking country, conducting international business, and other useful endeavors.

This dictionary will assist in the understanding of written French and English, too, and will provide an aid for the expansion of vocabulary in both languages. It will help in word games, in crossword puzzles, in writing and reading letters in French and English, and in reading signs and instructions. As a pocket dictionary, it will be invaluable in helping travelers obtain information, understand menus, and read magazines and newspapers in the foreign language-speaking country.

This edition reflects many of the new trends in foreign/second language learning. In particular, the author has included many of the goals of the national foreign language standards by using words and expressions in the functional contexts of communication, comparison of target language culture(s) through cultural notes and proverbs, etc., and a list of bilingual expressions for measurement to illustrate interdisciplinary connections. This edition contains many contemporary-usage words and expressions.

The pictures in this dictionary will help you clarify word meanings and expand your vocabulary by providing associations of pictures with words and phrases. The sentences will not only illustrate the use of the specific words and expressions, but will also serve as conversational expressions when communicating in the French-speaking or English-speaking community.

The third edition of the *Beginning French Bilingual Dictionary* reflects many of the new trends in foreign language learning, including the national foreign language standards. The standards deal with five goal areas: the five C's of Communication, Cultures, Connections, Comparisons, and Communities. Users of this dictionary will find words used in different contexts of communication; there are new cultural notes that will help to give dictionary users some insights into the various cultures of speakers of French; the sentences offer connections to everyday activities at home, at work, at school, at play, etc. By looking up words and expressions, dictionary users have an opportunity to compare words and expressions in French and English, as well as the differences in cultures. Finally, by seeing words and expressions in context in different aspects of life, dictionary users will find it easy to use French in French-speaking communities around the world.

The French pronunciation key will solve some of the mysteries of foreign language pronunciation. WELCOME TO THE WORLD OF LANGUAGES!

Basis of Word Selection

The selection of words in the French listing is based on a survey of basic words and idiomatic expressions used in beginning language programs, in FLES (K-8) and Level I, and simple reading materials. It may also be used at more advanced levels, when appropriate. The words in the English listing have been checked with the first thousand most frequently used words on the *Thorndike-Lorge Frequency List*, as well as with a survey of words and expressions used by young students and words found in juvenile literature. Both listings should be helpful in the development of new curricula, in test construction, and in the writing of new textbooks and readers to be used on this level.

The author would like to express appreciation to Claudine Jouannelle for her valuable suggestions.

G.C.L.

How to Use This Dictionary

The dictionary contains approximately 1300 entries in the French-English vocabulary listing and an equal number of English words and expressions in the English-French vocabulary listing. Each French entry consists of the following (whenever possible):

1. *French word*
2. *phonemic transcription**
3. *part of speech*
4. *gender*
5. *English definition(s)*
6. *use of word in French sentence*
7. *English translation of French sentence*

English entries consist of the following:

1. *English word*
2. *phonemic transcriptions of English*
3. *part of speech*
4. *French definition(s)*
5. *phonemic transcriptions of French*
6. *gender*
7. *use of word in English sentence*
8. *French translation of English sentence*

---

*The *phonemic* alphabet is based on a comparative analysis of English and French sounds; it uses only Roman letters, with minimal modifications. In contrast, the International Phonetic Alphabet is based on a comparison of several languages and uses some arbitrary symbols. For the English-speaking and -reading learner, the advantages of a phonemic system are obvious.

In addition, many word entries in both the English and French sections include an illustration.

To Find Verb Forms

Special mention should be made of the treatment of verbs in this dictionary. Since only the present tense is used actively in most beginning language programs, verb forms only in the present tense have been included in the dictionary, except for past participles used as adjectives and the conditional of *vouloir*. For regular verbs, only the infinitive is listed, with all the forms of the verb in the present tense included in the entry. There is no cross listing of the forms of regular verbs. For some irregular verbs, each form of the present tense is given (first, second, and third persons, singular and plural) in a separate listing with cross-reference to the infinitive. Here, too, under the infinitive listing, all the forms of the verb in the present tense are included in the entry. The following verbs have been treated in this detailed manner:

aller, avoir, boire, dire, être, faire, mettre, pouvoir, prendre, savoir, venir, voir, vouloir

All forms of irregular verbs also appear in the expanded French verb supplement.

Abbreviations Used in This Dictionary

fem.	*feminine*
fém.	*féminin*
masc.	*masculine, masculin*
pl.	*plural, pluriel*

French-English

(Français-Anglais)

French Pronunciation Key

Notes

1. Some French sounds do not have any English equivalent. (Shown by —)

2. Capital letters indicate the syllable that receives the emphasis. For example:
   a-bree-KOH.

3. Note difference between consonant "w" and phonemic symbol "w̲" for vowel sound for "oi" and "oui."

4. The sound systems of English and French are quite different. The pronunciation key is an attempt to approximate comparative sounds.

CONSONANTS

French Spelling	Phonemic Symbol
b	b
c	k, s
ç	s
ch	sh
d	d, t
f, ph	f
g	g, zh
h	—
j	zh
k	k
l	l
m	m
n	n
gne	n or N (as in onion)
p	p
qu, q	k
r	r
s	s, z
t, th	t
tion	syohn̸
v	v
w	v
x	gs, ks, s, z
y, ille	y (as in yes)
z, s, x	z

VOWELS			
French Spelling	French Example	Phonemic Symbol	Sounds Something Like English Word
a	(la)	a	at
â	(bâton)	ah	father
è, êt, ais	(mais, près)	eh	shelf
é, ai, er, ez	(école, j'ai)	ay	day (but it is a *very short* sound in French)
i, y	(si, pyjama)	ee	see
o	(robe)	uh	hut
ô	(hôtel)	oh	open
u	(mur)	~~ew~~	—
ou	(sous)	oo	too
eu	(deux)	eoh	—
e	(me)	~~e~~	the (book)
eu	(fleur)	euh	sir
an, am, en, em	(sans)	ah~~n~~	—
in, im, aim, ain, ein	(cinq)	ai~~n~~	—
on	(son)	oh~~n~~	—
un	(un)	uh~~n~~	—
oi	(bois)	wa	was
ui, oui	(bruit)	~~ew~~/ee	—

A

à [A] preposition **at, in, to**

Ils vont à Paris.
They are going to Paris.

---

l'abeille [a-BAY] noun, fem. **bee**

L'abeille aime la fleur.
The bee likes the flower.

---

l'abricot [a-bree-KOH] noun, masc. **apricot**

L'abricot est délicieux.
The apricot is delicious.

---

absent [ab-SAHN] adjective, masc. **absent**
absente [ab-SAHNT] fem.

Georges est absent aujourd'hui.
George is absent today.

---

accord [a-KUHR] noun, masc. **agreement**

d'accord! [da-KUHR] idiomatic expression **agreed!, O.K., all right**

Veux-tu jouer avec moi? D'accord!
Do you want to play with me? O.K.!

---

acheter [a-SHTAY] verb **to buy**

j'achète	nous achetons
tu achètes	vous achetez
il, elle achète	ils, elles achètent

Le garcon achète une balle.
The boy is buying a ball.

---

l'acteur [ak-TEUHR] noun, masc. **actor**
l'actrice [ak-TREES] fem. **actress**

L'acteur est beau.
The actor is handsome.

---

l'addition [a-dee-SYOHN] noun, fem. **addition; check (in restaurant)**

Après le dîner, papa demande l'addition.
After dinner, Dad asks for the check.

---

l'adresse [a-DREHS] noun, fem. **address**

Quelle est votre adresse?
What is your address?

---

l'aéroport [a-ay-ruh-PUHR] noun, masc. **airport**

Il y a tant d'avions à l'aéroport!
There are so many airplanes at the airport!

---

l'âge [AHZH] noun, masc. **age (used with "How old...?")**

Quel âge as-tu? J'ai huit ans.
How old are you? I am eight (years old). (See **avoir**)

---

l'agent (de police) **police officer**
[a-ZHAHN-dé-puh-LEES] noun, masc.

L'agent de police dirige la circulation.
The police officer directs traffic.

---

agréable [a-gray-ABL] adjective **pleasant, nice**

Le printemps est une saison agréable.
Spring is a pleasant season.

---

aider [eh-DAY] verb **to help, to aid**

j'aide	nous aidons
tu aides	vous aidez
il, elle aide	ils, elles aident

Jean aide sa soeur à porter les livres.
John helps his sister carry the books.

---

l'aiguille [ay-GWEEY] noun, fem. **needle**

Voici une aiguille à coudre.
Here is a sewing needle. (See **coudre**)

---

l'aile [EHL] noun, fem. **wing**

L'avion a deux ailes.
The airplane has two wings.

---

aimer [eh-MAY] verb **to like, to love**

j'aime	nous aimons
tu aimes	vous aimez
il, elle aime	ils, elles aiment

Maman aime ses enfants.
Mother loves her children.

---

ainsi [ain-SEE] adverb **(in) this way**

Ainsi dansent les petites marionettes.
The little marionettes dance this way.

---

l'air [EHR] noun, masc. **air, appearance, look**

Le tigre a l'air féroce.
The tiger has a ferocious look.

---

aller [a-LAY] verb **to go (also used with exp. of health)**

je vais	nous allons
tu vas	vous allez
il, elle va	ils, elles vont

Où allez-vous? Je vais chez moi.
Where are you going? I'm going home.

Comment allez-vous? Je vais très bien, merci.
How are you? I'm very well, thank you.

---

l'allumette [a-lew-MEHT] noun, fem. **match**

Les allumettes sont dangereuses pour les enfants.
Matches are dangerous for children.

---

l'alphabet [al-fa-BEH] noun, masc. **alphabet**

Il y a vingt-six lettres dans l'alphabet français.
There are twenty-six letters in the French alphabet.

---

l'ambulance [ahN-bew-LAHNS] noun, fem. **ambulance**

L'ambulance va à l'hôpital.
The ambulance is going to the hospital.

---

amener [am-NAY] verb **to bring (people)**

j'amène	nous amenons
tu amènes	vous amenez
il, elle amène	ils, elles amènent

Le garçon amène sa soeur à la maison.
The boy brings his sister home.

---

américain [a-may-ree-KAIN] adjective, masc. **American**
américaine [a-may-ree-KEHN] fem.

C'est un avion américain.
It's an American airplane.

---

l'ami [a-MEE] noun, masc. **friend**
l'amie fem.

Je suis ton amie.
I am your friend.

---

l'amour [a-MOOR] noun, masc. **love**

Le garçon a un grand amour pour son chien.
The boy loves his dog.

---

amusant [a-mew-ZAHN] adjective, masc. **amusing, funny**
amusante [a-mew-ZAHNT] fem.

Le clown est amusant.
The clown is funny.

---

s'amuser [sa-mew-ZAY] verb **to have a good time**

je m'amuse	nous nous amusons
tu t'amuses	vous vous amusez
il, elle, s'amuse	ils, elles s'amusent

Je m'amuse au cirque.
I have a good time at the circus.

---

l'an [AHN] noun, masc. **year**

J'ai neuf ans.
I'm nine years old.

le Jour de l'An **New Year's Day** (See **jour**)

---

l'ananas [a-na-NA] noun, masc. **pineapple**

L'ananas est gros.
The pineapple is big.

---

l'âne [AHN] noun, masc. **donkey**

L'âne a deux longues oreilles.
The donkey has two long ears.

---

l'anglais [ahN-GLEH] noun, masc. **English**

On parle anglais aux Etats-Unis.
They speak English in the United States.

---

l'animal [a-nee-MAL] noun, masc. **animal**
les animaux [a-nee-MOH] pl.

Les animaux sont dans la forêt.
The animals are in the forest.

l'animal favori **pet** (See **favori**)

---

l'anneau [a-NOH] noun, masc. **ring**

Quel joli anneau!
What a pretty ring! (See **bague**)

---

l'année [a-NAY] noun, fem. **year**

Il y a douze mois dans une année.
There are twelve months in a year.

---

l'anniversaire [a-nee-vehr-SEHR] noun, masc. **birthday, anniversary**

Joyeux anniversaire! Quel âge as-tu?
Happy Birthday! How old are you?

---

l'antenne de télévision **television antenna, aerial**
[ahn-tehn-de-tay-lay-vee-ZYOHN] noun, fem.

Les antennes de télévision sont sur le toit du bâtiment.
Television antennas are on the roof of the building.

---

août [oo] noun, masc. **August**

En août il fait chaud.
In August it is hot.

---

l'appareil photo [a-pa-RAY-fuh-TOH] noun, masc. **camera**

Regarde mon appareil. Il est nouveau.
Look at my camera. It is new.

---

l'appartement [a-par-te̸-MAHN̸] noun, masc. **apartment**

Mon appartement est au deuxième étage.
My apartment is on the third floor.

---

appeler [a-PLAY] verb **to call**

j'appelle	nous appelons
tu appelles	vous appelez
il, elle appelle	ils, elles appellent

J'appelle mon amie.
I call my friend.

---

s'appeler [sa-PLAY] verb **to be called, —name is**

je m'appelle	nous nous appelons
tu t'appelles	vous vous appelez
il, elle s'appelle	ils, elles s'appellent

Comment vous appelez-vous? Je m'appelle Henri.
What is your name? My name is Henry.

---

l'appétit [a-pay-TEE] noun, masc. **appetite**

Bon appétit!
Hearty appetite! (Enjoy your meal!)

---

apporter [a-puhr-TAY] verb **to bring**

j'apporte	nous apportons
tu apportes	vous apportez
il, elle apporte	ils, elles apportent

Ils apportent des valises à la colonie de vacances.
They bring valises to camp.

---

apprendre [a-PRAHN̸DR] verb **to learn**

j'apprends	nous apprenons
tu apprends	vous apprenez
il, elle apprend	ils, elles apprennent

Elle aime apprendre le français.
She likes to learn French.

---

après [a-PREH] preposition **after**

Septembre est le mois après août.
September is the month after August.

---

l'après-midi [a-preh-mee-DEE] noun, masc. **afternoon**

Il est deux heures de l'après-midi.
It is two o'clock in the afternoon.

---

l'aquarium [a-kwa-RYUHM] noun, masc. **aquarium, fish tank**

Il y a des poissons rouges dans l'aquarium.
There are some goldfish in the fish tank.

---

l'araignée [a-ray-NAY] noun, fem. **spider**

Qui a peur d'une araignée?
Who's afraid of a spider?

---

l'arbre [ARBR] noun, masc. **tree**

L'arbre a beaucoup de branches.
The tree has many branches.

---

l'arc-en-ciel [ar-kahn-SYEHL] noun, masc. **rainbow**

J'aime les couleurs de l'arc-en-ciel.
I like the colors of the rainbow.

---

l'argent [ar-ZHAHN] noun, masc. **silver; money**

Il n'a pas assez d'argent.
He doesn't have enough money.

en argent [ahn-nar-ZHAHN] **made of silver**

L'épingle est en argent.
The pin is made of silver.

---

l'armée [ar-MAY] noun, fem. **army**

Les soldats sont dans l'armée.
Soldiers are in the army.

---

l'armoire [ar-MWAR] noun, fem. **closet, cupboard**

L'armoire est vide.
The cupboard is empty (bare).

---

arranger [a-rahn-ZHAY] verb **to arrange**

j'arrange	nous arrangeons
tu arranges	vous arrangez
il, elle arrange	ils, elles arrangent

Le professeur arrange ses papiers.
The teacher arranges his papers.

---

arrêter [a-reh-TAY] verb **to stop; to arrest**

j'arrête	nous arrêtons
tu arrêtes	vous arrêtez
il, elle arrête	ils, elles arrêtent

L'agent de police arrête l'homme.
The policeman arrests the man.

L'agent arrête les autos.
The policeman stops the cars.

---

s'arrêter [sa-reh-TAY] verb **to stop (oneself; itself)**

je m'arrête	nous nous arrêtons
tu t'arrêtes	vous vous arrêtez
il, elle s'arrête	ils, elles s'arrêtent

Le train s'arrête à la gare.
The train stops at the station.

---

arrière [a-RYEHR] adjective **back, rear**
en arrière de [ahn-a-RYEHR-deh] preposition **behind**

Un garçon est en arrière des autres.
One boy is behind the others.

---

arriver [a-ree-VAY] verb **to arrive; to happen; to come**

j'arrive	nous arrivons
tu arrives	vous arrivez
il, elle arrive	ils, elles arrivent

Le facteur arrive à dix heures.
The postman arrives at ten o'clock.

Qu'est-ce qui arrive?
What is happening?

---

l'artiste [ar-TEEST] noun, masc. **artist**

Mon frère est artiste.
My brother is an artist.

---

l'aspirateur [as-pee-ra-TEUHR] noun, masc. **vacuum cleaner**

Pour nettoyer la maison, on emploie l'aspirateur.
We use the vacuum cleaner to clean the house.

---

s'asseoir [sa-SWAR] verb **to sit down**

je m'assieds	nous nous asseyons
tu t'assieds	vous vous asseyez
il, elle s'assied	ils, elles s'asseyent

Grand-mère s'assied sur une chaise.
Grandmother sits down on a chair.

---

assez [a-SAY] adverb — **enough**

As-tu assez de pommes de terre?
Do you have enough potatoes?

---

l'assiette [a-SYEHT] noun, fem. — **plate**

L'assiette est sur la table.
The plate is on the table.

---

assis [a-SEE] adjective, masc. — **seated**
assise [a-SEEZ] fem.

Il est assis dans un fauteuil.
He is seated in an armchair.

---

assister [a-sees-TAY] verb — **to attend**

j'assiste	nous assistons
tu assistes	vous assistez
il, elle assiste	ils, elles assistent

Nous assistons à un jeu de football.
We attend a soccer game.

---

l'astronaute [a-struh-NUHT] noun, masc. — **astronaut**

L'astronaute fait un voyage en fusée.
The astronaut takes a trip in a spaceship.

---

attendre [a-TAHNDR] verb — **to wait for**

j'attends	nous attendons
tu attends	vous attendez
il, elle attend	ils, elles attendent

Elle attend son amie.
She is waiting for her friend.

---

attention! [a-tahn-SYOHN] interjection — **take care!, be careful!**

Le professeur dit: "Attention!"
The teacher says, "Take care!"

Faites attention! [feh-tza-tahn-SYOHN] idomatic expression (See **faire**) — **Pay attention!**

---

attraper [a-tra-PAY] verb — **to catch**

j'attrape	nous attrapons
tu attrapes	vous attrapez
il, elle attrape	ils, elles attrapent

Bravo! Jean attrape la balle.
Hurray! John catches the ball.

---

au [OH] masc. (contraction of à + le) — **to the**
à la [a-la] fem.
aux [OH] pl. (contraction of à + les)

La petite fille donne du lait aux chats.
The little girl gives milk to the cats

---

aujourd'hui [oh-zhoor-DEW/EE] adverb — **today**

Aujourd'hui c'est le douze janvier.
Today is January 12th.

---

au revoir [uhr-VWAR] interjection — **good-bye**

Le matin Papa dit: "au revoir" à sa famille.
In the morning Father says "Good-bye" to his family.

---

aussi [oh-SEE] adverb — **too, also; as (used in comparisons)**

Moi aussi, je veux des bonbons!
I want some candy too!

Marc est aussi grand que Jacques.
Mark is as tall as Jack.

---

l'auto [uh-TOH] noun, fem. — **auto(mobile), car**

L'auto roule sur la route.
The car goes along the road.

en auto [ahn-nuh-TOH] — **by car**

---

l'autobus [uh-tuh-BEWS] noun, masc. **bus**

Les enfants vont à l'école en autobus.
The children go to school by bus.

---

l'automne [oh-TUHN] noun, masc. **autumn, fall**

En automne il fait frais.
In autumn it is cool.

---

autour de [oh-TOOR-deh] adverb **around**

Je voudrais faire un voyage autour du monde.
I would like to take a trip around the world.

---

autre [OHTR] adjective, pronoun **other, another**

Voici un autre crayon.
Here is another pencil.

l'autre [OHTR] pronoun, masc, fem. **the other**

Voici mon mouchoir. Les autres sont sur le lit.
Here is my handkerchief. The others are on the bed.

---

avant [a-VAHN] preposition **before**

Le professeur arrive avant les étudiants.
The teacher arrives before the students.

---

avec [a-VEHK] preposition **with**

Marie est à la plage avec ses amies.
Mary is at the beach with her friends.

avec soin **carefully** (See **soin**)

---

l'avenir [av-NEER] noun, masc. **future**

Je vais visiter la France dans l'avenir.
In the future I'm going to visit France.

---

l'aventure [a-vahn-TEWR] noun, fem. — **adventure**

J'aime lire les aventures d'Astérix.
I like to read the adventures of Astérix.

---

l'avenue [av-NEW] noun, fem. — **avenue**

L'Avenue des Champs-Elysées est à Paris.
The Avenue des Champs-Elysées is in Paris.

---

aveugle [a-VEUH-gl] adjective — **blind**

Cet homme est aveugle.
This man is blind.

---

l'avion [a-VYOHN] noun, masc. — **airplane**
en avion — **by air**
par avion — **airmail**
l'avion à réaction [a-vyohn-na-ray-a-KSOHN] noun, masc. — **jet plane**

L'avion à réaction va très vite.
The jet plane goes very fast.

le pilote d'avion — **(airplane) pilot**
(See **pilote**)

---

l'avocat [a-vuh-KA] noun, masc. — **lawyer**

Mon oncle est avocat.
My uncle is a lawyer.

---

avoir [a-VWAR] verb — **to have**

j'ai	nous avons
tu as	vous avez
il, elle a	ils, elles ont

Elle a un crayon.
She has a pencil.

Quel âge avez-vous? J'ai onze ans.
How old are you? I am 11 years old.

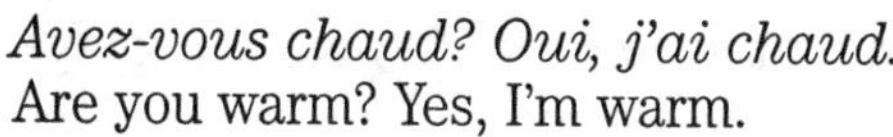

Qu'avez-vous? J'ai mal à la tête.
What's the matter? I have a headache.

Avez-vous chaud? Oui, j'ai chaud.
Are you warm? Yes, I'm warm.

As-tu peur? Oui, j'ai peur.
Are you afraid? Yes, I'm afraid

Pauvre bébé, il a sommeil.
The poor baby is sleepy.

Pauvre bébé, il a faim.
The poor baby is hungry.

Nous avons froid.
We are cold.

Marie a soif.
Mary is thirsty.

Papa a raison. Toi, tu as tort.
Father is right. You are wrong.

Elle a honte.
She is ashamed.

il y a [eel-YA] **there is, there are**
Y a-t-il? [ya-TEEL] **Is there, are there?**

Il y a trois enfants dans cette famille.
There are three children in this family.

---

avril [a-VREEL] noun, masc. **April**

Il pleut beaucoup en avril.
It rains a lot in April.

B

les bagages [ba-GAZH] noun, masc., pl. **baggage, luggage**

Les bagages sont prêts pour le voyage.
The baggage is ready for the trip.

---

la bague [BAG] noun, fem. **ring**

Hélène porte une jolie bague.
Helen is wearing a pretty ring.

---

le bain [BAIN] noun, masc. **bath**

Papa donne un bain à l'enfant.
Father is giving the baby a bath.

la salle de bain **bathroom** (See **salle**)
le bain de soleil **sunbath** (See **soleil**)

---

le baiser [beh-ZAY] noun, masc. **kiss**

Maman donne un baiser à l'enfant.
Mother is kissing the child.

---

baisser [beh-SAY] verb **to lower, to put down**

je baisse	nous baissons
tu baisses	vous baissez
il, elle baisse	ils, elles baissent

Le professeur dit: "Baissez les mains!"
The teacher says, "Put your hands down!"

---

le balai [ba-LAY] noun, masc. **broom**

On nettoie le plancher avec un balai.
We clean the floor with a broom.

---

la balançoire [ba-lahn̸-SWAR] noun, fem. **seesaw; swing**

Dans le parc les enfants s'amusent sur les balançoires.
In the park the children are having a good time on the swings (seesaws).

---

le balayeur des rues **street cleaner**
[ba-lay-yeuhr-day-REW] noun, masc.

Le balayeur des rues porte un balai.
The street cleaner is carrying a broom.

---

la balle [BAL] noun, fem. **ball**

La balle est ronde.
The ball is round.

---

le ballon [ba-LOHN̸] noun, masc. **balloon**

"Oh! Je perds mon ballon," crie la petite fille.
"Oh! I'm losing my balloon," cries the little girl.

---

la banane [ba-NAN] noun, fem. **banana**

La banane est mûre quand elle est jaune.
The banana is ripe when it is yellow.

---

la banque [BAHN̸K] noun, fem. **bank**

Avez-vous de l'argent à la banque?
Do you have any money in the bank?

---

la barbe [BARB] noun, fem. **beard**

Mon frère, qui est à l'université, a une barbe.
My brother, who is at the university, has a beard.

---

les bas [BAH] noun, masc. **stockings**

Les femmes portent des bas de nylon.
Women wear nylon stockings.

---

bas [BAH] adjective, masc. **low, short**
basse [BAHS] fem.

L'arbre à gauche est bas; l'arbre à droite est haut.
The tree at the left is short; the tree at the right is tall.

à voix basse [a-vwa-BAHS] **in a low voice**

Ma cousine parle à voix basse.
My cousin speaks in a low voice.

là bas **down there, over there**

---

le base-ball [behs-BUHL] noun, masc. **baseball**

Mon frère joue au base-ball.
My brother plays baseball.

---

le basket-ball [bas-keht-BUHL] noun, masc. **basketball**

Mon camarade joue au basket-ball.
My friend plays basketball.

---

le bateau [ba-TOH] noun, masc. **boat, ship**
les bateaux pl.

On traverse l'océan en bateau.
You cross the ocean by ship.

---

le bâtiment [bah-tee-MAHN] noun, masc. **building**

Les bâtiments sont très hauts dans la ville.
The buildings are very tall in the city.

---

le bâton [bah-TOHN] noun, masc. **stick**

L'agent de police porte un bâton.
The policeman carries a stick.

---

battre [BATR] verb **to hit**

je bats	nous battons
tu bats	vous battez
il, elle bat	ils, elles battent

Il me bat!
He's hitting me!

(se) battre [BATR] verb **to fight**

---

beau [BOH] adjective, masc. **beautiful, handsome,**
beaux [BOH] masc., pl. **good-looking**
belle [BEHL] fem.
bel [BEHL] masc., before a vowel

L'acteur est beau; l'actrice est belle.
The actor is handsome; the actress is beautiful.

Il fait beau **The weather is good** (See **faire**)

---

beaucoup de (d') [boh-KOO-deh] adverb **much, many, a lot (of)**

Berthe a beaucoup de livres.
Bertha has a lot of books.

---

le bébé [bay-BAY] noun, masc. **baby**

Marie joue avec le bébé.
Mary plays with the baby.

---

le bec [BEHK] noun, masc. **beak**

L'oiseau a un bec jaune.
The bird has a yellow beak.

---

le berceau [behr-SOH] noun, masc. **cradle**

Ma soeur est dans le berceau.
My sister is in the cradle.

---

besoin, avoir besoin de (d') **to need**
[be̸-ZWAIN̸], [a-vwar-be̸-ZWAIN̸É̸-de̸] idomatic expression

Le poisson a besoin d'eau.
The fish needs water.

---

bête [BEHT] adjective **silly, stupid**

Le petit chien est bête.
The puppy is silly.

---

la bête [BEHT] noun, fem. **beast, animal**

Le lion est une bête sauvage.
The lion is a wild animal.

---

le beurre [BUHR] noun, masc. **butter**

Passez-moi le beurre, s'il vous plaît.
Pass the butter, please.

---

la bibliothèque [bee-blyoh-TEHK] noun, fem. **library**

Il y a tant de livres dans la bibliothèque!
There are so many books in the library!

---

la bicyclette [bee-see-KLEHT] noun, fem. **bicycle**

Quand il fait beau Bernard va à bicyclette.
When the weather is good, Bernard rides his bicycle.

le vélo [vay-LOH] noun, masc. **bike, bicycle**

As-tu un vélo?
Do you have a bike?

---

bien [BYAIN] adverb **well**

Je vais très bien, merci.
I'm feeling very well, thank you.

bien sûr [byain-SEWR] interjection **of course**
bien entendu [byain-ahn-tahn-DEW] interjection **of course**

Aimez-vous les bonbons? Bien sûr (Bien entendu!)
Do you like candy? Of course!

bientôt [byahn-TOH] adverb **soon**

Le facteur arrive bientôt.
The mailman will come soon.

à bientôt [a-byahn-TOH] interjection **See you soon!**

Je vais faire des emplettes. À bientôt!
I am going shopping. See you soon!

---

le bifteck [beef-TEHK] noun, masc. **(beef)steak**

Le bifteck est bon.
The steak is good.

---

le bijou [bee-ZHOO] noun, masc. **jewel, jewelry**
les bijoux pl.

Il y a beaucoup de bijoux dans la malle.
There are many jewels in the trunk.

---

les billes [BEEY] noun, masc., pl. **marbles**

Les garçons aiment jouer aux billes.
Boys like to play marbles.

le stylo à bille **ballpoint pen** (See **stylo**)

---

le billet [bee-YAY] noun, masc. **ticket; note; bill (money)**

Voici mon billet, monsieur.
Here is my ticket, sir.

Je suis riche! J'ai un billet de dix francs!
I am rich! I have a ten-franc note!

---

bizarre [bee-ZAR] adjective **odd, strange**

Voici un animal bizarre!
Here is a strange animal!

---

blanc [BLAHN̸] adjective, masc. **white**
blanche [BLAHN̸SH] fem.

Mes souliers sont blancs.
My shoes are white.

---

le blé [BLAY] noun, masc. **wheat**

Je vois le blé dans les champs.
I see wheat in the fields.

---

bleu [BLEOH] adjective, masc. **blue**
bleue fem.

Le ciel est bleu, n'est-ce pas?
The sky is blue, isn't it?

---

blond [BLOHN̸] adjective, masc. **blonde**
blonde [BLOHN̸D] fem.

Avez-vous les cheveux blonds?
Do you have blond hair?

---

boire [BWAR] verb **to drink**

je bois	nous buvons
tu bois	vous buvez
il, elle boit	ils, elles boivent

L'enfant boit du lait.
The child is drinking milk.

le boisson [bwa-SOHN] noun, masc. **drink**

Le soda est un boisson.
Soda is a drink.

---

le bois [BWA] noun, masc. **woods, forest**

Je vais dans le bois.
I am going into the woods.

en bois [ahn-BWA] **made of wood, wooden**

La table est en bois.
The table is made of wood.

---

la boîte [BWAT] noun, fem. **box**
la boîte aux lettres [bwa-toh-LEHTR] noun, fem. **letter box, mailbox**

Il met la lettre dans la boîte aux lettres.
He puts the letter in the mailbox.

---

bon [BOHN] adjective, masc. **good**
bonne [BUHN] fem.

C'est un livre intéressant; c'est un bon livre.
It is an interesting book; it is a good book.

Bonne chance! **Good luck!** (See **chance**)
Bonne fête! **Happy birthday!** (See **fête**)

---

les bonbons [bohn-BOHN] noun, masc., pl. **candy**

Les enfants aiment les bonbons.
Children like candy.

---

le bonhomme de neige **snowman**
[buh-NUHM-dé-NEHZH] noun, masc.

Le bonhomme de neige porte un chapeau.
The snowman is wearing a hat.

---

bonjour [bohn-ZHOOR] interjection **Hello; Good morning; Good afternoon**

"Bonjour, mes enfants," dit le professeur.
"Good morning, children," says the teacher.

---

bon marché [bohn-mar-SHAY] **cheap(ly), inexpensive(ly)**
adjective, adverb

On vend le pain bon marché; il ne coûte pas cher.
Bread is cheap; it is not expensive.

---

bonne adjective, fem. (See **bon**)
de bonne heure (See **heure**)

---

la bonne [BUHN] noun, fem. **maid, cleaning woman**

La bonne nettoie la maison.
The maid cleans the house.

---

bonsoir [bohn-SWAR] interjection **Good evening!**

Quand Papa retourne à la maison à neuf heures, il dit: "Bonsoir!"
When Father returns home at nine o'clock, he says, "Good evening!"

---

le bord [BUHR] noun, masc. **edge; shore**

Je suis assis au bord du lac.
I am seated on the shore of the lake.

---

la botte [BUHT] noun, fem. **boot**

Quand il neige je mets mes bottes.
When it snows I put on my boots.

---

la bouche [BOOSH] noun, fem. **mouth**

L'enfant ouvre la bouche quand il pleure.
The child opens his mouth when he cries.

---

le boucher [boo-SHAY] noun, masc. **butcher**

Le boucher vend la viande.
The butcher sells meat.

---

la boucherie [boo-SHREE] noun, fem. **butcher shop**

On va à la boucherie pour acheter de la viande.
You go to the butcher shop to buy meat.

---

la boue [BOO] noun, fem. **mud**

Mes mains sont couvertes de boue!
My hands are covered with mud!

---

le boulanger [boo-lahn-ZHAY] noun, masc. **baker**

Le boulanger fait le pain.
The baker makes bread.

---

la boulangerie [boo-lahn-ZHREE] noun, fem. **bakery**

On va à la boulangerie pour acheter du pain.
You go to the bakery to buy bread.

---

le boulevard [bool-VAR] noun, masc. **boulevard, wide street**

Les étudiants se promènent sur le boulevard St-Michel à Paris.
Students walk on the Boulevard St. Michel in Paris.

---

le bouquet [boo-KEH] noun, masc. **bunch of flowers, bouquet**

"Voici un bouquet, Marthe," dit François.
"Here is a bunch of flowers, Martha," says Frank.

---

la bouteille [boo-TAY] noun, fem. **bottle**

Attention! La bouteille est en verre.
Be careful! The bottle is made of glass.

---

la boutique [boo-TEEK] noun, fem. **small store, shop**

Pardon. Où se trouve la boutique de monsieur Le Blanc?
Excuse me. Where is Mr. Le Blanc's shop?

---

le bouton [boo-TOHN] noun, masc. **button; (light)switch; doorknob; doorbell**

Ce manteau a seulement trois boutons.
This coat has only three buttons.

Nous voici à la porte de Virginie. Où est le bouton?
Here we are at Virginia's house. Where is the doorbell?

---

la branche [BRAHNSH] noun, fem. **branch**

L'arbre a beaucoup de branches.
The tree has many branches.

---

le bras [BRA] noun, masc. **arm**

L'homme a mal au bras.
The man has a sore arm.

---

bravo [bra-VOH] interjection **Well done! Hurray!**

Arnaud répond bien à la question.
Le professeur dit: "Bravo!"
Arnold answers the question well.
"Well done!" says the teacher.

---

la brioche [BRYUHSH] noun, fem. **roll**

Susanne prend une brioche pour le petit déjeuner.
Susan eats a roll for breakfast.

---

la brosse [BRUHS] noun, fem. **brush**

La brosse à cheveux est plus grande que la brosse à dents.
The hairbrush is bigger than the toothbrush.

---

se brosser [s~~e~~-bruh-SAY] verb **to brush (oneself)**

je me brosse	nous nous brossons
tu te brosses	vous vous brossez
il, elle se brosse	ils, elles se brossent

Laure se brosse les cheveux.
Laura is brushing her hair.

---

le brouillard [broo-YAR] noun, masc. **fog**

Il est difficile de voir à cause du brouillard.
It is difficult to see because of the fog.

---

le bruit [BR~~EW~~/EE] noun, masc. **noise**

Le tonnerre fait un grand bruit.
Thunder makes a loud noise.

---

brûler [br~~ew~~-lay] verb **to burn**

je brûle	nous brûlons
tu brûles	vous brûlez
il, elle brûle	ils, elles brûlent

On brûle du bois dans la cheminée.
We burn wood in the fireplace.

---

brun [BRUHN] adjective, masc. **brown**
brune [BREWN] fem.

Le garçon a les cheveux bruns.
The boy has brown hair.

---

le buffet [buh-FEH] noun, masc. **cupboard, sideboard**

Il y a des assiettes dans le buffet.
There are plates in the cupboard.

---

le bureau [bew-ROH] noun, masc. **desk; office**

Le bureau du professeur est grand.
The teacher's desk is big.

Voici le bureau d'une grande compagnie.
Here is the office of a large company.

le bureau de poste [bew-ROH-de-PUHST] noun, masc. **post office**

On va au bureau de poste pour mettre un colis à la poste.
You go to the post office to mail a package.

C

ça (See **cela**)

---

la cacahuète [ka-ka-WEHT] noun, fem. **peanut**

L'éléphant aime manger les cacahuètes.
The elephant likes to eat peanuts.

---

cacher [ka-SHAY] verb **to hide**

je cache | nous cachons
tu caches | vous cachez
il, elle cache | ils, elles cachent

Le garçon cache les fleurs derrière lui.
The boy is hiding the flowers behind him.

jouer à cache-cache [zhoo-AY-ah-kash-KASH] idiomatic expression **to play hide-and-seek**

(See **jouer**)

Les enfants jouent à cache-cache.
The children are playing hide-and-seek.

---

le cadeau [ka-DOH] noun, masc. **gift, present**
les cadeaux pl.

Voici un cadeau pour votre anniversaire.
Here is a birthday gift.

---

le café [ka-FAY] noun, masc. **coffee; café, small restaurant**

Voulez-vous du café?
Do you want some coffee?

Il y a un café au coin de la rue.
There is a café on the corner.

---

le cahier [ka-YAY] noun, masc. **notebook**

Elle écrit ses devoirs dans un cahier.
She writes her homework in a notebook.

---

le calendrier [ka-lahn-DRYAY] noun, masc. **calendar**

Selon le calendrier c'est aujourd'hui le 12 mai.
According to the calendar, today is May 12th.

---

le camarade [ka-ma-RAD] noun, masc. **close friend, pal**

Mon camarade et moi, nous allons jouer au parc.
My friend and I are going to the park to play.

---

le camion [ka-MYOHN] noun, masc. **truck**

Le camion fait beaucoup de bruit.
The truck makes a lot of noise.

---

la campagne [kahN-PAN] noun, fem. **country (opposite of city)**

Il fait beau. Allons à la campagne!
It's nice weather. Let's go to the country!

---

le canapé [ka-na-PAY] noun, masc. **sofa**

Le canapé est très confortable.
The sofa is very comfortable.

---

le canard [ka-NAR] noun, masc. **duck**

Voilà des canards sur le lac.
There are some ducks on the lake.

---

le canif [ka-NEEF] noun, masc. **pocketknife, jackknife**

Avez-vous un canif?
Do you have a pocketknife? (See **couteau**)

---

le caoutchouc [ka-oo-TSHOO] noun, masc. **rubber**

Il pleut. Il faut que je mette mes bottes en caoutchouc.
It is raining. I have to put on my rubbers.

en caoutchouc [ahN-ka-oo-TSHOO] **made of rubber**

---

la capitale [ka-pee-TAL] noun, fem. **capital**

Savez-vous le nom de la capitale de la France?
Do you know the name of the capital of France?

---

la carotte [ka-RUHT] noun, fem. **carrot**

Le lapins mangent des carottes.
Rabbits eat carrots.

---

carré [ka-RAY] adjective, masc. **square**
carrée fem.

La boite est carrée.
The box is square.

---

la carte [KART] noun, fem. **map; playing card; postcard; card; menu**

Avez-vous une carte des routes de la France?
Do you have a road map of France?

Savez-vous jouer aux cartes?
Do you know how to play cards?

Ces cartes postales sont jolies.
These postcards are pretty.

---

casser [ka-SAY] verb **to break**

je casse	nous cassons
tu casses	vous cassez
il, elle casse	ils, elles cassent

Attention! Ne casse pas l'assiette!
Be careful! Don't break the plate!

---

cause [KOHZ] noun, fem. **cause**
à cause de [a-KOHZ-d∉] **because of**

Je dois rester à la maison à cause de la neige.
I have to stay home because of the snow.

---

la cave [KAV] noun, fem. **basement, cellar**

Il y a plusieurs paquets dans la cave.
There are several packages in the cellar.

---

ce [SE] adjective, masc. **this**
cette [SEHT] fem.
ces [SAY] masc., pl.
cet [SEHT] masc. form before a vowel

Cette petite fille est sage.
This little girl is well behaved.

c'est [SEH] **it is, this is**

C'est aujourd'hui mercredi.
Today it is Wednesday.

c'est dommage (See **dommage**)
c'est triste (See **triste**)
ceci [se-SEE] pronoun **this**

Mmm, ceci est bon!
Mmm, this is good!

---

la ceinture [sain-TEWR] noun, fem. **belt**

Tiens! Tu portes une nouvelle ceinture!
Well! You're wearing a new belt!

---

cela [SLA] **that**

Je n'aime pas cela!
I don't like that!

---

célèbre [say-LEHBR] adjective **famous**

Le président des Etats-Unis est célèbre.
The President of the United States is famous.

---

le céleri [sayl-REE] noun, masc. **celery**

On fait une salade avec du céleri.
We make a salad with celery.

---

celui [SƏ-LEWEE] pronoun, masc. **the one that,**
ceux [SEOH] masc., pl. **the one who**
celle [SEHL] fem.
celles [SEHL] fem., pl.

Voici un stylo rouge. Celui de mon père est jaune.
Here is a red pen. The one that belongs to my father is yellow.

Voici une règle rouge. Celles qui sont sur la table sont jaunes.
Here is a red ruler. Those that are on the table are yellow.

---

cent [SAHN] adjective **one hundred**

Il y a cent personnes à la foire!
There are a hundred people at the fair!

---

le cerceau [sehr-SOH] noun, masc. **hoop**

Le garçon roule un grand cerceau.
The boy is rolling a big hoop.

---

le cercle [SEHRKL] noun, masc. **circle**

Les garçons forment un cercle pour jouer.
The boys form a circle to play.

---

le cerf-volant [sehr-vuh-LAHN] noun, masc. **kite**
les cerfs-volants pl.

Bon, il fait du vent. Allons jouer avec un cerf-volant.
Good, it's windy. Let's play with a kite.

---

la cerise [sə-REEZ] noun, fem. **cherry**

Je vais cueillir des cerises.
I am going to pick cherries.

---

chacun [sha-KUHN] pronoun, masc. **each one**
chacune [sha-KEWN] fem.

Voilà cinq jeunes filles; chacune a une fleur.
Here are five girls; each one has a flower.

"Chacun à son goût" is a popular proverb in French that means everyone has his or her own preference.

---

la chaise [SHEHZ] noun, fem. **chair**

Cette chaise est trop grande pour moi.
This chair is too big for me.

---

la chambre [SHAHNBR] noun, fem. **bedroom**

Cet appartement a trois chambres.
This apartment has three bedrooms.

---

le champ [SHAHN] noun, masc. **field**

C'est un champ de blé, n'est-ce pas?
It's a field of wheat, isn't it?

---

la chance [SHAHNS] noun, fem. **luck**
Bonne chance! [buhn-SHAHNS] interjection! Good luck!

Avant l'examen mon ami dit: "Bonne chance!"
Before the examination my friend says, "Good luck."

avoir de la chance **to be lucky** (See **avoir**)

Le garçon gagne un prix. Il a de la chance.
The boy wins a prize. He is lucky.

---

le chandail [shahn-DAHY] noun, masc. **sweater**

Je porte un chandail parce qu'il fait frais.
I am wearing a sweater because it is cool.

---

changer [shahn-ZHAY] verb **to change**

je change	nous changeons
tu changes	vous changez
il, elle change	ils, elles changent

Il faut changer de train.
We have to change to another train.

---

la chanson [shahn-SOHN] noun, fem. **song**

Quelle chanson préférez-vous?
Which song do you prefer?

---

chanter [shahn-TAY] verb **to sing**

je chante	nous chantons
tu chantes	vous chantez
il, elle chante	ils, elles chantent

Je chante et les oiseaux chantent.
I am singing and the birds are singing.

---

le chapeau [sha-POH] noun, masc. **hat**

Quel joli chapeau!
What a pretty hat!

---

chaque [SHAK] adjective **each, every**

Je mets une fourchette à chaque place.
I put a fork at each place.

---

le chasseur [sha-SEUHR] noun, masc. **hunter**

Le chasseur entre dans la forêt.
The hunter goes into the forest.

---

le chat [SHA] noun, masc. **cat**

Les chats aiment le lait.
Cats like milk.

> In French they say: "Quand le chat n'est pas là, les souris dansent." In English it is: "When the cat is away, the mice play."

le chaton [sha-TOHN] noun, masc. **kitten**

---

le château [sha-TOH] noun, masc. **castle, palace**

Le roi habite un grand château.
The king lives in a large palace.

---

chaud [SHOH] adjective, masc. **hot, warm**
chaude [SHOHD] fem.

Il fait chaud aujourd'hui. Allons nager. (See **faire**)
It's hot today. Let's go swimming.

Le garçon a chaud. Il va nager. (See **avoir**)
The boy is hot. He is going swimming.

---

le chauffeur [shoh-FEUHR] noun, masc. **driver**

Le chauffeur s'arrête quand le feu est rouge.
The driver stops when the light is red.

---

la chaussette [shoh-SEHT] noun, fem. **sock**

Je voudrais acheter une paire de chaussettes.
I would like to buy a pair of socks.

---

la chaussure [shoh-SEWR] noun, fem. **shoe**

Je n'aime pas ces chaussures!
I don't like these shoes!

---

le chef [SHEHF] noun, masc. **leader**

Mais non! Tu joues toujours le rôle du chef.
No! You're always playing the leader.

---

le chemin [SHMAIN] noun, masc. **road**

C'est le chemin de la ville?
Is this the road to town?

le chemin de fer [SHMAIN-de-FEHR] noun, masc. **railroad**

Pour aller à Marseille, je prends le chemin de fer.
To go to Marseilles, I take the railroad.

---

la cheminée [she-mee-NAY] noun, fem. **fireplace; chimney**

Les chaussures sont près de la cheminée.
The shoes are near the fireplace.

---

la chemise [SHMEEZ] noun, fem. **(man's) shirt**

Le garçon porte une chemise blanche.
The boy is wearing a white shirt.

---

cher [SHEHR] adjective, masc. **dear; expensive**
chère fem.

Je commence une lettre à Maman avec les mots: "Chère Maman."
I begin a letter to Mother with the words, "Dear Mother."

Cette bicyclette est trop chère.
This bicycle is too expensive.

---

chercher [shehr-SHAY] verb **to look for**

je cherche	nous cherchons
tu cherches	vous cherchez
il, elle cherche	ils, elles cherchent

Papa cherche toujours ses clefs.
Father is always looking for his keys.

---

le cheval [SHVAL] noun, masc. **horse**
les chevaux [SHVOH] pl.

Le soldat monte à cheval.
The solider rides on a horse.

---

le cheveu [SHVEOH] noun, masc. **hair**
les cheveux pl.

Les étudiants à l'université aiment les cheveux longs.
Students at the university like long hair.

---

la chèvre [SHEHVR] noun, fem. **goat**

Le fermier a une chèvre.
The farmer has a goat.

---

chez [SHAY] preposition **to (or at) the house of**

Je vais manger chez mon oncle.
I am going to eat at my uncle's house.

chez moi [shay-MWA] idiomatic expression **to (or at) my house**

Viens chez moi tout de suite.
Come to my house immediately.

---

le chien [SHYAIN] noun, masc. **dog**

As-tu un chien?
Do you have a dog?

le petit chien [ptee-SHYAIN] noun, masc. **puppy**

---

le chocolat [shuh-kuh-LA] noun, masc. **chocolate**

Comment? Tu n'aimes pas les chocolats?
What? You don't like chocolates?

---

choisir [shwa-ZEER] verb **to choose**

je choisis	nous choisissons
tu choisis	vous choisissez
il, elle choisit	ils, elles choisissent

Dans l'examen, choisissez la réponse correcte.
On the examination, choose the correct answer.

---

la chose [SHOHZ] noun, fem. **thing**

On vend toutes sortes de choses dans cette boutique.
They sell all kinds of things in this store.

---

le chou [SHOO] noun, masc. **cabbage**

Préférez-vous le chou ou les carottes?
Do you prefer cabbage or carrots?

---

le ciel [SYEHL] noun, masc. **sky**

Je vois la lune dans le ciel.
I see the moon in the sky.

---

la cigarette [see-ga-REHT] noun, fem. **cigarette**

Est-ce que ton oncle fume des cigarettes?
Does your uncle smoke cigarettes?

---

le cinéma [see-nay-MAH] noun, masc. **movies, film**

Il y a un bon film au cinéma.
There is a good film at the movies.

---

cinq [SAIN̸, SAIN̸K] adjective **five**

La main a cinq doigts. [SAIN̸]
The hand has five fingers.

Voici cinq enfants. [SAIN̸K]
Here are five children.

J'en ai cinq. [SAIN̸K]
I've got five.

---

cinquante [saiN̸-KAHN̸T] adjective **fifty**

Il y a cinquante états dans le Etats-Unis.
There are fifty states in the United States.

---

la circulation [seer-kew-la-SYOHN̸] noun, fem. **traffic**

La circulation s'arrête au feu rouge.
The traffic stops for the red light.

---

le cirque [SEERK] noun, masc. **circus**

Il ya a beaucoup d'animaux au cirque.
There are many animals at the circus.

---

les ciseaux [see-ZOH] noun, masc., pl. **scissors**

Je coupe le papier avec les ciseaux.
I cut the paper with scissors.

---

le citron [see-TROHN] noun, masc. **lemon**

Les citrons sont jaunes.
Lemons are yellow.

---

la citrouille [see-TROOY] noun, fem. **pumpkin**

C'est une grosse citrouille.
This is a big pumpkin.

---

clair [KLEHR] adjective, masc. **light, clear**
claire fem.

Quelle belle journée claire!
What a beautiful, clear day!

---

la classe [KLAS] noun, fem. **class**
la salle de classe noun, fem. **classroom** (See **salle**)

Nous sommes dans la salle de classe.
We are in the classroom.

---

la clef [KLAY] noun, fem. (sometimes spelled **clé**) **key**

Où est ma clef?
Where is my key?

---

la cloche [KLUHSH] noun, fem. **bell**

A midi la cloche sonne.
The bell rings at noon.

---

le clou [KLOO] noun, masc. **nail (metal)**

Mon frère joue avec des clous et un marteau.
My brother plays with nails and a hammer.

---

le clown [KLOON] noun, masc. **clown**

Quand je suis au cirque je dis "Bonjour" au clown.
When I am at the circus I say "Hello" to the clown.

---

le cochon [kuh-SHOHN̸] noun, masc. **pig**

Le fermier a trois cochons.
The farmer has three pigs.

---

le coeur [KEUHR] noun, masc. **heart**

Regardez tous les coeurs sur la carte!
Look at all the hearts on the (playing) card!

---

le coin [KWAIN̸] noun, masc. **corner**

Il faut traverser la rue au coin.
You must cross the street at the corner.

---

le colin-maillard [kuh-lain̸-mah-YAR] noun, masc. **blindman's buff**

jouer à colin-maillard [kuh-lain̸-mah-YAR] idiomatic expression **to play blindman's buff** (See **jouer**)

Oui, je voudrais jouer à colin-maillard.
Yes, I'd like to play blindman's buff.

---

le colis [kuh-LEE] noun, masc. **package**

Ah, bon! Un colis pour moi!
Oh, good! A package for me!

---

coller [kuh-LAY] verb **to paste, to glue**

je colle nous collons
tu colles vous collez
il, elle colle ils, elles collent

Je colle une image sur une page de mon cahier.
I glue a picture to a page of my notebook.

---

la colonie de vacances **camp**
[kuh-luh-need-va-KAHN̸S] noun, fem.

Mon cousin passe huit semaines à la colonie de vacances.
My cousin spends eight weeks at camp.

---

colorier [kuh-luh-ree-AY] verb **to color**

je colorie nous colorions
tu colories vous coloriez
il, elle colorie ils, elles colorient

Nous colorions avec les crayons de couleur.
We color with crayons.

---

combien [kohN̸-BYAIN̸] adverb **how much, how many**

Combien de jouets as-tu?
How many toys do you have?

---

commander [kuh-mahN̸-DAY] verb **to order, to command**

je commande nous commandons
tu commandes vous commandez
il, elle commande ils, elles commandent

Au restaurant Papa commande le dîner.
In the restaurant Father orders dinner.

---

comme [KUHM] preposition **for, as**

Comme dessert, elle prend une glace au chocolat.
For dessert she has chocolate ice cream.

---

commencer [kuh-mahn-SAY] verb **to begin, to start**

je commence nous commençons
tu commences vous commencez
il, elle commence ils, elles commencent

La classe de français commence à neuf heures.
The French class begins at nine o'clock.

---

comment [kuh-MAHN] adverb **how; what?**

Comment allez-vous?
How are you?

Comment?
What?

---

la compagnie [kohn-pa-NEE] noun, fem. **company**

La Compagnie Bardot se trouve au coin de la rue.
The Bardot Company is located on the corner (of the street).

---

la compétition [kohn-pay-tee-SYON] noun, fem. **contest**

Jeanne va gagner la compétition.
Jeanne is going to win the contest.

---

le complet [kohn-PLEH] noun, masc. **suit**

Papa porte un complet quand il va au travail.
Dad wears a suit when he goes to work.

---

comprendre [kohn-PRAHNDR] verb **to understand**

je comprends nous comprenons
tu comprends vous comprenez
il, elle comprend ils, elles comprennent

Tu comprends la leçon d'aujourd'hui?
Do you understand today's lesson?

---

compter [kohn-TAY] verb **to count**

je compte	nous comptons
tu comptes	vous comptez
il, elle compte	ils, elles comptent

Il sait compter de cinq à un: cinq, quatre, trois, deux, un.
He knows how to count from five to one: five, four, three, two, one.

---

le concours noun, masc. **contest** (See **compétition**)

---

conduire [kohn-DEW/EER] verb **to drive**

je conduis	nous conduisons
tu conduis	vous conduisez
il, elle conduit	ils, elles conduisent

Hélas! Je suis trop jeune pour conduire l'auto.
Too bad! I am too young to drive the car.

se conduire verb **to behave**

je me conduis	nous nous conduisons
tu te conduis	vous vous conduisez
il, elle se conduit	ils, elles se conduisent

Les enfants se conduisent bien à table.
The children behave well at the table.

---

la confiture [kohn-fee-TEWR] noun, fem. **jam**

Donnez-moi un morceau de pain avec de la confiture aux fraises, s'il vous plaît.
Please give me a piece of bread with strawberry jam.

---

confortable [kohn-fuhr-TABL] adjective **comfortable**

Mon lit est très confortable.
My bed is very comfortable.

---

le conseiller [kohn-say-YAY] noun, masc. **counselor**
la conseillère [kohn-say-YEHR] fem.

Mon conseiller s'appelle M. Blanc.
My counselor's name is Mr. Blanc.

---

le congé [kohn-ZHAY] noun, masc. **leave of absence**
un jour de congé **a day off** (See **jour**)

---

connaître [kuh-NEHTR] verb **to know, to be acquainted with**

je connais	nous connaissons
tu connais	vous connaissez
il, elle connaît	ils, elles connaissent

Connais-tu mon maître?
Do you know my teacher?

---

le conte [KOHNT] noun, masc. **story, tale**

Lisez-moi le conte des "Trois petits chatons."
Read me the story of the "Three Little Kittens."

le conte de fées **fairy tale** (See **la fée**)

---

content [kohn-TAHN] adjective, masc. **happy, glad**
contente [kohn-TAHNT] fem.

La petite fille n'est pas contente.
The little girl is not happy.

---

continuer [kohn-tee-new-AY] verb **to continue**

je continue	nous continuons
tu continues	vous continuez
il, elle continue	ils, elles continuent

Je continue à jouer du piano jusqu'à cinq heures.
I will continue to play the piano until five o'clock.

---

contre [KOHNTR] preposition **against**

Henri met le miroir contre le mur.
Henry puts the mirror against the wall.

---

copier [kuh-PYAY] to copy **verb**

je copie	nous copions
tu copies	vous copiez
il, elle copie	ils, elles copient

Il faut copier les phrases qui sont au tableau noir.
We have to copy the sentences that are on the blackboard.

---

le coq [KUHK] noun, masc. **rooster**

Le coq se lève de bonne heure.
The rooster gets up early.

---

le coquillage [kuhk-KYAZH] noun, masc. **shell**

Je cherche des coquillages à la plage.
I am looking for shells at the beach.

---

la corde [KUHRD] noun, fem. **rope**
sauter à la corde **to jump rope** (See **sauter**)

Marie, Jeanne, et moi, nous sautons à la corde.
Mary, Joan, and I are jumping rope.

---

correct [kuh-REHKT] adjective, masc. **correct**
correcte fem.

Le professeur dit: "Ecrivez la réponse correcte."
The teacher says, "Write the correct answer."

---

le côté [koh-TAY] noun, masc. **side**

à côté de [a-koh-TAY dɇ] preposition **next to, at the side of**

Dans le restaurant Pierre est assis à côté de Caroline.
At the restaurant Peter is seated next to Carolyn.

---

la côtelette [koh-TLEHT] noun, fem. **cutlet, chop**

Préfères-tu une côtelette de veau ou de mouton?
Do you prefer a veal cutlet or a lamb chop?

---

le coton [kuh-TOHN̸] noun, masc. **cotton**
en coton **made of cotton**

Il porte une chemise en coton.
He is wearing a cotton shirt.

---

le cou [KOO] noun, masc. **neck**

Ma grand'mère dit: "J'ai mal au cou."
My grandmother says, "My neck hurts."

---

se coucher [sɇ-koo-SHAY] verb **to go to bed; to set (sun)**

je me couche	nous nous couchons
tu te couches	vous vous couchez
il, elle se couche	ils, elles se couchent

Je n'aime pas me coucher de bonne heure.
I don't like to go to bed early.

Le soleil se couche.
The sun is setting.

---

coudre [KOODR] verb **to sew**

je couds	nous cousons
tu couds	vous cousez
il, elle coud	ils, elles cousent

l'aiguille à coudre **sewing needle** (See **l'aiguille**)

Maman coud avec une aiguille à coudre.
Mother sews with a sewing needle.

---

la couleur [koo-LEUHR] noun, fem. **color**

De quelle couleur est la banane?
What color is the banana?

blanc	**white**
bleu	**blue**
brun	**brown (for hair, eyes)**
gris	**gray**
jaune	**yellow**
marron	**brown**
noir	**black**
orange	**orange**
rose	**pink**
rouge	**red**
vert	**green**
violet	**purple, violet**

---

le coup [KOO] noun, masc. **blow; knock**

On frappe deux coups à la porte. Qui est là?
There are two knocks on the door. Who's there?

tout à coup **suddenly** (See **tout**)
le coup de pied [KOOD-PYAY] **kick**

Il donne un coup de pied à la balle.
He kicks the ball.

---

couper [koo-PAY] verb **to cut**

je coupe	nous coupons
tu coupes	vous coupez
il, elle coupe	ils, elles coupent

Papa coupe le pain avec un couteau.
Dad cuts the bread with a knife.

---

courageux [koo-ra-ZHEOH] adjective, masc. **courageous,**
courageuse [koo-ra-ZHEOHZ] fem. **brave**

Le prince est courageux quand il sauve la princesse.
The prince is brave when he saves the princess.

---

courir [koo-REER] verb **to run**

je cours nous courons
tu cours vous courez
il, elle court ils, elles courent

Ils courent à la gare parce qu'ils sont en retard.
They are running to the station because they are late.

---

court [KOOR] adjective, masc. **short**
courte [KOORT] fem.

Une règle est courte; l'autre est longue.
One ruler is short; the other is long.

---

le cousin [koo-ZAIN] noun, masc. **cousin**
la cousine [koo-ZEEN] fem.

Mon cousin Paul a dix ans et ma cousine Marie a dix-huit ans.
My cousin Paul is ten years old and my cousin Mary is eighteen.

---

le couteau [koo-TOH] noun, masc. **knife**
les couteaux pl.

Elle met un couteau à chaque place sur la table.
She puts a knife at each place at the table.

---

coûter [koo-TAY] verb **to cost**

il, elle coûte ils, elles coûtent

Combien coûte ce peigne?
How much does this comb cost?

---

couvert [koo-VEHR] adjective, masc. **covered**
couverte [koo-VEHRT] fem.

L'arbre est couvert de neige.
The tree is covered with snow.

Il est couvert.
It is cloudy.

mettre le couvert **to set the table** (See **mettre**)

---

la couverture [koo-vehr-TEWR] noun, fem. **cover, blanket**

En hiver j'aime une couverture chaude sur le lit.
In winter I like a warm blanket on my bed.

---

la craie [KREH] noun, fem. **chalk**

Le garçon écrit au tableau noir avec la craie.
The boy is writing on the blackboard with chalk.

---

la cravate [kra-VAT] noun, fem. **tie**

La cravate de Papa est trop grande pour moi.
Daddy's tie is too big for me.

---

le crayon [kray-YOHN] noun, masc. **pencil**

Donnez-moi un crayon, s'il vous plaît.
Please give me a pencil.

le crayon de couleur **crayon**
[kray-yohn-dkoo-LEUHR] noun, masc.

Je dessine avec les crayons de couleur.
I draw with crayons.

---

crier [kree-AY] verb **to shout, to scream**

je crie	nous crions
tu cries	vous criez
il, elle crie	ils, elles crient

Maman crie: "Viens vite!"
Mom shouts, "Come quickly!"

---

croire [KRWAR] verb **to believe**

je crois	nous croyons
tu crois	vous croyez
il, elle croit	ils, elles croient

Je crois que je peux aller au cinéma.
I believe I can go to the movies.

---

le croissant [krwa-SAHN] noun, masc. **croissant**

Henriette prend un croissant pour le petit déjeuner.
Harriet has a croissant for breakfast.

---

cueillir [keuh-YEER] verb **to pick, to gather**

je cueille	nous cueillons
tu cueilles	vous cueillez
il, elle cueille	ils, elles cueillent

Il va cueillir des pommes.
He is going to pick some apples.

---

la cuiller [kew/ee-YEHR] verb, fem. **spoon**
(sometimes spelled **cuillère**)

Je n'ai pas de cuiller.
I don't have a spoon.

---

le cuir [KEW/EER] noun, masc. **leather**
en cuir **made of leather**

La veste de mon frère est en cuir.
My brother's jacket is made of leather.

---

la cuisine [kew/ee-ZEEN] noun, fem. **kitchen**

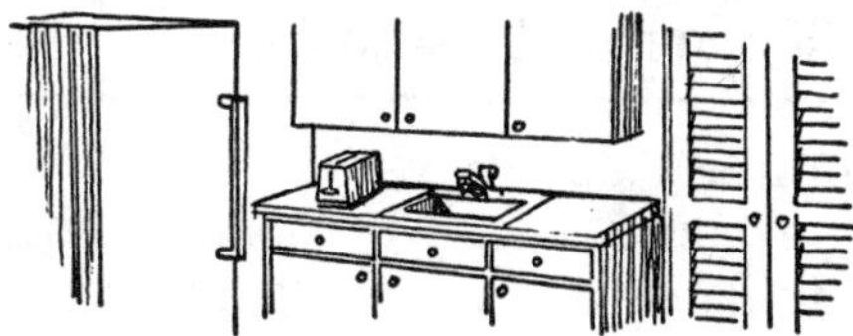

La cuisine est petite.
The kitchen is small.

faire la cuisine **to cook (See faire)**

---

curieux [kew-RYEOH] adjective, masc. **curious**
curieuse [kew-RYEOHZ] fem.

Elle est curieuse. Elle voudrait ouvrir le paquet.
She is curious. She would like to open the package.

D

la dactylo [dak-tee-LOH] noun, fem. **secretary, typist**

Il y a trois dactylos dans ce bureau.
There are three secretaries in this office.

---

la dame [DAHM] noun, fem. **lady**

Qui est cette dame?
Who is this lady?

jouer aux dames **to play checkers** (See **jouer**)

---

dangereux [dahn-ZHREOH] adjective, masc. **dangerous**
dangereuse [dahn-ZHREOHZ] fem.

Il est dangereux de courir dans la rue pour attraper une balle.
It is dangerous to run into the street to catch a ball.

---

dans [DAHN] preposition **in, into**

Ils entrent dans l'école.
They go into the school.

---

danser [dahn-SAY] verb **to dance**

je danse	nous dansons
tu danses	vous dansez
il, elle danse	ils, elles dansent

Ma soeur aime danser.
My sister likes to dance.

---

la date [DAT] noun, fem. **date**

Quelle ese la date?
What is the date?

---

de [de̸] preposition **from; of; some; any (also shows possession)**

du [DEW] masc. (contraction of de + le)
de la fem. [de̸-LA]
des [DAY] pl. (contraction of de + les)

Elle vient de Paris.
She comes from Paris.

Voulez-vous du pain?
Do you want any bread?

C'est le ballon de mon frère.
It's my brother's balloon.

Elle va acheter des pommes de terre.
She is going to buy some potatoes.

---

debout [dé-BOO] adverb **standing**

Dans la salle de classe la maîtresse est debout.
In the classroom the teacher is standing.

---

décembre [day-SAHNBR] noun, masc. **December**

Il fait froid en décembre.
It is cold in December.

---

décorer [day-kuh-RAY] verb **to decorate**

je décore	nous décorons
tu décores	vous décorez
il, elle décore	ils, elles décorent

Il décore sa bicyclette.
He is decorating his bicycle.

---

défense de [day-FAHNS-de] idiomatic expression **It is forbidden to, No. . .**

défense d'entrer [day-FAHNS-dahN-TRAY] idiomatic expression **No admittance**

Défense d'entrer. Nous ne pouvons pas entrer.
No admittance. We cannot enter.

défense de fumer [day-FAHNS-dé-few-MAY] idiomatic expression **No smoking**

Défense de fumer à l'école.
No smoking in school.

---

le défilé [day-fee-LAY] noun, masc. **parade**

Nous marchons dans le défilé.
We walk in the parade.

---

dehors [de̸-UHR] preposition **outside**

Mon ami m'attend dehors.
My friend is waiting for me outside.

---

déjà [day-ZHA] adverb **already**

Il est déjà l'heure de partir?
It is already time to leave?

---

le déjeuner [day-zheuh-NAY] noun, masc. **lunch**

Je prends le déjeuner à midi.
I eat lunch at noon.

le petit déjeuner [ptee-day-zheuh-NAY] noun, masc. **breakfast**

Je prends le petit déjeuner à sept heures et demie.
I eat breakfast at seven thirty.

---

délicieux [day-lee-SYEOH] adjective, masc. **delicious**
délicieuse [day-lee-SYEOHZ] fem.

Le gâteau est délicieux.
The cake is delicious.

---

demain [de̸-MAIN̸] adverb **tomorrow**

Demain je vais à la colonie de vacances.
Tomorrow I am going to camp.

---

demander [de̸-mahn̸-DAY] verb **to ask**

je demande	nous demandons
tu demandes	vous demandez
il, elle demande	ils, elles demandent

Je demande à Papa: "Je peux aller à la foire?"
I ask Father: "May I go to the fair?"

---

demeurer [dé-meuh-RAY] verb **to live**

je demeure	nous demeurons
tu demeures	vous demeurez
il, elle demeure	ils, elles demeurent

Où demeurez-vous?
Where do you live?

---

demi [dé-MEE] adjective, masc. **half**
demie fem.
la demi-heure [dé-mee-EUHR] noun, fem. **half an hour**

Voilà une demi-heure que je vous attends!
I have been waiting for you for half an hour!

---

la dent [DAHN] noun, fem. **tooth**

J'ai mal aux dents.
I have a toothache.

---

le dentifrice [dahn-tee-FREES] noun, masc. **toothpaste**

Maman, je n'aime pas ce dentifrice.
Mom, I don't like this toothpaste.

---

le dentiste [dahn-TEEST] noun, masc. **dentist**

Le dentiste dit: "Ouvre la bouche."
The dentist says, "Open your mouth."

---

dépasser [day-pah-SAY] verb **to pass**

je dépasse	nous dépassons
tu dépasses	vous dépassez
il, elle dépasse	ils, elles dépassent

L'auto dépasse le camion.
The car passes the truck.

---

se dépêcher [sɇ-day-peh-SHAY] verb **to hurry**

je me dépêche	nous nous dépêchons
tu te dépêches	vous vous dépêchez
il, elle se dépêche	ils, elles se dépêchent

Ils se dépêchent parce qu'ils sont en retard.
They hurry because they are late.

---

depuis [dɇ-PEW/EE] preposition **for**

Elle attend sa tante depuis une heure.
She has been waiting for her aunt for an hour.

---

de rien **you're welcome** (See **rien**)

---

dernier [dehr-NYAY] noun, adjective, masc. **last one; last**
dernière [dehr-NYEHR] fem.

Paul est le dernier à s'asseoir à table.
Paul is the last one to sit down at the table.

C'est mon dernier franc!
It is my last franc!

---

derrière [deh-RYEHR] preposition **behind**

Caroline est derrière la chaise.
Carolyn is behind the chair.

---

descendre [deh-SAHNDR] verb **to go down**

je descends nous descendons
tu descends vous descendez
il, elle descend ils, elles descendent

L'homme descend de la montagne.
The man goes down the mountain.

---

le désert [day-ZEHR] noun, masc. **desert**

Le désert est très sec.
The desert is very dry.

---

désirer [day-zee-RAY] verb **to wish, to want**

je désire nous désirons
tu désires vous désirez
il, elle désire ils, elles désirent

Monsieur désire?
What do you wish, sir?

---

le dessert [deh-SEHR] noun, masc. **dessert**

Comme dessert je désire une tarte aux fraises.
I would like to have a strawberry tart for dessert.

> There are delicious French desserts that are known all over the world, such as "mousse au chocolat" or "crêpes suzettes."

---

dessiner [deh-see-NAY] verb **to draw**

je dessine nous dessinons
tu dessines vous dessinez
il, elle dessine ils, elles dessinent

Va au tableau noir et dessine une maison.
Go to the blackboard and draw a house.

---

détester [day-tehs-TAY] verb **to hate, to detest**

je déteste	nous détestons
tu détestes	vous détestez
ile, elle déteste	ils, elles détestent

Il déteste les épinards.
He hates spinach.

---

deux [DEOH] adjective **two**

Je vois deux chats.
I see two cats.

deux fois **twice** (See **la fois**)

---

deuxième [deoh-ZYEHM] adjective **second**

Quel est le nom du deuxième mois de l'année?
What is the name of the second month of the year?

---

devant [dé-VAHN] preposition **in front of**

Il y a une table devant le canapé.
There is a table in front of the sofa.

---

devenir [dév-NEER] verb **to become**

je deviens	nous devenons
tu deviens	vous devenez
il, elle devient	ils, elles deviennent

Il voudrait devenir médecin.
He would like to become a doctor.

---

deviner [dé-vee-NAY] verb **to guess**

je devine	nous devinons
tu devines	vous devinez
il, elle devine	ils, elles devinent

Tu peux deviner combien d'argent j'ai dans la main?
Can you guess how much money I have in my hand?

---

le devoir [dé-VWAR] noun, masc. **homework; duty**

Nous allons faire nos devoirs ensemble.
We are going to do our homework together.

---

devoir [dé-VWAR] verb **to have to**

je dois	nous devons
tu dois	vous devez
il, elle doit	ils, elles doivent

Je dois me laver les mains.
I have to wash my hands.

---

le dictionnaire [deek-syohn-NEHR] noun, masc. **dictionary**

Ce dictionnaire est très lourd.
This dictionary is very heavy.

---

différent [dee-fay-RAHN] adjective, masc. **different**
différente [dee-fay-RAHNT] fem.

Ces pains sont différents.
These loaves of bread are different.

---

difficile [dee-fee-SEEL] adjective **difficult**

Il est difficile de lire cette lettre.
It is difficult to read this letter.

---

le dimanche [dee-MAHNSH] noun, masc. **Sunday**

Le dimanche nous allons au parc.
We go to the park on Sundays.

---

la dinde [DAIND] noun, masc. **turkey**

Tu aimes manger la dinde?
Do you like to eat turkey?

---

le dîner [dee-NAY] noun, masc. **dinner**

Nous prenons le dîner à huit heures.
We eat dinner at eight o'clock.

---

dire [DEER] verb **to say**

je dis nous disons
tu dis vous dites
il, elle dit ils, elles disent

Le professeur dit "Bonjour" chaque matin.
The teacher says "Good Morning" each morning.

vouloir dire [voo-lwar-DEER] verb **to mean**

Que veut dire ce mot?
What does this word mean?

---

diriger [dee-ree-ZHAY] verb **to direct**

je dirige nous dirigeons
tu diriges vous dirigez
il, elle dirige ils, elles dirigent

Mon frère dirige le jeu.
My brother is directing the game.

---

le disque [DEESK] noun, masc. **computer disk**

(See **l'ordinateur**)

J'utilise des disques pour l'ordinateur Apple.
I use disks for the Apple computer.

---

dix [DEES, DEEZ, DEE] adjective **ten**

Combien de doigts avez-vous? Dix. [DEES]
How many fingers do you have? Ten.

Il a dix abricots. [DEEZ] *(before a vowel)*
He has ten apricots.

Il a dix ballons. [DEE] *(before a consonant)*
He has ten balloons.

---

dix-huit [dee-ZEW/EET] adjective **eighteen**

Elle a dix-huit ans.
She is eighteen years old.

---

dix-neuf [deez-NEOHF] adjective **nineteen**

C'est aujourd'hui le dix-neuf septembre.
Today is September 19th.

---

dix-sept [dee-SEHT] adjective **seventeen**

Neuf et huit font dix-sept.
Nine and eight are seventeen.

---

le docteur [duhk-TEUHR] noun, adjective **doctor**

Maman dit: "Tu es malade. Je vais appeler le docteur."
Mother says, "You are sick. I am going to call the doctor."

---

le doigt [DWA] noun, masc. **finger**

Le bébé a dix petits doigts.
The baby has ten little fingers.

---

le dollar [duh-LAR] noun, masc. **dollar**

Voilà un dollar pour toi.
Here is a dollar for you.

---

les dominos [doh-mee-NOH] noun, masc., pl. **dominoes**

Mon cousin joue bien aux dominos.
My cousin plays dominoes well.

---

dommage [doh-MAHZH] noun, masc. **pity**
C'est dommage! [seh-doh-MAHZH] interjection **That's too bad!**

Vous n'aimez pas le chocolat? C'est dommage!
You don't like chocolate? That's too bad!

---

donner [duh-NAY] verb **to give**

je donne nous donnons
tu donnes vous donnez
il, elle donne ils, elles donnent

Donne-moi l'appareil, s'il te plaît.
Please give me the camera.

---

dormir [duhr-MEER] verb **to sleep**

je dors nous dormons
tu dors vous dormez
il, elle dort ils, elles dorment

Tu dors? Je voudrais te parler.
Are you sleeping? I would like to talk to you.

---

le dos [DOH] noun, masc. **back**

C'est Robert? Je ne sais pas. Je vois seulement son dos.
Is it Robert? I don't know. I see only his back.

---

doucement [doos-MAHN] adverb **softly, gently**

Marche doucement. Maman a mal à la tête.
Walk softly. Mother has a headache.

---

la douche [DOOSH] noun, fem. **shower**

Je prends une douche chaque matin.
I take a shower every morning.

---

doux [DOO] adjective, masc. **sweet, soft, gentle**
douce [DOOS] fem.

Ce manteau est très doux.
This coat is very soft.

---

la douzaine [doo-ZEHN] noun, fem. **dozen**

Elle achète une douzaine de poires.
She is buying a dozen pears.

---

douze [DOOZ] adjective — **twelve**

Il y a douze bananes dans une douzaine.
There are twelve bananas in a dozen.

---

le drapeau [dra-POH] noun, masc. — **flag**
les drapeaux pl.

Voilà deux drapeaux dans la salle de classe.
There are two flags in the classroom.

---

droit [DRWA] adjective, masc. — **right**
droite [DRWAT] fem.
la main droite [main-DRWAT] noun, fem. — **right hand**

Je lève la main droite.
I raise my right hand.

à droite [a-DRWAT] preposition — **to the right**

L'arbre est à droite de la maison.
The tree is to the right of the house.

---

drôle [DROHL] adjective — **funny; odd**

Les marionnettes sont drôles.
The marionettes are funny.

---

dur [DEWR] adjective, masc. — **hard**
dure fem.

Cette pomme est trop dure.
This apple is too hard.

E

l'eau [OH] noun, fem. — **water**
les eaux pl.

Il y a de l'eau dans la piscine.
There is water in the swimming pool.

échecs [ay-SHEHK] noun, masc., pl. **chess**
jouer aux échecs **to play chess** (See **jouer**)

---

l'éclair [ay-KLEHR] noun, masc. **lightning**

J'ai peur de l'éclair.
I am afraid of lightning.

---

l'école [ay-KUHL] noun, fem. **school**

Le jeudi nous n'allons pas à l'école.
We don't go to school on Thursdays.

écouter [ay-koo-TAY] verb **to listen**

j'écoute	nous écoutons
tu écoutes	vous écoutez
il, elle écoute	ils, elles écoutent

Le garçon écoute la radio.
The boy is listening to the radio.

écrire [ay-KREER] verb **to write**

j'écris	nous écrivons
tu écris	vous écrivez
il, elle écrit	ils, elles écrivent

La maîtresse dit: "Écrivez la date au tableau noir."
The teacher says, "Write the date on the blackboard."

la machine à écrire **typewriter** (See **machine**)

---

effacer [eh-fa-SAY] verb **to erase**

j'efface	nous effaçons
tu effaces	vous effacez
il, elle efface	ils, elles effacent

Oh, une faute! Je dois effacer ce mot.
Oh, a mistake! I have to erase this word.

---

effrayant [eh-fray-YAHN] adjective, masc. **frightening**
effrayante [eh-fray-YAHNT] fem.

Le tonnerre est effrayant.
Thunder is frightening.

égal [ay-GAL] adjective, masc. **equal, all the same**
égale fem.
égaux [ay-GOH] pl.

Tu veux la glace ou le gâteau?
Oh, cela m'est égal.
Do you want ice cream or cake?
Oh, it doesn't make any difference.
(Oh, it's all the same to me.)

---

l'église [ay-GLEEZ] noun, fem. **church**

Il y a une grande église dans la ville.
There is a big church in the city.

électrique [ay-lehk-TREEK] adjective, masc. or fem. **electric**

Regarde! On vend des machines à écrire électriques.
Look! They sell electric typewriters.

---

l'éléphant [ay-lay-FAHN] noun, masc. **elephant**

Il y a un grand éléphant dans le jardin zoologique.
There is a big elephant in the zoo.

---

l'élève [ay-LEV] noun, masc. or fem. **pupil**
les élèves [leh-zay-LEV] pl.

Les élèves sont dans la salle de classe.
The pupils are in the classroom.

---

elle [EHL] pronoun, fem. **she, her, it**
elles pl. **they**

Elles sont assises.
They are seated.

Donnez le crayon à elle, pas à moi.
Give the pencil to her, not to me.

Où est ma chaussure? Elle est sous le lit.
Where is my shoe? It's under the bed.

---

l'émission [ay-mee-syoṅ] noun, fem. **broadcast**

Aimez-vous l'émission de Paris?
Do you like the broadcast from Paris?

---

l'emplettes [ahṅ-pleht] noun, fem. **purchase**
faire des emplettes **to go shopping** (See **faire**)

---

employer [ahṅ-plwa-YAY] verb **to use**

j'emploie	nous employons
tu emploies	vous employez
il, elle emploie	ils, elles emploient

Elle emploie les ciseaux pour couper le ruban.
She uses scissors to cut the ribbon.

---

emprunter [ahṅ-pruhṅ-TAY] verb **to borrow**

j'emprunte	nous empruntons
tu empruntes	vous empruntez
il, elle emprunte	ils, elles empruntent

Je peux emprunter la gomme?
May I borrow the eraser?

---

en [AHṄ] preposition **in, into**

En juillet nous allons aux Etats-Unis.
In July we are going to the United States.

---

encore [ahn-KUHR] adverb **again; more; still**

Lisez la lettre encore une fois.
Read the letter once again.

Tu désires encore du pain?
Do you want more bread?

Es-tu encore à la maison?
Are you still at home?

---

l'enfant [ahn-FAHN] noun, masc. or fem. **child**
les enfants [leh-zahn-FAHN] pl. **children**

Les enfants sont au lit.
The children are in bed.

---

enfin [ahn-FAIN] adverb **finally**

Il fait beau, enfin!
It is good weather, finally!

---

ennuyé [ahn-newee-YAY] adjective, masc. **annoyed**
ennuyée fem.

Maman est ennuyée quand je fais trop de bruit.
Mother is annoyed when I make too much noise.

---

enseigner [ahn-seh-NYAY] verb **to teach**

j'enseigne	nous enseignons
tu enseignes	vous enseignez
il, elle enseigne	ils, elles enseignent

Qui enseigne la musique dans cette classe?
Who teaches music to this class?

---

ensemble [ahn-SAHNBL] adverb **together**

Nous allons à l'épicerie ensemble.
We are going to the grocery store together.

---

ensuite [ahn-SEW/EET] adverb **then**

Je lis le livre; ensuite je rends le livre à la bibliothèque.
I read the book; then I return the book to the library.

---

entendre [ahn-TAHNDR] verb **to hear**

j'entends	nous entendons
tu entends	vous entendez
il, elle entend	ils, elles entendent

J'entends le téléphone qui sonne.
I hear the telephone ringing.

bien entendu **of course** (See **bien**)

---

entier [ahn-TYAY] adjective, masc. **whole**
entière [ahn-TYEHR] fem.

Bien sûr je voudrais manger le gâteau entier!
Of course I would like to eat the whole cake!

---

entre [AHNTR] preposition **between**

Quel est le numéro entre quatorze et seize?
What is the number between fourteen and sixteen?

---

l'entrée [ahn-TRAY] noun, fem. **entrance, admission**

Il faut payer à l'entrée.
One must pay at the entrance.

---

entrer [ahn-TRAY] verb **to enter, to come into, to go into**

j'entre	nous entrons
tu entres	vous entrez
il, elle entre	ils, elles entrent

Ils entrent dans la maison.
They go into the house.

défense d'entrer **No admittance** (See **défense de . . .**)

---

l'enveloppe [ahn-VLUHP] noun, fem. **envelope**

Le facteur me donne une enveloppe.
The mailman gives me an envelope.

---

l'envie [ahn-VEE] noun, fem. **desire, longing**
avoir envie de [a-vwahr-ahn-VEE-de] **to have the wish to**
idiomatic expression

Il a envie de lire.
He feels like reading.

---

envoyer [ahn-vwa-YAY] verb **to send**

j'envoie	nous envoyons
tu envoies	vous envoyez
il, elle envoie	ils, elles envoient

Mon oncle va m'envoyer un cadeau.
My uncle is going to send me a present.

épais [ay-PEH] adjective, masc. **thick**
épaisse [ay-PEHS] fem.

La peau du citron est très épaisse.
The lemon's skin is very thick.

---

l'épaule [ay-POHL] noun, fem. **shoulder**

La balle frappe l'épaule de Claude.
The ball hits Claude's shoulder.

---

l'épicerie [ay-pee-SREE] noun, fem. **grocery store**

On va à l'épicerie pour acheter du sucre.
You go to the grocery store to buy sugar.

---

l'épicier [ay-pee-SYAY] noun, masc. **grocer**

L'epicier vend du sel et de la confiture.
The grocer sells salt and jam.

---

les épinards [ay-pee-NAR] noun, masc., pl. **spinach**

Les épinards sont verts.
Spinach is green.

---

l'épingle [ay-PAIN̸GL] noun, fem. **pin**

Quelle jolie épingle en forme de fleurs!
What a pretty flower pin!

épouser [ay-poo-ZAY] verb **to marry**

j'épouse	nous épousons
tu épouses	vous épousez
il, elle épouse	ils, elles épousent

Le prince épouse la princesse.
The prince marries the princess.

---

l'équipe [ay-KEEP] noun, fem. **team**

Nous sommes tous membres de la même équipe.
We are all members of the same team.

---

l'escalier [ehs-ka-LYAY] noun, masc. **staircase**

J'aime sauter la dernière marche de l'escalier.
I like to jump over the last step of the staircase.

---

l'espace [ehs-PAS] noun, masc. **space**

Les astronautes voyagent dans l'espace.
The astronauts travel in space.

---

espérer [ehs-pay-RAY] verb **to hope**

j'espère	nous espérons
tu espères	vous espérez
il, elle espère	ils, elles espèrent

J'espère avoir une bonne note en histoire.
I hope to have a good mark in history.

---

essayer [eh-say-YAY] verb **to try**

j'essaye	nous essayons
tu essayes	vous essayez
il, elle essaye	ils, elles essayent

Elle essaye de porter le paquet lourd.
She tries to carry the heavy package.

---

l'essence [eh-SAHNS] noun, fem. **gasoline**

Papa dit: "Nous n'avons pas assez d'essence."
Daddy says, "We don't have enough gasoline."

---

l'est [EHST] noun, masc. **east**

Quand je vais de Paris à Strasbourg, je vais vers l'est.
When I go from Paris to Strasbourg, I go toward the east.

---

est-ce que [ehs-KUH] **(one form of asking a question)**

Est-ce que tu viens avec moi?
(or: Tu viens avec moi?)
(or: Viens-tu avec moi?)
Are you coming with me?

---

et [AY] conjunction **and**

André et son ami jouent ensemble.
Andrew and his friend are playing together.

---

l'étage [ay-TAZH] noun, masc. **floor (of a building)**

À quel étage est votre appartement?
On what floor is your apartment?

---

l'état [ay-TA] noun, masc. **state**

De quel état venez-vous?
From which state do you come?

---

l'été [ay-TAY] noun, masc. **summer**

Préférez-vous l'été ou l'hiver?
Do you prefer summer or winter?

éteindre [ay-TAIN̸DR] verb **to turn off**

j'éteins	nous éteignons
tu éteins	vous éteignez
il, elle éteint	ils, elles éteignent

J'éteins la lumière.
I turn off the light.

éternuer [ay-tehr-n~~ew~~/-AY] verb **to sneeze**

j'éternue	nous éternuons
tu éternues	vous éternuez
il, elle éternue	ils, elles éternuent

Tu éternues. Tu as un rhume?
You're sneezing. Do you have a cold?

---

l'étoile [ay-TWAL] noun, fem. **star**

Combien d'étoiles y a-t-il dans le ciel?
How many stars are there in the sky?

étonnant [ay-tuh-NAHN̸] adjective, masc. **surprising**
étonnante [ay-tuh-NAHN̸T] fem.

Il est étonnant de recevoir une lettre d'une actrice.
It is surprising to receive a letter from an actress.

étranger [ay-trahn-ZHAY] noun, adjective, masc. **stranger, foreign**
étrangère [ay-trahn-ZHEHR] fem.

Maman dit: "Ne parlez pas aux étrangers."
Mother says, "Don't speak to strangers."

C'est un livre étranger.
It is a foreign book.

être [EHTR] verb **to be**

je suis	nous sommes
tu es	vous êtes
il, elle est	ils, elles sont

Papa, où sommes-nous?
Dad, where are we?

étroit [ay-TRWA] adjective, masc. **narrow, tight**
étroite [ay-TRWAT] fem.

Le tiroir est trop étroit pour les papiers.
The drawer is too narrow for the papers.

---

l'étudiant [ay-tew-DYAHN] noun, masc. **student**
l'étudiante [ay-tew-DYAHNT] fem.

Mon cousin est étudiant à l'université.
My cousin is a student at the university.

étudier [ay-tew-DYAY] verb **to study**

j'étudie	nous étudions
tu étudies	vous étudiez
il, elle étudie	ils, elles étudient

Je dois étudier ce soir. J'ai un examen demain.
I have to study this evening. I have an examination tomorrow.

---

eux [EOH] pronoun, masc., pl. **them**

Je vais à l'école avec eux.
I go to school with them.

---

l'examen [eh-gza-MAIN] noun, masc. **examination, test**

Tu as une bonne note à l'examen?
Do you have a good mark on the examination?

---

excellent [eh-kseh-LAHN] adjective, masc. **excellent**
excellente [eh-kseh-LAHNT] fem.

Le professeur dit: "Ce travail est excellent."
The teacher says, "This work is excellent."

---

excusez-moi [eh-kskew-zay-MWA] **excuse me**
idiomatic expression

Excusez-moi. Voici vos paquets.
Excuse me. Here are your packages.

---

expliquer [eh-ksplee-KAY] verb **to explain**

j'explique	nous expliquons
tu expliques	vous expliquez
il, elle explique	ils, elles expliquent

Jeanne, tu peux m'expliquer cette phrase?
Joan, can you explain this sentence to me?

---

exprès [eh-KSPREH] adverb **on purpose, intentionally**

Mon frère me taquine exprès.
My brother teases me on purpose.

---

extraordinaire **unusual; wonderful;**
[eh-kstra-uhr-dee-NEHR] adjective **extraordinary**

Nous allons faire un voyage extraordinaire en fusée.
We are going to take an unusual trip in a rocket ship.

F

fâché [fah-SHAY] adjective, masc. **angry, displeased**
fâchée fem.

Quand je taquine ma soeur, Maman est fâchée.
When I tease my sister, Mom is angry.

---

facile [fa-SEEL] adjective **easy**

Il est facile de faire mes devoirs.
It is easy to do my homework.

---

le facteur [fak-TUHR] noun, masc. **mail carrier, postman**

Le facteur apporte des lettres et des paquets.
The mail carrier brings letters and packages.

---

faible [FEHBL] adjective **weak**

Le pauvre garçon est faible parce qu'il est malade.
The poor boy is weak because he is sick.

---

la faim [FAIN] noun, fem. **hunger**
avoir faim [a-vwar-FAIN] **to be hungry**
idiomatic expression

Avez-vous faim? Oui, j'ai faim.
Are you hungry? Yes, I'm hungry. (See **avoir**)

---

faire [FEHR] verb **to make; to do**

je fais	nous faisons
tu fais	vous faites
il, elle fait	ils, elles font

Il fait ses devoirs.
He does his homework.

faire des emplettes idiomatic expression **to go shopping**

Maman fait des emplettes.
Mom goes shopping.

faire beau idiomatic expression **to be nice weather**

Il fait beau aujourd'hui, n'est-ce pas?
It's nice weather today, isn't it?

faire du vent idiomatic expression **to be windy**

Il fait du vent aujourd'hui.
It's windy today.

faire un voyage idiomatic expression **to take a trip**

Je vais faire un voyage dans deux semaines.
I am going to take a trip in two weeks.

faire une promenade idiomatic expression **to take a walk**

Le soir Papa fait une promenade avec Maman.
In the evening Dad and Mom take a walk.

faire attention idiomatic expression **to pay attention**

Quand le professeur dit "Faites attention," je ferme le livre.
When the teacher says "Pay attention," I close the book.

faire la cuisine idiomatic expression **to cook**

Qui fait la cuisine?
Who is cooking?

(l'addition)

Cinq et huit font treize.
Five and eight are thirteen.

faire un pique-nique (See **pique-nique**)

---

la famille [fa-MEEY] noun, fem. **family**

Combien de personnes y a-t-il dans votre famille?
How many people are there in your family?

le nom de famille **family name, surname**
[nohn-de-fa-MEEY] noun, masc.

---

fatigué [fa-tee-GAY] adjective, masc. **tired**
fatiguée fem.

Après deux heures de travail dans le jardin, je suis fatigué.
After two hours of work in the garden, I am tired.

---

faut, il faut [FOH] idiomatic expression **it is necessary; one must; you have to**

Il faut aller à l'école.
It is necessary to go to school.
(We have to go to school.)
(Everyone has to go to school.)
(You have to go to school.)

---

la faute [FOHT] noun, fem. **error, mistake**

Je fais des fautes quand j'écris en français.
I make mistakes when I write in French.

---

le fauteuil [foh-TUHY] noun, masc. **armchair**

J'aime m'asseoir dans le fauteuil.
I like to sit in the armchair.

---

faux [FOH] adjective, masc. **false**
fausse [FOHS] fem.

Il a six ans, vrai ou faux?
He is six years old, true or false?

---

favori [fa-voh-REE] adjective, masc. **favorite**
favorite [fa-voh-REET] fem.

Quel est ton jouet favori?
What is your favorite toy?

l'animal favori [a-nee-mal-fa-voh-REE] noun, masc. **pet**

Mon chien est mon animal favori.
My dog is my pet.

---

la fée [FAY] noun, fem. **fairy**
le conte de fées [kohn̸t-dé̸-FAY] noun, masc. **fairy tale**

Lisez-moi ce conte de fées.
Read this fairy tale to me.

---

la femme [FAM] noun, fem. **woman, wife**

Ces deux femmes vont faire des emplettes.
These two women are going shopping.

---

la fenêtre [fé̸-NEHTR] noun, fem. **window**

Le chien aime regarder par la fenêtre.
The dog likes to look out the window.

---

le fer [FEHR] noun, masc. **iron; iron (metal)**

Le fer ne marche pas. Je ne peux pas repasser cette robe.
The iron is not working. I can't iron this dress.

en fer [ahn̸-FEHR] **made of iron**

Le fourneau est en fer.
The stove is made of iron.

---

la ferme [FEHRM] noun, fem. **farm**

Il y a des vaches et des chevaux à la ferme.
There are cows and horses on the farm.

---

fermer [fehr-MAY] verb **to close**

je ferme	nous fermons
tu fermes	vous fermez
il, elle ferme	ils, elles ferment

Fermez la fenêtre, s'il vous plaît.
Please close the window.

---

la fermier [fehr-MYAY] noun, masc. **farmer**

Mon grand-père est fermier.
My grandfather is a farmer.

---

féroce [fay-RUHS] adjective **ferocious, fierce, wild**

Qui a peur d'un tigre féroce?
Who is afraid of a ferocious tiger?

---

la fête [FEHT] noun, fem. **holiday; birthday; party**

Le jour de la fête est le dix-huit juillet?
The party is July 18th?

Bonne fête [buhn-FEHT] interjection **Happy birthday**

---

le feu [FEOH] noun, masc. **fire; light (traffic)**

Le feu est chaud.
The fire is hot.

On traverse la rue quand on voit le feu vert.
You cross the street when you see the green light.

---

la feuille [FUHY] noun, fem. **leaf, sheet of paper**

Les feuilles sont vertes en été.
The leaves are green in summer.

Donne-moi une feuille de papier, s'il te plaît.
Give me a sheet of paper, please.

---

février [fay-VRYAY] noun, masc. **February**

Combien de jours y a-t-il en février?
How many days are there in February?

---

la ficelle [fee-SEHL] noun, fem. **string**

Je cherche une ficelle pour mon cerf-volant.
I am looking for a string for my kite.

---

la fièvre [FYEHVR] noun, fem. **fever**

Je dois rester au lit. J'ai de la fièvre.
I have to stay in bed. I have a fever.

---

la figure [fee-GEWR] noun, fem. **face**

Elle se lave la figure.
She is washing her face.

---

la fille [FEEY] noun, fem. **girl; daughter**

La petite fille joue avec sa poupée.
The little girl plays with her doll.

Je vous présente ma fille, Aimée.
I should like to introduce my daughter, Amy.

---

le film [FEELM] noun, masc. **film, movie**

On joue un bon film au cinéma?
Are they playing a good film at the movies?

---

le fils [FEES] noun, masc. **son**

Je vous présente mon fils, Georges.
I should like to introduce my son, George.

---

la fin [FAIN] noun, fem. **end**

C'est la fin de la leçon.
It is the end of the lesson.

---

finir [fee-NEER] verb **to finish**

je finis nous finissons
tu finis vous finissez
il, elle finit ils, elles finissent

Je vais finir mon travail avant de sortir.
I am going to finish my work before going out.

---

la fleur [FLUHR] noun, fem. **flower**

Nous avons beaucoup de fleurs dans le jardin.
We have many flowers in the garden.

---

le foin [FWAIN] noun, masc. **hay**

Le fermier donne du foin aux chevaux.
The farmer gives hay to the horses.

---

la foire [FWAR] noun, fem. **fair**

Nous allons à la foire pour nous amuser.
We are going to the fair to have a good time.

---

la fois [FWA] noun, fem. **time**

On frappe trois fois à la porte.
They knock three times at the door.

encore une fois [ahn-kuh-rewn-FWA] **again**
idiomatic expression

Répétez encore une fois.
Repeat once again.

---

foncé [fohn-SAY] adjective, masc. **dark**
foncée fem.

Elle porte une robe bleu foncé.
She is wearing a dark blue dress.

---

le football [fuht-BUHL] noun, masc. **soccer**

Savez-vous jouer au football?
Do you know how to play soccer?

---

la forêt [fuh-REH] noun, fem. **forest, woods**

Il y a cent arbres dans la forêt!
There are a hundred trees in the forest!

---

former [fuhr-MAY] verb **to form, to make**

je forme	nous formons
tu formes	vous formez
il, elle forme	ils, elles forment

Je forme une balle avec la neige.
I make a snowball with the snow.

en forme de (d') [ahn̸-fuhrm-de̸] idiomatic expression **in the form of, shaped like**

Le petit gâteau est en forme d'étoile.
The cookie is in the form of a star.

---

formidable [fuhr-mee-DABL] interjection **Great!, Marvelous!, Wonderful!**

Tu vas au cirque? Formidable!
You are going to the circus? Great!

---

fort [FUHR] adjective, masc. **strong**
forte [FUHRT] fem.

Mon père est très fort.
My father is very strong.

---

fort [FUHR] adverb **loudly**

Il joue trop fort du tambour.
He plays the drum too loudly.

---

fou [FOO] adjective, masc. **mad, crazy**
folle [FUHL] fem.

Le chien est fou.
The dog is mad.

---

la fourchette [foor-SHEHT] noun, fem. **fork**

Je mange la viande avec une fourchette.
I eat meat with a fork.

---

la fourmi [foor-MEE] noun, fem. **ant**

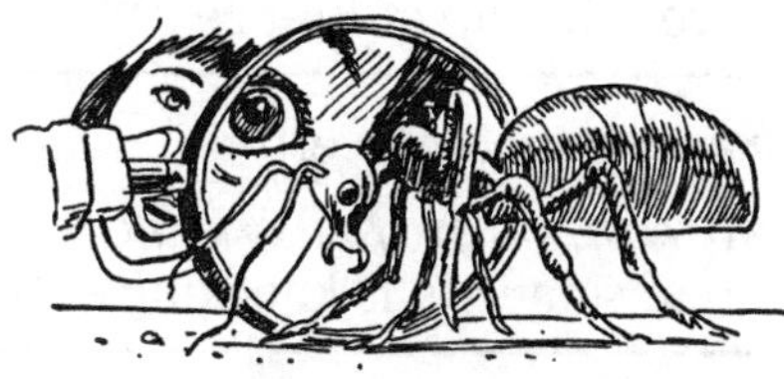

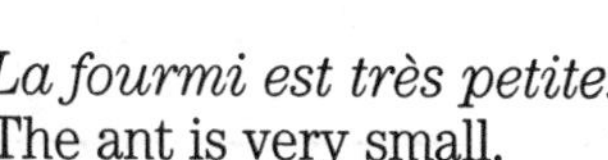

La fourmi est très petite.
The ant is very small.

---

le fourneau [foor-NOH] noun, masc. **stove**

Attention! Le fourneau est chaud.
Careful! The stove is hot.

---

frais [FREH] adjective, masc. **cool; fresh**
fraîche [FREHSH] fem.

Il fait frais à la plage.
It is cool at the beach.

---

la fraise [FREHZ] noun, fem. **strawberry**

Le fraises sont rouges.
Strawberries are red.

---

le franc [FRAHN̸] noun, masc. **franc (French monetary unit)**

Voici un billet de cinq francs.
Here is a five-franc note.

---

français [frahn̸-SEH] adjective, masc. **French**
française [frahn̸-SEHZ] fem.

Je lis un livre français.
I am reading a French book.

---

la France [FRAHN̸S] noun, fem. **France**

Voici une carte de la France.
Here is a map of France.

---

frapper [fra-PAY] verb **to hit; to knock**

Maman, on frappe à la porte.
Mom, someone is knocking at the door.

---

le frère [FREHR] noun, masc. **brother**

Je suis petit, mais mon frère est grand.
I am little, but my brother is big.

---

le froid [FRWAH] noun, masc. **cold**

Quand il fait froid en hiver, j'ai froid.
When it is cold in winter, I am cold.

il fait froid **it is cold** (See **faire**)
avoir froid **to be cold** (See **avoir**)

---

le fromage [fruh-MAHZH] noun, masc. **cheese**

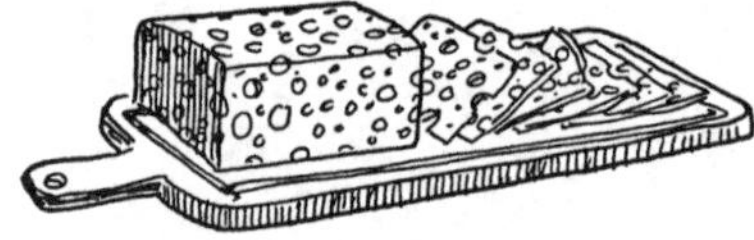

Ma soeur prend du fromage comme dessert.
My sister has cheese for dessert.

---

les fruits [FR~~EW~~/EE] noun, masc. **fruit**

Voici des fruits. Préférez-vous une poire ou une banane?
Here is some fruit. Do you prefer a pear or a banana?

---

fumer [f~~ew~~-MAY] verb **to smoke**

je fume	nous fumons
tu fumes	vous fumez
il, elle fume	ils, elles fument

Papa dit qu'il est dangereux de fumer.
Dad says that it is dangerous to smoke.

défense de fumer **no smoking**
(See **défense...**)

la fumée [f~~ew~~-MAY] noun, fem. **smoke**

---

la fusée [f~~ew~~-ZAY] noun, fem. **spaceship**

On va à la lune en fusée.
They are going to the moon in a spaceship.

---

le fusil [f~~ew~~-ZEE] noun, masc. **gun**

Le chasseur porte un fusil.
The hunter carries a gun.

G

gagner [ga-NAY] verb **to earn; to win**

je gagne	nous gagnons
tu gagnes	vous gagnez
il, elle gagne	ils, elles gagnent

C'est notre équipe qui gagne!
Our team wins!

le gagnant [ga-NAHN] noun, masc. **winner**
la gagnante [ga-NAHNT] fem.

Qui est le gagnant?
Who is the winner?

---

gai [GAY] adjective, masc. **gay, cheerful**
gaie fem.

Ma soeur est toujours gaie.
My sister is always cheerful.

---

le gant [GAHN] noun, masc. **glove**

Elle porte des gants blancs.
She is wearing white gloves.

---

le garage [ga-RAZH] noun, masc. **garage**

Où est la voiture? Elle n'est pas dans le garage.
Where is the car? It isn't in the garage.

---

le garçon [gar-SOHN] noun, masc. **boy; waiter**

Le garçon joue avec sa soeur.
The boy is playing with his sister.

---

garder [gar-DAY] verb **to guard; to keep**

je garde	nous gardons
tu gardes	vous gardez
il, elle garde	ils, elles gardent

L'agent de police garde la banque.
The policeman is guarding the bank.

---

la gare [GAR] noun, fem. **station**

Le train est en gare.
The train is in the station.

---

le gâteau [gah-TOH] noun, masc. **cake**
le petit gâteau [ptee-gah-TOH] noun, masc. **cookie**

Voici un petit gâteau pour Thérèse et un morceau de gâteau pour Guillaume.
Here is a cookie for Theresa and a piece of cake for William.

---

gauche [GOHSH] adjective **left**
la main gauche [maiɴ-GOHSH] noun, fem. **left hand**

Je lève la main gauche.
I raise my left hand.

à gauche [a-GOHSH] idiomatic expression **to the left**

L'arbre est à gauche de la maison.
The tree is to the left of the house.

---

le gaz [GAZ] noun, masc. **gas**

Tu as une cuisinière à gaz? Nous avons un fourneau électrique!
You have a gas stove? We have an electric stove!

---

le géant [zhay-AHɴ] noun, masc. **giant**

Lis-moi le conte "Jacques et le géant."
Read me the story of "Jack and the Giant."

---

le genou [ZHNOO] noun, masc. **knee**
les genoux pl.

Tu as mal au genou? C'est triste.
You have a sore knee? That's too bad!

---

les gens [ZHAHɴ] noun, masc., pl. **people**

Beaucoup de gens sont dans le magasin.
Many people are in the store.

---

gentil [zhahɴ-TEE] adjective, masc. **gentle, kind, nice**
gentille [zhahɴ-TEEY] fem.

La maîtresse est gentille. Elle ne gronde pas.
The teacher is nice. She doesn't scold.

---

la glace [GLAS] noun, fem. **ice cream; ice; mirror**

Tu aimes la glace à la vanille?
Do you like vanilla ice cream?

Allons patiner sur la glace.
Let's go ice skating.

Est-ce que vous avez une glace?
Do you have a mirror?

le patin à glace **ice skate** (See **patin**)

---

glisser [glee-SAY] verb **to slide; to slip**

je glisse	nous glissons
tu glisses	vous glissez
il, elle glisse	ils, elles glissent

Nous glissons sur la glace en hiver.
We slip on the ice in winter.

---

la gomme [GUHM] noun, fem. **eraser**

Je dois effacer cette phrase avec la gomme.
I have to erase this sentence with the eraser.

---

la gorge [GUHRZH] noun, fem. **throat**

La maîtresse dit doucement:
"J'ai mal à la gorge."
The teacher says softly,
"I have a sore throat."

---

le goûter [goo-TAY] noun, masc. **snack**

Bonjour Maman. Tu as un goûter pour nous?
Hello, Mom. Do you have a snack for us?

---

grand [GRAHN] adjective, masc. **big, tall, high,**
grande [GRAHND] fem. **large; great**

Voici un grand arbre et un petit arbre.
Here is a big tree and a little tree.

Madame Curie est une grande savante.
Madame Curie is a great scientist.

---

la grand-mère [grahn̸-MEHR] noun, fem. **grandmother**

Dimanche nous allons chez ma grand-mère.
We are going to my grandmother's house on Sunday.

le grand-père [grahn̸-PEHR] noun, masc. **grandfather**

Mon grand-père aime conduire la voiture.
My grandfather likes to drive the car.

les grands-parents [grahn̸-pa-RAHN̸] noun, masc. and fem., pl. **grandparents**

---

le gratte-ciel [gra-TSYEHL] noun, masc. **skyscraper**

La ville de New York a beaucoup de gratte-ciel.
New York City has many skyscrapers.

---

gratuit [gra-TWEE] adjective, masc. **free**
gratuite [gra-TWEET] fem.

L'entrée est gratuite.
Admission is free.

---

la grenouille [gruh-NOOY] noun, fem. **frog**

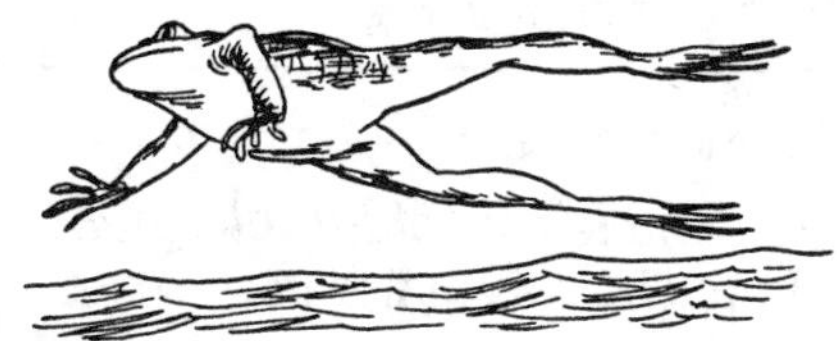

J'essaye d'attraper une grenouille.
I am trying to catch a frog.

---

grimper [grain̸-PAY] verb **to climb**

je grimpe	nous grimpons
tu grimpes	vous grimpez
il, elle grimpe	ils, elles grimpent

Le chat grimpe sur l'arbre.
The cat climbs the tree.

---

gris [GREE] adjective, noun **gray**
grise [GREEZ] fem.

La souris est grise.
The mouse is gray.

---

gronder [grohn-DAY] verb **to scold**

je gronde	nous grondons
tu grondes	vous grondez
il, elle gronde	ils, elles grondent

Il a honte parce que sa mère le gronde.
He is ashamed because his mother is scolding him.

---

gros [GROH] adjective, masc. **big, fat**
grosse [GROHS] fem.

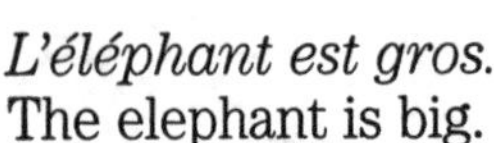

L'éléphant est gros.
The elephant is big.

---

la guerre [GEHR] noun, fem. **war**

Mon oncle est soldat à la guerre.
My uncle is a soldier in the war.

---

la guitare [gee-TAR] noun, fem. **guitar**

Je sais jouer de la guitare.
I know how to play the guitar.

H

s'habiller [sa-bee-YAY] verb **to get dressed, to dress**

je m'habille nous nous habillons
tu t'habilles vous vous habillez
il, elle s'habille ils, elles s'habillent

Je me lève, je m'habille, je vais à l'école.
I get up, I get dressed. I go to school.

---

habiter [a-bee-TAY] verb **to live (dwell)**

j'habite nous habitons
tu habites vous habitez
il, elle habite ils, elles habitent

Où habitez-vous?
Where do you live?

---

haricots [a-ree-KOH] noun, masc., pl. **beans**
les haricots verts [leh-a-ree-koh-VEHR] noun, masc., pl. **string beans**

Nous avons des haricots verts pour le dîner.
We have string beans for dinner.

---

haut [OH] adjective, masc. **high; tall; loud**
haute [OHT] fem.

La Tour Eiffel est très haute.
The Eiffel Tower is very tall.

à haute voix [a-oh-VWA] idiomatic expression **in a loud voice, aloud**

La maîtresse dit: "Parlez à haute voix."
The teacher says, "Speak in a loud voice."

en haut [ahn-OH] adverb **upstairs**

Où es-tu? En haut.
Where are you? Upstairs.

Hélas! [ay-LAHS] interjection **What a pity!**

Hélas! Tu ne peux pas venir avec moi.
What a pity! You can't come with me.

---

l'hélicoptère [lay-lee-kuhp-TEHR] noun, masc. **helicopter**

Qu'est-ce que c'est? Un hélicoptère.
What is it? A helicopter.

---

l'herbe [LEHRB] noun, fem. **grass**

L'herbe est verte.
Grass is green.

---

l'heure [LEUHR] noun, fem. **hour; o'clock, time**

Quelle heure est-il?
What time is it?

C'est l'heure du dîner. Il est sept heures et demie.
It is dinner time. It is seven thirty.
(It is half past seven.)

de bonne heure [dø-buh-NEUHR] adverb **early**

Le soleil se lève de bonne heure.
The sun rises early.

la demi-heure (See **demi**)
tout à l'heure **in a little while** (See **tout**)

---

heureux [uh-REOH] adjective, masc. **happy, glad,**
heureuse [uh-REOHZ] fem. **delighted**

Tout le monde est heureux à une fête.
Everyone is happy at a party.

---

le hibou [lø-ee-BOO] noun, masc. **owl**
hiboux pl.

On entend le hibou pendant la nuit.
You hear the owl during the night.

---

hier [YEHR] adverb **yesterday**

C'est aujourd'hui le dix mai; hier, le neuf mai.
Today is May 10; yesterday (was) May 9.

---

l'histoire [lees-TWAR] noun, fem. **story; history**

Tu aimes l'histoire "Les trois ours"?
Do you like the story of "The Three Bears"?

---

l'hiver [lee-VEHR] noun, masc. **winter**

En hiver il fait froid.
It is cold in winter.

---

l'homme [LUHM] noun, masc. **man**

L'homme vient pour réparer le téléviseur.
The man comes to fix the television set.

---

l'honneur [luh-NUHR] noun, masc. **honor**
en l'honneur de [ahn-luh-NUHR-de] idiomatic expression **in honor of**

Nous dînons au restaurant en l'honneur de ma fille.
We are dining in a restaurant in honor of my daughter.

---

l'honte [LOHNT] noun, fem. **shame**
avoir honte [OHNT] idiomatic expression **to be ashamed**

Il a honte parce qu'il est méchant.
He is ashamed because he is naughty.

---

l'hôpital [loh-pee-TAL] noun, masc. **hospital**

L'infirmière travaille à l'hôpital.
The nurse works at the hospital.

---

l'horloge [luhr-LUHZH] noun, fem. **clock**

L'horloge sonne deux fois. Il est deux heures.
The clock strikes twice. It is two o'clock.

---

l'hôtel [loh-TEHL] noun, masc. **hotel**

Quel est le nom de cet hôtel?
What is the name of this hotel?

---

l'hôtesse [loh-TEHS-de-LEHR] noun, fem. **flight attendant**

L'hôtesse nous sert un bon repas.
The flight attendant serves us a good meal.

---

l'huile [LEW/EEL] noun, fem. **oil**

Maman, tu mets de l'huile dans la salade?
Mother, are you putting oil in the salad?

---

huit [EW/EET] [EW/EE] adjective **eight**

J'ai huit insectes. [EW/EET] (before a vowel)
I have eight insects.

Je vois huit cuillers. [EW/EE] (before a consonant)
I see eight spoons.

---

humide [ew-MEED] adjective **humid, moist, damp**

Mon maillot est humide.
My bathing suit is damp.

I

ici [ee-SEE] adverb **here**

Viens ici, Pierrot.
Come here, Pierrot.

---

l'idée [ee-DAY] noun, fem. **idea**

Quelle bonne idée d'aller nager!
What a good idea it is to go swimming!

---

l'île [EEL] noun, fem. **island**

La Corse est une île française.
Corsica is a French island.

---

il [EEL] pronoun, masc. **he; it**
ils pl. **they**

Ils sont assis. Il est assis.
They are seated. He is seated.

Voici le crayon. Il est jaune.
Here is the pencil. It is yellow.

il y a [eel-YA] **there is, there are**
(See **avoir**)

il n'y a pas de quoi **You're welcome.**
[eel-nee-ya-pa-dé-KWAH] idiomatic expression

---

l'image [ee-MAHZH] noun, fem. **picture**

Il y a beaucoup d'images dans ce livre.
There are many pictures in this book.

---

l'imperméable [ain-pehr-may-ABL] noun, masc. **raincoat**

Il porte son imperméable parce qu'il pleut.
He is wearing his raincoat because it is raining.

---

important [ain-puhr-TAHN] adjective **important**

Il est important de manger des légumes.
It is important to eat vegetables.

---

importer [ain̸-puhr-TAY] verb **to be of importance**
N'importe! [nain̸-PUHRT] **No matter!—Never mind**

Le train n'est pas en gare? N'importe. Il vient bientôt.
The train is not at the station? Never mind! It will come soon.

---

impossible [ain̸-puh-SEEBL] adjective **impossible**

Il est impossible de rouler ce rocher.
It is impossible to roll this rock.

---

indiquer [ain̸-dee-KAY] verb **to point to, to indicate**

j'indique	nous indiquons
tu indiques	vous indiquez
il, elle indique	ils, elles indiquent

L'agent de police indique qu'il faut aller par cette route.
The policeman indicates that we must go by this road.

---

l'infirmière [ain̸-feer-MYEHR] noun, fem. **nurse**

Ma voisine est infirmière.
My neighbor is a nurse.

---

l'ingénieur [ain̸-zhay-NYUHR] noun, masc. **engineer**

Je voudrais devenir ingénieur.
I would like to become an engineer.

---

l'insecte [ain̸-SEHKT] noun, masc. **insect**

Je déteste les insectes!
I hate insects!

---

intelligent [ain̸-teh-lee-ZHAHN̸] **intelligent**
adjective, masc.
intelligente [ain̸-teh-lee-ZHAHN̸T] fem.

Le professeur dit: "Quelle classe intelligente!"
The teacher says, "What an intelligent class!"

---

intéressant [ain̸-tay-reh-SAHN̸] **interesting**
adjective, masc.
intéressante [ain̸-tay-reh-SAHN̸T] fem.

Tu trouves que le film est intéressant?
Do you think the film is interesting?

---

inviter [ain̸-vee-TAY] verb **to invite**

j'invite	nous invitons
tu invites	vous invitez
il, elle invite	ils, elles invitent

Ma tante m'invite chez elle.
My aunt invites me to her house.

J

jamais [zha-MEH] adverb **never**

Je ne veux jamis jouer avec toi!
I never want to play with you!

---

la jambe [ZHAHN̸B] noun, fem. **leg**

L'homme a deux jambes; l'animal a quatre pattes.
Man has two legs; animals have four paws.

---

le jambon [zhahn̸-BOHN̸] noun, masc. **ham**

Vous prenez du jambon dans votre sandwich?
Will you have some ham in your sandwich?

---

janvier [zhahn-VYAY] noun, masc. **January**

Le six janvier est un jour de fête en France.
January sixth is a holiday in France.

---

le jardin [zhar-DAIN] noun, masc. **garden**

Le jardin est plein de fleurs au mois de juin.
The garden is full of flowers in June.

le jardin zoologique **zoo**
[zhar-dain-zuh-uh-luh-ZHEEK] noun, masc.

Les animaux féroces sont au jardin zoologique.
Ferocious animals are at the zoo.

---

jaune [ZHOHN] adjective **yellow**

Le maïs est jaune.
Corn is yellow.

---

je [je] pronoun **I**

Je parle à mes amis.
I am speaking to my friends.

---

jeter [je-TAY] verb **to throw**

je jette	nous jetons
tu jettes	vous jetez
il, elle jette	ils, elles jettent

Il jette une pierre dans l'eau.
He throws a stone into the water.

---

le jeu [ZHEOH] noun, masc. **game**
les jeux pl. **games**

Quel jeu préfères-tu?
Which game do you prefer?

---

jeudi [zheoh-DEE] noun, masc. **Thursday**

Jeudi est mon anniversaire.
My birthday is Thursday.

---

jeune [ZHEUHN] adjective **young**

Toujours on me dit: "Tu es trop jeune!"
They always say to me, "You're too young!"

---

je vous en prie [zhe-voo-zahn-PREE] idiomatic expression **you're welcome**

Merci, mademoiselle. Je vous en prie, monsieur.
Thank you, miss. You're welcome, sir.

---

joli [zhuh-LEE] adjective, masc. **pretty, good-looking**
jolie fem.

Quel joli chandail! Il est neuf?
What a pretty sweater! Is it new?

---

jouer [zhoo-AY] verb **to play**

je joue	nous jouons
tu joues	vous jouez
il, elle joue	ils, elles jouent

Jouons à la balle.
Let's play ball.

Laure joue du piano.
Laura plays the piano.

jouer aux dames [zhoo-ay-oh-DAM] idiomatic expression **to play checkers**

Mon ami et moi, nous jouons aux dames.
My friend and I play checkers.

jouer aux échecs [zhoo-ay-oh-zay-SHEHK] idiomatic expression **to play chess**

Mon père et mon oncle jouent aux échec.
My father and my uncle play chess.

---

le jouet [zhoo-AY] noun, masc. **toy**

Quelle sorte de jouets as-tu?
What kind of toys do you have?

---

le jour [ZHOOR] noun, masc. **day**

Quel jour de la semaine est-ce?
What day of the week is it?

un jour de congé [zhoor-de̸-kohn̸-ZHAY] noun, masc. **a day off**

Le jeudi est un jour de congé pour les élèves français.
Thursday is a day off for French students.

le Jour de l'An [zhoor-de̸-LAHN̸] noun, masc. **New Year's Day**

Le premier janvier est le Jour de l'An.
January 1st is New Year's Day.

tous le jours [too-leh-ZHOOR] adverb **every day**

Je lis tous les jours.
I read every day.

---

le journal [zhoor-NAL] noun, masc. **newspaper**
les journaux [zhoor-NOH] pl.

Après le dîner mon oncle lit le journal.
After dinner my uncle reads the newspaper.

---

la journée [zhoor-NAY] noun, fem. **day**

Je vais passer la journée chez ma cousine.
I am going to spend the day at my cousin's house.

---

juillet [zhew̸ee-YAY] noun, masc. **July**

Le quatorze juillet est la fête nationale française.
July 14th is the French national holiday.

---

juin [ZHWAI~~N~~] noun, masc. **June**

Combien de jours y a-t-il en juin?
How many days are there in June?

---

la jupe [ZH~~EW~~P] noun, fem. **skirt**

Je ne peux pas choisir. Quelle jupe préfères-tu?
I can't choose. Which skirt do you prefer?

---

le jus [ZH~~EW~~] noun, masc. **juice**
le jus d'orange [zh~~ew~~-duh-RAH~~N~~ZH] noun, masc. **orange juice**

J'aime le jus d'orange.
I like orange juice.

---

jusqu'à [zh~~ew~~-SKA] preposition **until**

Nous sommes à l'école jusqu'à trois heures.
We are in school until three o'clock.

---

juste [ZH~~EW~~ST] adjective **fair; correct**

Mais c'est mon tour. Ce n'est pas juste!
But it's my turn. It isn't fair!

K

le kangourou [kah~~n~~-goo-ROO] noun, masc. **kangaroo**

Le kangourou est un animal bizarre.
The kangaroo is a strange animal.

---

le kilomètre [kee-loh-MEHTR] noun, masc. **kilometer**

J'habite à cinq kilomètres de l'école.
I live five kilometers from the school.

L

l' adverb **the** (See **le**)
l' **it; him** (See **le**)
la **the** (See **le**)
la **it; her** (See **le**)
là [LA] **there**

---

là-bas [la-BA] adverb **down there; over there**

Tu vois ton frère qui arrive, là-bas?
Do you see your brother coming, down there?

---

le lac [LAK] noun, masc. **lake**

Je vais à la pêche au bord du lac.
I go fishing at the lake shore.

---

laid [LEH] adjective, masc. **ugly**
laide [LEHD] fem.

Je n'aime pas ce chapeau; il est laid.
I don't like this hat; it's ugly.

---

la laine [LEHN] noun, fem. **wool**
en laine [ahn̸-LEHN] **made of wool, woolen**

Mon manteau est en laine.
My coat is made of wool.

---

laisser [leh-SAY] verb **to leave; to let; to permit**

je laisse	nous laissons
tu laisses	vous laissez
il, elle laisse	ils, elles laissent

Je laisse souvent mes livres chez Michel.
I often leave my books at Michael's house.

Mon frère me laisse laver la voiture.
My brother lets me wash the car.

---

le lait [LEH] noun, masc. **milk**

Je bois du lait et Papa boit du café au lait.
I drink milk and Dad drinks coffee with milk.

---

la laitue [leh-TEW] noun, fem. **lettuce**

On prépare une salade avec la laitue.
We make a salad with lettuce.

---

la lampe [LAHNP] noun, fem. **lamp**

La lampe est dans le salon.
The lamp is in the living room.

---

lancer [lahn-SAY] verb **to throw**

je lance	nous lançons
tu lances	vous lancez
il, elle lance	ils, elles lancent

Il me lance un oreiller!
He's throwing a pillow at me!

---

la langue [LAHNG] noun, fem. **tongue**

Je me brûle la langue avec la soupe chaude.
I burn my tongue with hot soup.

---

le lapin [la-PAIN] noun, masc. **rabbit**

Le lapin est mignon.
The rabbit is cute.

---

large [LARZH] adjective **broad, wide**

Le boulevard est une rue large.
The boulevard is a wide street.

---

la larme [LARM] noun, fem. **tear**

Grand-père dit: "Assez de larmes!"
Grandpa says, "Enough tears!"

---

le lavabo [la-va-BOH] noun, masc. **washstand, bathroom sink**

Le lavabo est dans la salle de bain.
The washstand is in the bathroom.

---

laver [la-VAY] verb **to wash (something or someone)**

je lave	nous lavons
tu laves	vous lavez
il, elle lave	ils, elles lavent

Nous lavons le chien.
We are washing the dog.

se laver [sǝ-la-VAY] verb **to wash (oneself)**

je me lave	nous nous lavons
tu te laves	vous vous lavez
il, elle se lave	ils, elles se lavent

Je me lave les mains avant de manger.
I wash my hands before eating.

la machine à laver **washing machine**
(See **machine**)

---

le [lǝ] article, masc. **the**
l' (before a vowel)
la [LA] fem.
les [LEH] pl., masc. and fem.

Le chat, la souris, l'ours et l'éléphant sont des animaux.
The cat, the mouse, the bear and the elephant are animals.

---

le [lǝ] pronoun, masc. **it; him**
l' (before a vowel)
la [LA] fem.
les [LEH] pl., masc. and fem. **them**

Je l'aime.
I like him (her) (it).

Je la vois.
I see her (it).

Je les vois.
I see them.

---

la leçon [le-SOHN] noun, fem. **lesson**

La leçon d'aujourd'hui est difficile, n'est-ce pas?
Today's lesson is difficult, isn't it?

---

le lecteur de CD [lehk-TER-de-SAY-DAY] noun, masc. **CD player**

J'ai un nouveau lecteur de CD.
I have a new CD player.

---

léger [lay-ZHAY] adjective, masc. **light**
légère [lay-ZHEHR] fem.

Cette boîte est légère.
This box is light.

---

le légume [lay-GEWM] noun, masc. **vegetable**

Les légumes sont délicieux avec la viande.
Vegetables are delicious with meat.

---

lentement [lahnt-MAHN] adverb **slowly**

Grand-père marche lentement.
Grandfather walks slowly.

---

le léopard [lay-oh-PAR] noun, masc. **leopard**

Le léopard est dans la forêt.
The leopard is in the forest.

---

les **the** (See **le**, article)
les **them** (See **le**, pronoun)

---

la lettre [LEHTR] noun, fem. **letter**

Je mets la lettre dans l'enveloppe.
I put the letter in the envelope.

la boîte aux lettres **mailbox** (See **boîte**)

---

leur [LEUHR] adjective, masc. and fem. **their**
leurs pl.

Mes cousins partent. Où sont leurs valises?
My cousins are leaving. Where are their valises?

---

leur [LEUHR] pronoun **to them, them**

Je leur donne une carte.
I give them a card.

---

se lever [se-le-VAY] verb **to get up, to stand up**

je me lève	nous nous levons
tu te lèves	vous vous levez
il, elle se lève	ils, elles se lèvent

Lève-toi, Edouard. Tu es en retard.
Get up, Edward. You're late.

---

lever [le̸-VAY] verb **to raise**

je lève	nous levons
tu lèves	vous levez
il, elle lève	ils, elles lèvent

L'agent de police lève la main droite.
The policeman raises his right hand.

---

la lèvre [LEHVR] noun, fem. **lip**

Regarde! La poupée ouvre les lèvres.
Look! The doll is opening its lips.

---

la librairie [lee-bray-ree] noun, fem. **bookstore**

Combien de livres y a-t-il dans la librairie?
How many books are there in the bookstore?

---

le lion [LYOHN] noun, masc. **lion**

Le lion n'est pas un animal doux.
The lion is not a gentle animal.

---

lire [LEER] verb **to read**

je lis	nous lisons
tu lis	vous lisez
il, elle lit	ils, elles lisent

Nous allons lire dans la bibliothèque.
We are going to read in the library.

---

le lit [LEE] noun, masc. **bed**

Le chat est dans mon lit.
The cat is in my bed.

---

le livre [LEEVR] noun, masc. **book**

Nous cherchons des livres intéressants.
We are looking for some interesting books.

---

loin (de) [LWAIN] adverb **far (from), distant (from)**

Est-ce que Paris est loin de Washington?
Is Paris far from Washington?

---

long [LOHN] adjective, masc. **long**
longue [LOHNG] fem.

Le pantalon du garçcon est long.
The boy's pants are long.

---

le loup [LOO] noun, masc. **wolf**

Qui a peur du méchant loup?
Who is afraid of the bad wolf?

---

lourd [LOOR] adjective, masc. **heavy**
lourde [LOORD] fem.

La valise est très lourde.
The valise is very heavy.

---

la luge [LEWZH] noun, fem. **sled**

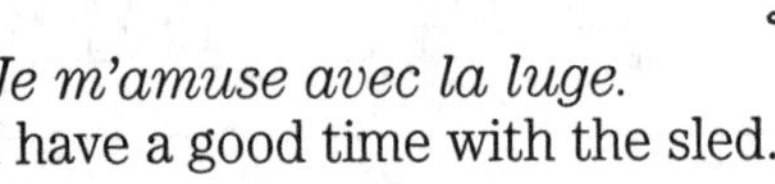

Je m'amuse avec la luge.
I have a good time with the sled.

---

lui [LEW/EE] pronoun **to him, to her; him, her**

Elle lui donne un café.
She is giving him a cup of coffee.

---

la lumière [lew-MYEHR] noun, fem. **light**

La lune ne donne pas beaucoup de lumière.
The moon does not give much light.

---

lundi [luhn-DEE] noun, masc. **Monday**

Que faites-vous le lundi?
What do you do on Mondays?

---

la lune [LEWN] noun, fem. **moon**

L'astronaute marche sur la lune.
The astronaut walks on the moon.

---

les lunettes [lew-NEHT] noun, fem., pl. **glasses**

Attention! Tu vas casser tes lunettes.
Be careful! You are going to break your glasses.

M

ma [MA] **my** (See **mon**)

---

la machine [ma-SHEEN] noun, fem. **machine**
la machine à écrire [ma-shee-na-ay-KREER] noun, fem. **typewriter**

Dorothée désire une machine à écrire pour son anniversaire.
Dorothy wants a typewriter for her birthday.

la machine à laver [ma-shee-na-la-VAY] noun, fem. **washing machine**

Maman désire une machine à laver.
Mother wants a washing machine.

---

madame [ma-DAM] noun, fem. **Mrs.**
mesdames [meh-DAM] pl. **ladies**

Dis "Bonjour, Madame" à ta maîtresse.
Say "Good morning" to your teacher.

---

mademoiselle [ma-dmwa-ZEHL] noun, fem. **Miss**
mesdemoiselles [meh-dmwa-ZEHL] pl. **young ladies**

Mademoiselle Duval? Elle est un bon professeur.
Miss Duval? She is a good teacher.

---

le magasin [ma-ga-ZAIN] noun, masc. **store**

Je vais au magasin avec mon amie.
I'm going to the store with my friend.

---

le magnétophone [ma-nay-tuh-FUHN] noun, masc. **tape recorder**

Le professeur emploie un magnétophone dans la classe.
The teacher uses a tape recorder in class.

---

mai [MAY] noun, masc. **May**

Il y a trente et un jours au mois de mai.
There are thirty-one days in May.

---

maigre [MEHGR] adjective **thin, skinny**

Vous êtes trop maigre. Il faut manger.
You are too thin. You must eat.

---

le maillot [ma-YOH] noun, masc. **bathing suit**

Tu aimes mon nouveau maillot?
Do you like my new bathing suit?

---

la main [MAIN] noun, fem. **hand**

J'ai les mains sales!
My hands are dirty!

la main droite [main-DRWAT] **right hand** (See **droit**)
la main gauche [main-GOHSH] **left hand** (See **gauche**)

---

maintenant [main-TNAHN] adverb **now**

Tu dois prendre un bain maintenant!
You have to take a bath now!

---

mais [MEH] conjunction **but**

Je veux aller au parc mais Papa dit "non."
I want to go to the park but Daddy says "no."

---

le maïs [ma-EES] noun, masc. **corn**

Mmm, le maïs est bon!
Mmm, the corn is good!

---

la maison [meh-ZOHN] noun, fem. **house, home**

Voici la maison de mon oncle.
Here is my uncle's house.

la maison de poupée **dollhouse**
[meh-zohn-de-poo-PAY] (See **poupée**)

---

la maîtresse [meh-TREHS] noun, fem. **teacher**
le maître [MEHTR] noun, masc.

La maîtresse est gentille.
The teacher is kind.

---

le mal [MAL] noun, masc. **sore, evil, harm**
avoir mal à [a-vwar-mal-la] **to have a sore . . .;**
idiomatic expression **to have a pain in the . . .;**
to hurt . . . (See **avoir**)

Je suis malade. J'ai mal à la tête.
I am sick. I have a headache.

Pierre a mal au pied.
Peter has a sore foot.

---

malade [ma-LAD] adjective **sick**

Qu'as-tu? Je suis malade.
What's the matter? I am sick.

---

malheureux [ma-luh-REOH] adjective, masc. **unhappy, sad**
malheureuse [ma-luh-REOHZ] fem.

Il est malheureux parce qu'il ne peut pas jouer à la balle.
He is unhappy because he can't play ball.

---

la malle [MAL] noun, fem. **trunk, suitcase**

Il est difficile de porter cette malle.
It is difficult to carry this trunk.

---

maman [ma-MAHN] noun, fem. **Mother, Mom, Mama, Mommy**

Maman, où sont mes chaussettes?
Mom, where are my socks?

---

le manège [ma-NEZH] noun, masc. **merry-go-round**

Regarde les chevaux du manège!
Look at the horses on the merry-go-round!

---

manger [mahn-ZHAY] verb **to eat**

je mange nous mangeons
tu manges vous mangez
il, elle mange ils, elles mangent

Le dimanche nous mangeons la dinde.
On Sundays we eat turkey.

---

le manteau [mahn-TOH] noun, masc. **coat**

Elle porte un manteau chaud en hiver.
She wears a warm coat in winter.

---

la marche [MARSH] noun, fem. **step**

Il y a beaucoup de marches devant ce bâtiment.
There are many steps in front of this building.

---

le marché [mar-SHAY] noun, masc. **market, store**

Qu'est-ce qu'on vend au marché?
What do they sell at the market?

le supermarché [sew-pehr-mar-SHAY] noun, masc. **supermarket**

Le supermarché est un grand marché.
The supermarket is a large market.

---

marcher [mar-SHAY] verb **to walk, to work (things), to operate**

je marche nous marchons
tu marches vous marchez
il, elle marche ils, elles marchent

Nous marchons dans la rue.
We are walking on the street.

Cette lampe ne marche pas.
This lamp is not working.

---

mardi [mar-DEE] noun, masc. **Tuesday**

Est-ce que mardi est un jour de congé?
Is Tuesday a day off?

---

la marelle [ma-REHL] noun, fem. **hopscotch**
jouer à la marelle **to play hopscotch**
[zhoo-ay-a-la-ma-REHL] idiomatic expression (See **jouer**)

Je ne sais pas jouer à la marelle.
I don't know how to play hopscotch.

---

le mari [ma-REE] noun, masc. **husband**

Le mari de ma tante est mon oncle.
My aunt's husband is my uncle.

---

la marionnette [ma-ryoh-NEHT] noun, fem. **marionette**

Les marionnettes sont drôles.
The marionettes are amusing.

---

marron [ma-ROHN̸] adjective **brown**

Le tapis est marron.
The rug is brown.

---

mars [MARS] noun, masc. **March**

Il fait du vent en mars.
It is windy in March.

---

le marteau [mar-TOH] noun, masc. **hammer**

Albert travaille avec un marteau.
Albert is working with a hammer.

---

le matin [ma-TAIN] noun, masc. **morning**

Que mangez-vous le matin?
What do you eat in the morning?

---

mauvais [moh-VEH] adjective, masc. **bad**
mauvaise [moh-VEHZ] fem.

Il fait mauvais aujourd'hui.
The weather is bad today.

---

me [me] pronoun **me; to me; myself**

Je m'habille le matin.
I get dressed in the morning.

Il me donne du pain.
He gives me some bread.

---

le mécanicien [may-ka-nee-SYAIN] noun, masc. **mechanic**

Je voudrais devenir mécanicien.
I would like to become a mechanic.

---

méchant [may-SHAHN] adjective, masc. **naughty**
méchante [may-SHAHNT] fem.

Robert ne peut pas sortir. Il est méchant.
Robert cannot go out. He is naughty.

---

le médecin [may-TSAIN] noun, masc. **doctor**

Le médecin entre dans l'hôpital.
The doctor enters the hospital.

---

le médicament [may-dee-ka-MAHN] noun, masc. **medicine**

Je n'aime pas ce médicament!
I don't like this medicine!

---

meilleur [may-YEUHR] adjective, masc. **better**
meilleure fem.

Je pense que les cerises sont meilleures que les fraises.
I think that cherries are better than strawberries.

---

mélanger [may-lahn-ZHAY] verb **to mix**

je mélange	nous mélangeons
tu mélagnes	vous mélangez
il, elle mélange	ils, elles mélangent

Quand on joue aux dominos, on mélange les dominos.
When you play dominoes, you mix the dominoes.

---

le membre [MAHNBR] noun, masc. **member**

Il est membre de notre équipe.
He is a member of our team.

---

même [MEHM] adjective, adverb **same; even**

Mon amie et moi, nous portons la même robe.
My friend and I are wearing the same dress.

Elle pleure même quand elle est heureuse.
She cries even when she is happy.

moi-même [mwa-MEHM] pronoun **myself**

Je veux faire le gâteau moi-même!
I want to make the cake myself!

---

mener [m~~e~~-NAY] verb **to lead**

je mène	nous menons
tu mènes	vous menez
il, elle mène	ils, elles mènent

Il mène son chien dehors.
He leads his dog outside.

---

le mensonge [mah~~n~~-SOH~~N~~ZH] noun, masc. **lie**

Il dit des mensonges!
He tells lies!

---

le menton [mah~~n~~-TOH~~N~~] noun, masc. **chin**

Voici le menton de la poupée.
Here is the doll's chin.

---

la mer [MEHR] noun, fem. **sea**

Est-ce qu'il y a beaucoup de poissons dans la mer?
Are there many fish in the sea?

---

merci [mehr-SEE] noun, masc. **thank you**

Quand ma grand-mère me donne un petit gâteau je dis: "Merci."
When my grandmother gives me a cookie I say, "Thank you."

---

mercredi [mehr-kr~~e~~-DEE] noun, masc. **Wednesday**

C'est aujourd'hui mercredi—on sert du poulet.
Today is Wednesday—they are serving chicken.

---

la mère [MEHR] noun, fem. **mother**

C'est l'anniversaire de ma mère aujourd'hui.
Today is my mother's birthday.

---

mes (See **mon**)

---

mesdames (See **madame**)

---

mesdemoiselles (See **mademoiselle**)

---

messieurs (See **monsieur**)

---

le métro [may-TROH] noun, masc. **subway**

Pour aller au musée nous prenons le métro.
We take the subway to go to the museum.

---

mettre [MEHTR] verb **to put, to put on; to set**

je mets	nous mettons
tu mets	vous mettez
il, elle met	ils, elles mettent

Ma soeur met ses gants.
My sister puts on her gloves.

Ma mère met le couvert.
My mother sets the table.

---

mettre une lettre à la poste **to mail**
[meh-trewn-le-tra-la-PUHST] idiomatic expression

Mon frère met une lettre à la poste.
My brother mails a letter.

---

midi [mee-DEE] noun, masc. **noon**

Il est midi. C'est l'heure du déjeuner.
It is noon. It's time for lunch.

---

mignon [mee-NYOHN] adjective, masc. **cute, darling**
mignonne [mee-NYUHN] fem.

Le bébé est mignon.
The baby is cute.

---

le milieu [mee-LYEOH] noun, masc. **middle**
au milieu de [oh-mee-LYEOH-de] preposition **in the middle of**

Maman met les bonbons au milieu de la table.
Mom puts the candy in the middle of the table.

---

mille [MEEL] adjective **thousand**

Combien coûte une auto? Mille francs?
How much does a car cost? A thousand francs?

---

le mille [MEEL] noun, masc. **mile**

Mon ami demeure à un mille d'ici.
My friend lives one mile from here.

---

le million [mee-LYOHN] noun, masc. **million**

Combien de livres as-tu? Un million!
How many books do you have? A million!

---

minuit [mee-NEW/EE] noun, masc. **midnight**

Il est minuit. Pourquoi ne dors-tu pas?
It is midnight. Why aren't you sleeping?

---

la minute [mee-NEWT] noun, fem. **minute**

Combien de minutes y a-t-il dans une heure?
How many minutes are there in an hour?

---

le miroir [mee-RWAR] noun, masc. **mirror**

La petite fille se regarde dans le miroir.
The little girl is looking at herself in the mirror.

---

moi [MWAH] pronoun **me, to me**

Qui frappe à la porte? C'est moi, Michel.
Who is knocking at the door? It's me, Michael.

moi-même [mwa-MEHM] **myself** (See **même**)

---

moins [MWAIN] adverb **less; to (in time expressions)**

Nous partons à deux heures moins vingt.
We are leaving at twenty minutes to two.

---

le mois [MWA] noun, masc. **month**

Nous avons deux mois de vacances.
We have two months of vacation.

---

la moitié [mwa-TYAY] noun, fem. **half**

Donnez-moi la moitié de la poire, s'il vous plait.
Give me half of the pear, please.

---

le moment [muh-MAHN] noun, masc. **moment**

J'entre dans la poste pour un moment.
I am going into the post office for a moment.

---

mon [MOHN] adjective, masc. **my**
ma [MA] fem.
mes [MEH] masc., fem., pl.

Mon frère est beau.
My brother is handsome.

Ma soeur est jolie.
My sister is pretty.

Mes cousins sont toujours gais.
My cousins are always cheerful.

---

le monde [MOHND] noun, masc. **world**

Combien de nations y a-t-il dans le monde?
How many nations are there in the world?

tout le monde **everyone, everybody**
(See **tout**)

---

la monnaie [muh-NAY] noun, fem. **change (money)**

Le boucher dit: "Voici la monnaie de trente francs."
The butcher says, "Here is the change from 30 francs."

---

monsieur [muh-SYE] noun, masc. **Mr., sir, gentleman**
messieurs [meh-SYEOH] pl. **gentlemen**

L'épicier s'appelle monsieur Montand.
The grocer's name is Mr. Montand.

---

la montagne [mohN-TAN] noun, fem. **mountain**

Les montagnes près de l'Espagne sont les Pyrénées.
The mountains near Spain are the Pyrenees.

---

monter [mohň-TAY] verb **to go up; to ride**

Le cerf-volant monte dans le ciel.
The kite goes up into the sky.

Il monte à cheval.
He rides a horse.

Je monte à bicyclette.
I go bicycle riding.

---

la montre [MOHŇTR] noun, fem. **watch**

Hélas, ma montre ne marche pas.
What a shame, my watch doesn't work.

---

montrer [mohň-TRAY] verb **to show**

je montre	nous montrons
tu montres	vous montrez
il, elle montre	ils, elles montrent

Montre-moi ton nouveau stylo.
Show me your new pen.

---

le morceau [muhr-SOH] noun, masc. **piece**

Je désire un morceau de fromage.
I want a piece of cheese.

---

mordre [MUHRDR] verb **to bite**

je mords	nous mordons
tu mords	vous mordez
il, elle mord	ils, elles mordent

Les chats ne mordent pas.
Cats do not bite.

---

mort [MUHR] adjective, masc. **dead**
morte [MUHRT] fem.

Tu pleures? Oui, ma tortue est morte.
You're crying? Yes, my turtle is dead.

---

le mot [MOH] noun, masc. **word**

Je pense à un mot qui commence avec la lettre "a."
I'm thinking of a word that begins with the letter "a."

---

la mouche [MOOSH] noun, fem. **fly**

Il y a des mouches dans la cuisine!
There are flies in the kitchen!

---

le mouchoir [moo-SHWAR] noun, masc. **handkerchief**

J'emploie un mouchoir quand j'eternue.
I use a handkerchief when I sneeze.

---

mouillé [moo-YAY] adjective, masc. **wet**
mouillée fem.

Mon cahier tombe dans l'eau. Oh, il est mouillé!
My notebook is falling into the water. Oh, it is wet!

---

le moustique [moos-TEEK] noun, masc. **mosquito**

Papa, attrape le moustique! Il va me piquer.
Daddy, catch the mosquito! It's going to bite me.

---

le mouton [MOO-TOHN] noun, masc. **sheep**

Le mouton est dans le champ.
The sheep is in the field.

---

le mur [MEWR] noun, masc. **wall**

Il y a une image d'une fusée au mur de ma chambre.
There is a picture of a spaceship on my bedroom wall.

---

mûr [MEWR] adjective, masc. **ripe**
mûre fem.

Quand la banane est jaune, elle est mûre.
When the banana is yellow, it is ripe.

---

le musée [mew-ZAY] noun, masc. **museum**

Le musée est ouvert de deux heures jusqu'à cinq heures.
The museum is open from two to five o'clock.

---

le musicien [mew-zee-SYAIN] noun, masc. **musician**

Le garçon désire devenir musicien.
The boy wants to become a musician.

---

la musique [mew-ZEEK] noun, fem. **music**

Est-ce que vous savez lire les notes de musique?
Do you know how to read musical notes?

N

nager [na-ZHAY] verb **to swim**

je nage	nous nageons
tu nages	vous nagez
il, elle nage	ils, elles nagent

Je vais nager en été.
I go swimming in summer.

---

la nappe [NAP] noun, fem. **tablecloth**

Ma tante met la nappe sur la table.
My aunt puts the tablecloth on the table.

---

la nation [na-SYOHN] noun, fem. **nation**

Il y a beaucoup de nations dans le monde.
There are many nations in the world.

les Nations Unies [na-syohn-zew-NEE] noun, fem., pl. **United Nations**

Le bâtiment des Nations Unies est intéressant.
The United Nations building is interesting.

---

national [na-syoh-NAL] adjective, masc. **national**
nationale fem.

Le quatre juillet est la fête nationale des Etats-Unis.
The Fourth of July is the national holiday of the United States.

---

ne . . . jamais [nǝ . . . zha-MEH] adverb **never** (See **jamais**)

Je vais à l'école. Ma soeur ne va jamais à l'école.
I go to school. My sister never goes to school.

---

ne . . . pas [nǝ . . . pa] adverb **not**

Je vais à l'école. Mon grand-père ne va pas à l'école.
I go to school. My grandfather does not go to school.

---

ne . . . plus [nǝ . . . plew] adverb **no longer**

Je vais à l'école. Mon frère ne va plus à l'ècole.
I go to school. My brother no longer goes to school.

---

né [NAY] adjective, masc. **born**
née fem.

Je suis né le deux mars.
I was born on March 2nd.

---

la neige [NEHZH] noun, fem. **snow**

J'aime jouer dans la neige.
I like to play in the snow.

le bonhomme de neige **snowman** (See **bonhomme**)

neiger [neh-ZHAY] verb **to snow**

Il va neiger demain?
Is it going to snow tomorrow?

Il neige. [eel-NEHZH] idiomatic expression **It is snowing.**

Regardez par la fenêtre. Il neige!
Look out the window. It's snowing!

---

n'est-ce pas? [nehs-PA] idiomatic expression — **Isn't that true? Isn't that so? Don't you agree? Aren't you? (etc.)**

Il fait mauvais, n'est-ce pas?
The weather is bad, isn't it?

Mon professeur est beau, n'est-ce pas?
My teacher is handsome, don't you agree?

---

nettoyer [neh-twa-YAY] verb — **to clean**

je nettoie	nous nettoyons
tu nettoies	vous nettoyez
il, elle nettoie	ils, elles nettoient

Tu aides ta mère à nettoyer la maison?
Do you help your mother clean the house?

---

neuf [NEUHF, NEUHV] adjective — **nine**

Combien font neuf et deux? [NEUHF]
How much are nine and two?

J'ai neuf ans. [NEUHV]
I am nine years old.

---

neuf [NEUHF] adjective, masc. — **new**
neuve [NEUHV] fem.

Ma bicyclette est neuve.
My bicycle is new.

---

le neveu [nø-VEOH] noun, masc. — **nephew**

Il est le neveu de monsieur Duval.
He is Mr. Duval's nephew.

---

le nez [NAY] noun, masc. — **nose**

Le nez de ma poupée est mignon.
My doll's nose is cute.

---

le nid [NEE] noun, masc. **nest**

Combien d'oeufs vois-tu dans le nid?
How many eggs do you see in the nest?

---

la nièce [NYEHS] noun, fem. **niece**

Elle est la nièce de l'avocat.
She is the lawyer's niece.

N'importe! [nain-PUHRT] idiomatic expression **No matter!**

Vous n'avez pas de stylo? N'importe. Voici un crayon.
You don't have a pen? No matter! Here is a pencil.

Noël [no-ehl] noun, masc. **Christmas**

Le lumières de Noël sont belles.
Christmas lights are beautiful.

---

noir [NWAR] adjective, masc. **black**
noire fem.

Je porte mes souliers noirs.
I am wearing my black shoes.

le tableau noir **chalkboard, blackboard** (See **tableau**)

---

le nom [NOHN] noun, masc. **name**

Quel est le nom de ce bâtiment?
What is the name of this building?

le nom (de famille) [nohn-de-fa-MEEY] noun, masc. **surname**

---

le nombre [NOHNBR] noun, masc. **number (quantity)**

Tu as un grand nombre de livres!
You have a great number of books!
(See **numéro**)

---

non [NOHN] adverb **no**

Lève-toi! Non, je ne veux pas me lever!
Get up! No, I don't want to get up!

---

le nord [NUHR] noun, masc. **north**

Quand je vais de Marseille à Paris, je vais vers le nord.
When I go from Marseilles to Paris, I go toward the north.

---

la note [NUHT] noun, fem. **mark (in school); musical note**

Tu as de bonnes notes?
Do you have good marks?

---

notre [NUHTR] adjective **our**
nos [NOH] masc., fem., pl.

Notre maîtresse nous gronde aujourd'hui.
Our teacher is scolding us today.

---

nous [NOO] pronoun, pl. **we; us, to us**

Nous allons à la plage.
We are going to the beach.

---

nouveau [noo-VOH] adjective, masc. **new**
nouveaux masc., pl.
nouvel [noo-VEHL] masc. (before a vowel)
nouvelle [noo-VEHL] fem.

Regarde ma nouvelle tortue!
Look at my new turtle!

---

novembre [nuh-VAHNBR] noun, masc. **November**

Novembre n'est pas le dernier mois de l'année.
November is not the last month of the year.

---

le nuage [NEWAZH] noun, masc. **cloud**

Le soleil est derrière un nuage.
The sun is behind a cloud.

Il est couvert.
It is cloudy.

---

la nuit [NEW/EE] noun, fem. **night, at night**

La nuit on peut voir de étoiles.
At night you can see the stars.

---

le numéro [new-may-ROH] noun, masc. **number**

Quel est votre numéro de téléphone?
What is your telephone number? (See **nombre**)

O

obéir [oh-bay-EER] verb **to obey**

j'obéis	nous obéissons
tu obéis	vous obéissez
il, elle obéit	ils, elles obéissent

Quand je suis sage, j'obéis à mes parents.
When I am well behaved, I obey my parents.

---

occupé [uh-kew-PAY] adjective, masc. **busy, occupied**
occupée fem.

Mon frère est occupé maintenant; il fait ses devoirs.
My brother is busy now; he is doing his homework.

---

l'océan [un-say-AHN] noun, masc. **ocean**

L'océan Atlantique est à l'ouest de la France?
Is the Atlantic Ocean to the west of France?

---

octobre [uhk-TUHBR] noun, masc. **October**

Il fait frais en octobre.
It is cool in October.

---

l'oeil [EUHY] noun, masc. **eye**
les yeux [leh-ZYEOH] pl.

De quelle couleur sont vos yeux?
What color are your eyes?

---

l'oeuf [UHF] noun, masc. **egg**
les oeufs [les-ZEOH] pl.

Maman demande: "Tu veux un oeuf ce matin?"
Mother asks, "Do you want an egg this morning?"

---

l'oignon [uhn-NYOHN] noun, masc. **onion**

Je vais au marché pour acheter des oignons.
I am going to the store to buy some onions.

---

l'oiseau [wah-ZOH] noun, masc. **bird**

L'oiseau chante très bien.
The bird sings very well.

---

l'ombre [OHNBR] noun, fem. **shadow**

L'ombre danse avec moi.
My shadow dances with me.

---

on [OHN] pronoun **one; people; you; we; they; somebody**

Quand on regarde par la fenêtre, on voit la Tour Eiffel.
When you look out of the window, you see the Eiffel Tower.

---

l'oncle [OHNKL] noun, masc. **uncle**

Mon oncle est le frère de ma mère.
My uncle is my mother's brother.

---

l'ongle [OHNGL] noun, masc. **(finger) nail**

J'ai honte. Mes ongles sont sales.
I am ashamed. My fingernails are dirty.

---

onze [OHNZ] adjective **eleven**

Le fermier a onze poulets.
The farmer has eleven chickens.

---

l'or [UHR] noun, masc. **gold**
en or [ahn-NUHR] **made of gold**

Je voudrais avoir une bague en or.
I would like to have a gold ring.

---

l'orage [uh-RAZH] noun, masc. **storm**

Il n'y a pas de classes à cause de l'orage.
There are no classes because of the storm.

---

orange [uh-RAHNZH] adjective **orange**

J'ai besoin d'une jupe orange.
I need an orange skirt.

---

l'orange [uh-RAHNZH] noun, fem. **orange**

De quelle couleur est l'orange?
What color is the orange?

---

l'ordinateur [uhr-dee-na-TEUHR] noun, masc. **computer**

As tu un ordinateur?
Do you have a computer?

le disque [DEESK] noun, masc. **(computer) disk**

le technicien [TEK-nee-SYAIN] noun, masc. **(computer) technician**

la technicienne [tek-nee-SYEHN] fem.

---

l'oreille [uh-RAY] noun, fem. **ear**

Les oreilles du loup sont longues.
The wolf's ears are long.

---

l'oreiller [uh-ray-YAY] noun, masc. **pillow**

Où est l'oreiller de Raoul?
Where is Ralph's pillow?

---

l'orteil [uhr-TEHY] noun, masc. **toe**

Le bébé regarde ses orteils.
The baby looks at his toes.

---

oser [oh-ZAY] verb **to dare (to)**

j'ose	nous osons
tu oses	vous osez
il, elle ose	ils, elles osent

Tu oses me battre?
You dare to hit me?

ôter [oh-TAY] verb **to take off, to remove**

j'ôte	nous ôtons
tu ôtes	vous ôtez
il, elle ôte	ils, elles ôtent

Ôte le chapeau dans la maison.
Take off your hat in the house.

---

ou [oo] conjunction **or**

Que désirez-vous, des pêches ou des pommes?
What would you like, peaches or apples?

---

où [oo] adverb **where**

Où sont mes lunettes?
Where are my glasses?

---

oublier [oo-BLYAY] verb **to forget**

j'oublie	nous oublions
tu oublies	vous oubliez
il, elle oublie	ils, elles oublient

Elle oublie toujours son billet.
She always forgets her ticket.

---

l'ouest [WEHST] noun, masc. **west**

Quand je vais de Lyon à Bordeaux, je vais vers l'ouest.
When I go from Lyons to Bordeaux, I go toward the west.

---

oui [WEE] adverb **yes**

Veux-tu des bonbons? Oui, bien sûr!
Do you want some candy? Yes, of course!

---

l'ours [OORS] noun, masc. **bear**

Les ours jouent dans l'eau.
The bears are playing in the water.

---

ouvert [oo-VEHR] adjective, masc. **open**
ouverte [oo-VEHRT] fem.

La fenêtre est ouverte.
The window is open.

---

ouvrir [oo-VREER] verb **to open**

j'ouvre nous ouvrons
tu ouvres vous ouvrez
il, elle ouvre ils, elles ouvrent

J'ouvre mon pupitre pour chercher une gomme.
I open my desk to look for an eraser.

P

la page [PAHZH] noun, fem. **page**

La carte de la France est à la page dix.
The map of France is on page ten.

---

le pain [PAIN] noun, masc. **(loaf of) bread**

On voit beaucoup de pain dans la boulangerie.
You see a lot of bread in the bakery.

le petit pain [ptee-PAIN] noun, masc. **roll**

Un petit pain, s'il vous plaît.
A roll, please.

le pain grillé [pain-gree-YAY] noun, masc. **toast**

Ma soeur préfère le pain grillé.
My sister prefers toast.

---

la paire [PEHR] noun, fem. **pair**

Je voudrais acheter une paire de gants.
I would like to buy a pair of gloves.

---

le palais [pa-LEH] noun, masc. **palace**

Le roi arrive au palais.
The king arrives at the palace.

---

le pamplemousse [pahn̸-ple̸-MOOS] noun, masc. **grapefruit**

Le pamplemousse n'est pas doux.
The grapefruit is not sweet.

---

le panier [pa-NYAY] noun, masc. **basket**

Il y a des pommes dans le panier.
There are apples in the basket.

---

le pantalon [pahn̸-ta-LOHN̸] noun, masc. **pants, trousers**

Le pantalon du garçon est sale.
The boy's pants are dirty.

---

papa [pa-PA] noun, masc. **Father, Dad, Papa, Daddy**

Papa, j'ai peur!
Daddy, I'm afraid!

---

le papier [pa-PYAY] noun, masc. **paper**

Il y a du papier dans mon cahier.
There is some paper in my notebook.

---

le paquebot [pak-BOH] noun, masc. **steamship, ocean liner**

Le paquebot traverse l'océan Atlantique.
The steamship crosses the Atlantic Ocean.

---

le paquet [pa-KEH] noun, masc. **package**

Qu'est-ce qu'il y a dans le paquet?
What's in the package?

---

par [PAR] preposition **by, through, out of**

Mon grand-père regarde par la fenêtre.
My grandfather looks out of the window.

---

le parachute [pa-ra-SH~~EW~~T] noun, masc. **parachute**

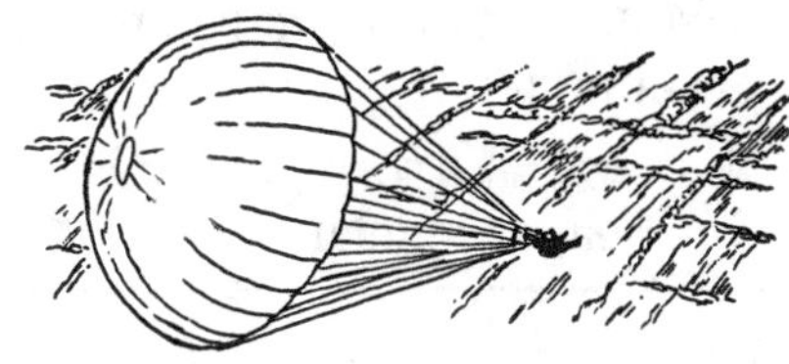

Est-ce qu'il est dangereux de sauter en parachute?
Is it dangerous to jump with a parachute?

---

le parapluie [pa-ra-PL~~EW~~/EE] noun, masc. **umbrella**

N'oublie pas ton parapluie.
Don't forget your umbrella.

---

le parc [PARK] noun, masc. **park**

Le parc est tout près d'ici.
The park is near here.

---

parce que [pars-k~~e~~] conjunction **because**

Je ne vais pas au cinéma parce que je n'ai pas d'argent.
I am not going to the movies because I don't have any money.

---

pardon [par-DOHN] idiomatic expression — **I beg your pardon, pardon me, excuse me, forgive me**

Pardon! C'est votre sac, n'est-ce pas?
Excuse me! It's your pocketbook, isn't it?

---

pareil [pa-RAY] adjective, masc. — **similar, alike**
pareille fem.

Nos cravates sont pareilles.
Our ties are similar.

---

les parents [pa-RAHN] noun, masc., pl. — **parents, relatives**

Mes parents vont au travail le matin.
My parents go to work in the morning.

---

paresseux [pa-reh-SEOH] adjective, masc. — **lazy**
paresseuse [pa-reh-SEOHZ] fem.

Ma maîtresse dit que je suis paresseuse.
My teacher says I am lazy.

---

parler [par-LAY] verb — **to speak, to talk**

je parle	nous parlons
tu parles	vous parlez
il, elle parle	ils, elles parlent

Nous parlons du film à la télévision.
We are talking about the movie on television.

---

partager [par-ta-ZHAY] verb — **to share**

je partage	nous partageons
tu partages	vous partagez
il, elle partage	ils, elles partagent

Partageons le gâteau.
Let's share the cake!

---

partir [par-TEER] verb **to leave, to go**

je pars nous partons
tu pars vous partez
il, elle part ils, elles partent

Ma tante part à cinq heures.
My aunt is leaving at five o'clock.

---

partout [par-TOO] adverb **all over, everywhere**

Je cherche ma montre partout.
I look everywhere for my watch.

---

le passager [pa-sa-ZHAY] noun, masc. **passenger**
la passagère [pa-sa-ZHEHR] fem.

Il y a quatre passagers dans la voiture.
There are four passengers in the car.

---

passer [pa-SAY] verb **to pass, to spend (time)**

je passe nous passons
tu passes vous passez
il, elle passe ils, elles passent

Elle passe deux semaines à la campagne.
She spends two weeks in the country.

---

la pastèque [pas-TEHK] noun, fem. **watermelon**

La pastèque est un fruit délicieux.
Watermelon is a delicious fruit.

---

le patin [pa-TAIN] noun, masc. **skate**
le patin (à glace) [pa-tain-(a-GLAS)] noun, masc. **ice skate**
le patin à roulettes [pa-tain-a-roo-LEHT] noun, masc. **roller skate**

Avez-vous des patins à glace ou des patins à roulettes?
Do you have ice skates or roller skates?

---

patiner [pa-tee-NAY] verb **to skate**

je patine	nous patinons
tu patines	vous patinez
il, elle patine	ils, elles patinent

Allons patiner!
Let's go skating!

---

la patte [PAT] noun, fem. **paw**

Le chien a quatre pattes.
The dog has four paws.

---

pauvre [POHVR] adjective **poor**

Ce garçon pauvre n'a pas beaucoup d'argent.
This poor boy does not have much money.

---

payer [pay-YAY] verb **to pay, to pay for**

je paye	nous payons
tu payes	vous payez
il, elle paye	ils, elles payent

Maman paye la viande au boucher.
Mother pays the butcher for the meat.

---

le pays [pay-EE] noun, masc. **country**

Quel est le nom du pays à l'est de la France?
What is the name of the country to the east of France?
(See **campagne**)

---

la peau [POH] noun, fem. **skin**

Le soleil me brûle la peau quand je prends un bain de soleil.
The sun burns my skin when I take a sunbath.

---

la pêche [PEHSH] noun, fem. **peach; fishing**

On mange des pêches en été.
People eat peaches in summer.

aller à la pêche [a-lay-a-la-PEHSH] idiomatic expression **to go fishing**

Nous allons à la pêche.
We are going fishing. (See **aller**)

---

le peigne [PEHN] noun, masc. **comb**

Où est mon peigne?
Where is my comb?

---

se peigner [sé-peh-NAY] verb **to comb (one's hair)**

je me peigne	nous nous peignons
tu te peignes	vous vous peignez
il, elle se peigne	ils, elles se peignent

Avant de sortir de la maison, je me peigne.
Before leaving the house, I comb my hair.

---

peindre [PAIN̸DR] verb **to paint**

je peins	nous peignons
tu peins	vous peignez
il, elle peint	ils, elles peignent

Ma soeur est une artiste. Elle aime peindre.
My sister is an artist. She likes to paint.

---

la pelle [PEHL] noun, fem. **shovel**

Mon frère joue avec une pelle.
My brother plays with a shovel.

---

pendant [pahn̸-DAHN̸] preposition **during**

Je dors pendant la nuit.
I sleep during the night.

---

penser [pahn̸-SAY] verb **to think**

je pense	nous pensons
tu penses	vous pensez
il, elle pense	ils, elles pensent

Je pense que je vais chez mon ami. D'accord?
I think I'll go to my friend's house. All right?

---

perdre [PEHRDR] verb **to lose**

je perds	nous perdons
tu perds	vous perdez
il, elle perd	ils, elles perdent

Jacques perd toujours son chapeau.
Jack always loses his hat.

---

le père [PEHR] noun, masc. **father**

Mon père est facteur.
My father is a mail carrier.

> There is a famous French proverb, "Tel père, tel fils." In English it is: "Like father, like son."

---

la permission [pehr-mee-SYOHN] noun, fem. **permission**

Tu as la permission d'aller à la campagne?
Do you have permission to go to the country?

---

le perroquet [peh-ruh-KAY] noun, masc. **parrot**

Un perroquet est mon animal favori.
A parrot is my pet.

---

la perruche [peh-REWSH] noun, fem. **parakeet**

Nous avons deux jolies perruches.
We have two pretty parakeets.

---

la personne [pehr-SUHN] noun, fem. **person**
les personnes fem., pl. **people**

Il y a sept personnes dans ma famille.
There are seven people in my family.

---

petit [PTEE] adjective, masc. **small, little; short**
petite [PTEET] fem.

L'oiseau est petit.
The bird is small.

le petit déjeuner **breakfast** (See **déjeuner**)
la petite-fille [pteet-FEEY] noun, fem. **granddaughter**

Je suis la petite-fille de l'ingénieur.
I am the engineer's granddaughter.

le petit-fils [ptee-FEES] noun, masc. **grandson**

Je suis le petit-fils du boucher.
I am the butcher's grandson.

le petit pain **roll** (See **pain**)
les petits pois noun, masc., pl. **peas**

---

un peu [PEOH] adverb **a little**

Voulez-vous de la soupe? Un peu, s'il vous plaît.
Do you want any soup? A little, please.

---

la peur [PEUHR] noun, fem. **fear**

avoir peur [PEUHR] idiomatic expression **to be afraid, to be frightened, to fear** (See **avoir**)

Avez-vous peur de l'orage?
Are you afraid of the storm?

---

peut-être [peoh-TEHTR] adverb **maybe, perhaps**

Nous montons à cheval ce matin? Peut-être.
Are we going horseback riding this morning? Maybe.

---

la pharmacie [far-ma-SEE] noun, fem. **pharmacy, drugstore**

La pharmacie se trouve près du parc.
The pharmacy is located close to the park.

---

la photo [fuh-TOH] noun, fem. **photograph, picture**

Regarde ma photo! Elle est drôle, n'est-ce pas?
Look at my picture. It's funny, isn't it?

---

la phrase [FRAZ] noun, fem. **sentence**

J'écris une phrase dans mon cahier.
I am writing a sentence in my notebook.

---

le piano [pya-NOH] noun, masc. **piano**
jouer du piano idiomatic expression **to play the piano**

Qui joue du piano dans votre famille?
Who plays the piano in your family?

---

la pièce [PYEHS] noun, fem. **room**

Il y a deux pièces dans notre appartement.
There are two rooms in our apartment.

---

le pied [PYAY] noun, masc. **foot**
aller à pied [a-lay-a-PYAY] verb **to walk, to go on foot**

Nous allons au musée à pied.
We walk to the museum.

avoir mal au pied **to have a sore foot**
[a-vwar-ma-loh-PYAY] verb (See **avoir**)

---

la pierre [PYEHR] noun, fem. **stone**

Il y a beaucoup de pierres dans le terrain de jeux.
There are many stones in the playground.

---

le pilote (d'avion) [pee-luht-da-VYOHN] **(airplane) pilot**
noun, masc.

Mon cousin est pilote d'avion.
My cousin is an airplane pilot.

---

le pique-nique [peek-NEEK] noun, masc. **picnic**
faire un pique-nique [feh-ruhn-peek-NEEK] (See **faire**)

Nous faisons un pique-nique à la campagne.
We have a picnic in the country.

---

piquer [pee-KAY] verb **to bite (insect); to sting**

il, elle pique ils, elles piquent

Les moustiques aiment me piquer.
The mosquitoes like to bite me.

---

la piscine [pee-SEEN] noun, fem. **swimming pool**

J'ai la permission d'aller à la piscine avec vous.
I have permission to go to the pool with you.

---

le placard [pla-KAR] noun, masc. **closet, poster**

Le placard est fermé.
The closet is closed.

---

la place [PLAS] noun, fem. **place; seat; setting (table)**

Ma cousine met un couteau à chaque place.
My cousin puts a knife at each setting.

Je vais au tableau nor et je retourne à ma place.
I go to the blackboard and I return to my seat.

---

le plafond [pla-FOHN] noun, masc. **ceiling**

Le plafond du château est très intéressant.
The ceiling of the chateau is very interesting.

---

la plage [PLAZH] noun, fem. **beach**

Noun allons à la plage en été.
We go to the beach in summer.

---

se plaindre [sé-PLAINDR] verb **to complain**

je me plains	nous nous plaignons
tu te plains	vous vous plaignez
il, elle se plaint	ils, elles se plaignent

Mon amie dit que je me plains toujours!
My friend says that I always complain!

---

le plaisir [pleh-ZEER] noun, masc. **pleasure**

Tu viens avec nous? Avec plaisir!
Are you coming with us? With pleasure!

---

le plancher [plahn-SHAY] noun, masc. **floor**

Le stylo tombe sur le plancher.
The pen falls to the floor.

---

la planète [pla-NEHT] noun, fem. **planet**

Savez-vous les noms de toutes les planètes?
Do you know the names of all the planets?

---

la plante [PLAHNT] noun, fem. **plant**

Il y a cinq plantes dans la salle de classe.
There are five plants in the classroom.

---

plat [PLA] adjective, masc. **flat**
plate [PLAT] fem.

Le champ est plat.
The field is flat.

---

plein [PLAIN] adjective, masc. **full**

pleine [PLEHN] fem.

La valise est pleine de vêtements.
The valise is full of clothes.

---

pleurer [pleuh-RAY] verb **to cry, to weep**

je pleure	nous pleurons
tu pleures	vous pleurez
il, elle pleure	ils, elles pleurent

Je pleure quand on me taquine.
I cry when somebody teases me.

---

pleuvoir [pleuh-VWAR] verb **to rain**

Vous pensez qu'il va pleuvoir?
Do you think it's going to rain?

Il pleut. [eel-PLEUH] **It is raining. It rains.**
idiomatic expression

Il pleut beaucoup au mois d'avril.
It rains a lot in the month of April.

---

plus [PLEW] adverb **more, ...er** (comparative of adjectives)

Mon amie est plus grande que moi.
My friend is taller than I.

ne...plus **no longer** (See **ne...plus**)
plus tard **later** (See **tard**)
plusieurs [plew-ZYEUHR] adjective **several**

Il y a plusieurs autos sur la route.
There are several cars on the road.

---

la poche [PUHSH] noun, fem. **pocket**

J'ai des billes dans la poche.
I have some marbles in my pocket.

---

la poire [PWAR] noun, fem. **pear**

Est-ce que la poire est mûre?
Is the pear ripe?

---

le pois [PWA] noun, masc. **pea**
les petits pois [ptee-PWA] noun, masc., pl. **peas**

J'aime bien manger les petits pois.
I like to eat peas.

---

le poisson [pwah-SOHN] noun, masc. **fish**

Il y a beaucoup de poissons dans ce lac.
There are many fish in this lake.

le poisson rouge [pwah-sohn-ROOZH] noun, masc. **goldfish**

J'ai cinq poissons rouges.
I have five goldfish.

---

poli [puh-LEE] adjective **polite**

Maman dit: "L'enfant poli ne parle pas la bouche pleine."
Mother says, "A polite child does not speak with a full mouth."

---

la police [puh-LEES] noun, fem. **police**
l'agent de police **police officer** (See **agent...**)

---

la pomme [PUHM] noun, fem. **apple**

Je mange une pomme tous les jours.
I eat an apple every day.

---

la pomme de terre [puhm-de-TEHR] noun, fem. **potato**

Aimez-vous les pommes de terre?
Do you like potatoes?

---

la pompe à incendie **fire truck**
[pohn-pa-ain-sahn-DEE] noun, fem.

La pompe à incendie fait beaucoup de bruit.
The fire truck makes a lot of noise.

---

le pompier [pohn-PYAY] noun, masc. **fireman**

Le pompier est très fort.
The fireman is very strong.

---

le pont [POHN] noun, masc. **bridge**

Où est le pont d'Avignon?
Where is the Avignon bridge?

---

la porte [PUHRT] noun, fem. **door**

Fermez la porte, s'il vous plaît.
Please close the door.

---

porter [puhr-TAY] verb **to carry; to wear**

je porte	nous portons
tu portes	vous portez
il, elle porte	ils, elles portent

Il porte ses livres.
He is carrying his books.

Elle porte un chapeau.
She is wearing a hat.

se porter [sǝ-puhr-TAY] idiomatic expression **to be (state of health), to feel**

Comment vous portez-vous?
How are you?

---

la poste **post office** (See **le bureau de poste**)

le bureau de poste **post office** (See **le bureau**)

mettre une lettre à la poste **to mail a letter** (See **mettre**)

---

le poulet [poo-LAY] noun, masc. **chicken**

Qu'est-ce qu'on mange ce soir? Du poulet.
What are we eating this evening? Chicken.

---

la poupée [poo-PAY] noun, fem. **doll**

Ma poupée s'appelle Sylvie.
My doll's name is Sylvia.

la maison de poupée **dollhouse**
[meh-sohn-dǝ-poo-PAY] noun, fem.

---

pour [POOR] preposition **for, in order to, to**

Elle va au magasin pour acheter des chemises.
She is going to the store to buy shirts.

---

le pourboire [poor-BWAR] noun, masc. **tip**

L'homme laisse un pourboire pour le garçon.
The man leaves a tip for the waiter.

---

pourquoi [poor-KWAH] adverb **why?**

Pourquoi êtes-vous en retard?
Why are you late?

---

pousser [poo-SAY] verb **to push, to grow**

je pousse	nous poussons
tu pousses	vous poussez
il, elle pousse	ils, elles poussent

Il me pousse!
He's pushing me!

Les fleurs poussent dans le jardin.
Flowers are growing in the garden.

---

pouvoir [poo-VWAR] verb **to be able, (can, may)**

je peux	nous pouvons
tu peux	vous pouvez
il, elle peut	ils, elles pouvent

Je ne peux pas faire mes devoirs. Les leçons sont trop difficiles.
I can't do my homework. The lessons are too difficult.

Puis-je aller à la pêche?
May I go fishing?

---

préférer [pray-fay-RAY] verb **to prefer**

je préfère	nous préférons
tu préfères	vous préférez
il, elle préfère	ils, elles préfèrent

Préfères-tu la ville ou la campagne?
Do you prefer the city or the country?

---

premier [prẹ́-MYAY] adjective, masc. **first**
première [prẹ́-MYEHR] fém.

Le petit déjeuner est le premier repas de la journée.
Breakfast is the first meal of the day.

---

prendre [PRAHNDR] verb **to take; to have (food)**

je prends	nous prenons
tu prends	vous prenez
il, elle prend	ils, elles prennent

Nous prenons un bain de soleil à la plage.
We take a sun bath at the beach.

Maman prend un croissant pour le petit déjeuner.
Mom has a croissant for breakfast.

---

préparer [pray-pa-RAY] verb **to prepare**

je prépare	nous préparons
tu prépares	vous préparez
il, elle prépare	ils, elles préparent

Ma soeur prépare la salade.
My sister prepares the salad.

---

près de [PREH] preposition **near, close to**

Bordeaux est près de l'océan Atlantique.
Bordeaux is near the Atlantic Ocean.

---

présent [pray-ZAHN] adjective, masc. **present, here**
présente [pray-ZAHNT] fem.

Mon amie Jeanne est présente; mon amie Suzanne est absente.
My friend Joan is present; my friend Susan is absent.

---

présenter [pray-sahn-TAY] verb **to introduce**

je présente	nous présentons
tu présentes	vous présentez
il, elle présente	ils, elles présentent

Je jous présente mon petit-fils.
I would like to introduce my grandson to you.

---

le président [pray-zee-DAHN] noun, masc. **president**

Qui est le président de la France?
Who is the president of France?

---

presque [PREHSK] adverb **almost**

Il est presque six heures.
It is almost six o'clock.

---

prêt [PREH] adjective, masc. **ready**
prête [PREHT] fem.

Es-tu prêt? Nous sommes en retard.
Are you ready? We are late.

---

prêter [preh-TAY] verb **to lend**

je prête	nous prêtons
tu prêtes	vous prêtez
il, elle prête	ils, elles prêtent

Peux-tu me prêter ta bicyclette?
Can you lend me your bicycle?

---

je vous en prie [zhe-voo-zahn-PREE] **you're welcome**
idiomatic expression

Merci, mademoiselle.
Thank you, miss.

Je vous en prie, monsieur.
You're welcome, sir.

---

le prince [PRAINS] noun, masc. **prince**
la princesse [PRAIN-SEHS] fem.

Le prince joue dans le jardin.
The prince is playing in the garden.

---

le printemps [prain-TAHN] noun, masc. **spring**

Au printemps on voit beaucoup de fleurs.
You see a lot of flowers in the spring.

---

le prix [PREE] noun, masc. **price**

Quel est le prix de ce livre?
What is the price of this book?

---

prochain [pro-SHAIN] noun, masc. **next**
prochaine [proh-SHEHN] fem.

Le professeur dit: "La semaine prochaine nous avons un examen."
The teacher says, "Next week we will have an examination."

---

le professeur [pruh-feh-SUHR] noun, masc. **teacher**

Le professeur est dans la salle de classe.
The teacher is in the classroom.

---

profond [pruh-FOHN] adjective, masc. **deep**
profonde [pruh-FOHND] fem.

Est-ce que la piscine est profonde?
Is the pool deep?

---

se promener [seh-pruhm-NAY] **to walk**
verb, idiomatic expression

je me promène	nous nous promenons
tu te promènes	vous vous promenez
il, elle se promène	ils, elles se promènent

Elles se promènent dans le parc.
They are walking in the park.

faire une promenade **to take a walk**
[feh-rewn-pruhm-NAD]
idiomatic expression

Ils vont faire une promenade.
They are going to take a walk.

---

promettre [pruh-MEHTR] verb **to promise**

je promets	nous promettons
tu promets	vous promettez
il, elle promet	ils, elles promettent

Je promets de faire mes devoirs.
I promise to do my homework.

---

propre [PRUHPR] adjective **clean; own**

Mes mains sont propres.
My hands are clean.

Ce n'est pas le livre de ma soeur; c'est mon propre livre.
It is not my sister's book; it is my own book.

---

puis [PEW-EE] adverb **then**

J'écris une lettre; puis, je vais chez mon ami.
I write a letter; then I go to my friend's house.

---

punir [pew-NEER] verb **to punish**

je punis	nous punissons
tu punis	vous punissez
il, elle punit	ils, elles punissent

Quand je suis méchant, maman me punit.
When I am naughty, Mom punishes me.

---

le pupitre [pew-PEETR] noun, masc. **desk (pupil's)**

Son pupitre est trop petit.
His desk is too small.

---

le pyjama [pee-zha-MA] noun, masc. **pajamas**

Je mets le pyjama à dix heures du soir.
I put on my pajamas at ten o'clock at night.

Q

quand [KAHN] adverb **when**

Je lis un livre quand il pleut.
I read a book when it rains.

---

quarante [ka-RAHNT] adjective **forty**

Connaissez-vous l'histoire des quarante voleurs?
Do you know the story of the forty thieves?

---

le quart [KAR] noun, masc. **quarter**

Il est sept heures et quart.
It is a quarter after seven.

---

quatorze [ka-TUHRZ] adjective **fourteen**

Le quatorze juillet est la fête nationale française.
July 14th is the French national holiday.

---

quatre [KATR] adjective **four**

Il y a quatre personnes dans ma famille.
There are four people in my family.

---

quatre-vingt-dix [ka-tre-vain-DEES] adjective **ninety**

Quelqu'un a quatre-vingt-dix ans?
Somebody is ninety years old?

---

quatre-vingts [ka-tre-VAIN] adjective **eighty**

J'ai quatre-vingts billes!
I have eighty marbles!

---

que [ke] pronoun **that; which; what; whom**
qu' (before a vowel)

Voici la lettre que j'écris.
Here is the letter that I am writing.

La femme que je vois est ma tante.
The woman whom I see is my aunt.

Qu'as-tu? [ka-TEW], **Qu'avez-vous?** [ka-vay-voo] interjection — **What's the matter?**

quel [KEHL] adjective, pronoun, masc.
quelle fem. — **what, which; what a ...!**

Quel drapeau est le drapeau français?
Which flag is the French flag?

Quelle belle robe!
What a beautiful dress!

---

quelque [KEHL-ke] adjective — **any; some; several**

Il y a quelques chaises dans le salon.
There are several chairs in the living room.

---

quelque chose [kehl-ke-SHOHZ] pronoun — **something, anything**

Est-ce qu'il y a quelque chose dans ce tiroir?
Is there something in this drawer?

---

quelquefois [kehl-ke-FWA] adverb — **sometimes**

Quelquefois je ne suis pas sage.
Sometimes I am not well-behaved.

---

quelqu'un [kehl-KUHN] pronoun, masc.
quelqu'une [kehl-KEWN] fem. — **someone, somebody**

Quelqu'un est dans le restaurant.
Somebody is in the restaurant.

---

la querelle [ke-REHL] noun, fem. — **quarrel**

Quelquefois, mon père se querelle avec ma mère.
My father sometimes has a quarrel with my mother.

---

la question [kehs-TYOHN] noun, fem. **question**

Le professeur demande: "Est-ce qu'il y a des questions?"
The teacher asks, "Are there any questions?"

---

la queue [KEOH] noun, fem. **tail**

Mon chien remue la queue quand je rentre à la maison.
My dog wags his tail when I return home.

---

qui [KEE] pronoun **who, which, that**

Qui vient chez nous?
Who is coming to visit us?

Je cherche mon stylo qui est sur le tapis.
I am looking for my pen which is on the rug.

---

quinze [KAINZ] adjective **fifteen**

C'est aujourd'hui le quinze janvier, l'anniversaire de Martin Luther King.
Today is January 15th, the birthday of Martin Luther King.

---

quitter [kee-TAY] verb **to leave, to take off**

je quitte	nous quittons
tu quittes	vous quittez
il, elle quitte	ils, elles quittent

Nous quittons le musée à cinq heures.
We leave the museum at five o'clock.

---

quoi [KWA] interjection **what**

Quoi? Tu n'as pas la monnaie pour l'autobus?
What? You don't have the change for the bus?

il n'y a pas de quoi. **You're welcome. (polite)**
[eel-nee-a-pa-dé-KWA] idiomatic expresion
or
Je vous en prie. [zhé-voo-zahn-PREE] idiomatic expression

R

raconter [ra-kohn-TAY] verb **to tell**

je raconte nous racontons
tu racontes vous racontez
il, elle raconte ils, elles racontent

Raconte-moi une histoire, maman.
Tell me a story, Mom.

---

la radio [ra-DYOH] noun, fem. **radio**

La radio ne marche pas.
The radio is not working.

---

le raisin [reh-ZAIN] noun, masc. **grape**

Mmm, nous avons des raisins!
Mmm, we have grapes!

> La Fontaine is a famous writer who wrote such fables as "The Fox and the Grapes" ("Le Renard et les raisins").

---

la raison [reh-ZOHN] noun, fem. **reason, right**
avoir raison [reh-ZOHN] idiomatic expression **to be right**
(See **avoir**)

Grand-mère a toujours raison.
Grandmother is always right.

---

le rang [RAHN] noun, masc. **row**

La maîtress dit: "Les enfants du premier rang, levez-vous."
The teacher says, "Children in the first row, stand."

---

rapide [ra-PEED] adjective **rapid, fast**

Le chien est rapide quand il court après un chat.
The dog is fast when he runs after a cat.

---

se rappeler [sɇ-ra-PLAY] verb **to remember**

je me rappelle	nous nous rappelons
tu te rappelles	vous vous rappelez
il, elle se rappelle	ils, elles se rappellent

Je ne peux pas me rappeller le nom de ce bâtiment.
I cannot remember the name of this building.

---

le rat [RA] noun, masc. **rat**

J'ai peur des rats!
I am afraid of rats!

---

recevoir [rɇ-sɇ-VWAR] verb **to receive, to get**

je reçois	nous recevons
tu reçois	vous recevez
il, elle reçoit	ils, elles reçoivent

Je reçois une carte postale de ma soeur toutes les semaines.
I receive a postcard from my sister every week.

---

le réfrigérateur [ray-free-zhay-ra-TUHR] noun, masc. **refrigerator**

Le réfrigérateur est dans la cuisine.
The refrigerator is in the kitchen.

---

regarder [rɇ-gar-DAY] verb **to look at, to watch**

je regarde	nous regardons
tu regardes	vous regardez
il, elle regarde	ils, elles regardent

J'aime regarder la télévision.
I like to watch television.

se regarder [sé-ré-gar-DAY] **to look at oneself**
idiomatic expression

je me regarde	nous nous regardons
tu te regardes	vous vous regardez
il, elle se regarde	ils, elles regardent

Le singe se regarde dans la glace.
The monkey looks at itself in the mirror.

---

la règle [REHGL] noun, fem. **ruler; rule**

La règle est longue.
The ruler is long.

Il faut obéir aux règles à l'école et à la maison.
We have to obey the rules at school and at home.

---

la reine [REHN] noun, fem. **queen**

La reine est assise près du roi.
The queen is seated near the king.

---

remplir [rahn-PLEER] verb **to fill**

je remplis	nous remplissons
tu remplis	vous remplissez
il, elle remplit	ils, elles remplissent

Etienne remplit la boîte de papier.
Stephen fills the box with paper.

---

remeur [ré-mew-AY] verb **to move, to shake, to wag**

je remue	nous remuons
tu remues	vous remuez
il, elle remue	ils, elles remuent

Elle remue vite ses doigts quand elle joue du piano.
She moves her fingers quickly when she plays the piano.

---

le renard [ré-NAR] noun, masc. **fox**

Le renard court très vite.
The fox runs very fast.

---

rencontrer [rahn-kohn-TRAY] verb **to meet**

je rencontre	nous rencontrons
tu rencontres	vous rencontrez
il, elle rencontre	ils, elles rencontrent

Qui rencontre Le Petit Chaperon Rouge dans la forêt?
Who meets Little Red Riding Hood in the forest?

---

le rendez-vous [rahn-day-voo] noun, masc. **appointment**

A quelle heure est votre rendez-vous avec le médecin?
What time is your appointment with the doctor?

---

rendre [RAHNDR] verb **to give back, to return**

je rends	nous rendons
tu rends	vous rendez
il, elle rend	ils, elles rendent

Il me rend mes patins à roulettes.
He returns my roller skates.

---

rentrer [rahn-tray] verb **to return**

je rentre	nous rentrons
tu rentres	vous rentrez
il, elle rentre	ils, elles rentrent.

Je rentre chez moi.
I return home.

---

renverser [rahn-vehr-SAY] verb **to spill, to overturn**

je renverse	nous renversons
tu renverses	vous renversez
il, elle renverse	ils, elles renversent

Le bébé renverse l'assiette.
The baby overturns the plate.

---

réparer [ray-pa-RAY] verb **to repair, to fix**

je répare	nous réparons
tu répares	vous réparez
il, elle répare	ils, elles réparent

Mon frère répare la machine.
My brother is fixing the machine.

---

le repas [re̸-PA] noun, masc. **meal**

Quel repas préférez-vous?
Which meal do you prefer?

---

repasser [re̸-pa-SAY] verb **to iron**

je repasse	nous repassons
tu repasses	vous repassez
il, elle repasse	ils, elles repassent

Ma mère repasse la chemise de Papa avec un fer.
My mother irons Dad's shirt with an iron.

---

répéter [ray-pay-TAY] verb **to repeat**

je répète	nous répétons
tu répètes	vous répétez
il, elle répète	ils, elles répètent

Le maître dit: "Répétez après moi."
The teacher says, "Repeat after me."

---

répondre [ray-POHN̸DR] verb **to answer, to reply**

je réponds	nous répondons
tu réponds	vous répondez
il, elle répond	ils, elles répondent

La petite fille ne peut pas répondre à la question.
The little girl cannot answer the question.

---

la réponse [ray-POHN̸S] noun, fem. **answer**

J'écris la réponse correcte dans mon cahier.
I write the correct answer in my notebook.

---

se reposer [sɇ-rɇ-poh-SAY] verb **to rest**

je me repose	nous nous reposons
tu te reposes	vous vous reposez
il, elle se repose	ils, elles se reposent

L'enfant court. Il ne veut pas se reposer.
The child runs. He does not want to rest.

---

le restaurant [rehs-tuh-RAHN̸] noun, masc. **restaurant**

Le garçon travaille dans ce restaurant.
The waiter works in this restaurant.

---

rester [rehs-TAY] verb **to stay, to remain**

je reste	nous restons
tu restes	vous restez
il, elle reste	ils, elles restent

Je voudrais rester chez ma grand-mère.
I would like to stay at my grandmother's house.

---

retard [rɇ-TAR] noun, masc. **delay**
en retard [ahn̸-rɇ-TAR] adverb **late**

François arrive en retard à l'école.
Frank comes late to school.

---

retourner [rɇ-toor-NAY] verb **to return, to go back**

je retourne	nous retournons
tu retournes	vous retournez
il, elle retourne	ils, elles retournent

Il va au tableau noir et puis il retourne à sa place.
He goes to the blackboard and then he returns to his seat.

---

réussir [ray-ew-SEER] verb **to succeed, to be successful**

je réussis	nous réussissons
tu réussis	vous réussissez
il, elle réussit	ils, elles réussissent

Il réussit à attraper un poisson.
He succeeds in catching a fish.

---

le réveille-matin [ray-vay-ma-TAIN] **alarm clock**
noun, masc.

Le réveille-matin sonne trop fort.
The alarm clock rings too loudly.

---

se réveiller [se-ray-vay-YAY] verb **to wake up**

je me réveille	nous nous réveillons
tu te réveilles	vous vous réveillez
il, elle se réveille	ils, elles se réveillent

Nous nous réveillons de bonne heure.
We wake up early.

---

rêver [reh-VAY] verb **to dream**

je rêve	nous rêvons
tu rêves	vous rêvez
il, elle rêve	ils, elles rêvent

Je rêve d'aller sur la lune!
I dream of going to the moon!

le rêve [REHV] noun, masc. **dream**

---

revoir [re-VWAR] verb **to see again**

je revois	nous revoyons
tu revois	vous revoyez
il, elle revoit	ils, elles revoient

Je vais revoir le film.
I am going to see the film again.

au revoir **good-bye** (See **au revoir**)

---

le rez-de-chaussée **ground floor**
[rayd-shoh-SAY] noun, masc.

Notre appartement est au rez-de-chaussée.
Our apartment is on the ground floor.

---

le rhume [REWM] noun, masc. **cold (illness)**

Tu ne peux pas sortir. Tu as un rhume.
You cannot go out. You have a cold.

---

riche [REESH] adjective **rich, wealthy**

La femme riche porte des bijoux.
The rich lady wears jewels.

---

le rideau [ree-DOH] noun, masc. **curtain**
les rideaux pl.

Les rideaux dans ma chambre sont trop longs.
The curtains in my room are too long.

---

rien [RYAIN] pronoun **nothing, none**

Qu'est-ce que tu as dans la poche? Rien!
What do you have in your pocket? Nothing!

De rien. [de-RYAIN] idiomatic expression **You're welcome.**

Je lui donne une banane. Il dit: "Merci."
Je réponds: "De rien."
I give him a banana. He says, "Thanks."
I answer, "You're welcome."

---

rire [REER] verb **to laugh**

je ris	nous rions
tu ris	vous riez
il, elle rit	ils, elles rient

Il rit quand il regarde les ours.
He laughs when he looks at the bears.

---

rivaliser [ree-va-lee-zay] verb **to compete**

Nous rivalisons dans le concours.
We compete in the contest.

---

la rivière [ree-VYEHR] noun, fem. **river**

Comment peut-on traverser la rivière?
How can we cross the river?

---

le riz [REE] noun, masc. **rice**

Le riz est délicieux.
The rice is delicious.

---

la robe [RUHB] noun, fem. **dress**

La robe de ma poupée est sale.
My doll's dress is dirty.

---

le rocher [ruh-SHAY] noun, masc. **rock**

Quel grand rocher là-bas!
What a large rock over there!

---

le roi [RWA] noun, masc. **king**

Est-ce qu'il y a un roi en France? Non, il y a un président.
Is there a king in France? No, there is a president.

---

le rôle [ROHL] noun, masc. **role, part**

Je veux jouer le rôle du prince.
I want to play the part of the prince.

---

rond [ROHN] adjective, masc. **round**
ronde [ROHND] fem.

L'assiette est ronde.
The plate is round.

---

le rosbif [ruhz-BEEF] noun, masc. **roast beef**

Je voudrais un sandwich de rosbif, s'il vous plaît.
I would like a roast beef sandwich, please.

---

rose [ROHZ] adjective **pink**

J'aime porter mon ruban rose dans les cheveux.
I like to wear my pink ribbon in my hair.

---

la roue [ROO] noun, fem. **wheel**

Mon oncle répare la roue de ma bicyclette.
My uncle fixes the wheel of my bicycle.

---

rouge [ROOZH] adjective **red**

Les voitures s'arrêtent quand le feu est rouge.
The cars stop when the light is red.

---

rouler [ROO-LAY] verb **to roll, to go**

je roule	nous roulons
tu roules	vous roulez
il, elle roule	ils, elles roulent

Le patin à roulettes roule dans la rue.
The roller skate is rolling into the street.

---

la route [ROOT] noun, fem. **road, route, highway**

Quel est le nom de cette route?
What's the name of this road?

---

le ruban [rew-BAHN] noun, masc. **ribbon**

Elle porte un joli ruban.
She is wearing a pretty ribbon.

---

la rue [REW] noun, fem. **street**

Il est dangereux de jouer à la balle dans la rue.
It is dangerous to play ball in the street.

---

rusé [rew-ZAY] adjective, masc. **clever, cunning**
rusée fem.

Le voleur est rusé; il grimpe sur un arbre.
The thief is clever; he climbs a tree.

S

sa (See **son**)

---

le sable [SABL] noun, masc. **sand**

A la plage, je m'assieds sur le sable.
At the beach I sit on the sand.

---

le sac [SAK] noun, masc. **bag, sack, purse**
le sac à main [sa-ka-MAIN] noun, masc. **handbag, pocketbook**

J'achète un sac à main pour ma mère.
I am buying a handbag for my mother.

---

sage [SAZH] adjective, noun, masc. **well-behaved; wise, wise person**

Les petites filles sont plus sages que les petits garçons.
Little girls are better behaved than little boys.

Grand-père est un sage.
Grandfather is wise.

---

sain et sauf [sain-ay-SOHF] idiomatic expression **safe and sound**

Je retourne à la maison sain et sauf.
I come home safe and sound.

---

la saison [seh-ZOHN] noun, fem. **season**

Combien de saisons y a-t-il?
How many seasons are there?

---

la salade [sa-LAD] noun, fem. **salad**

Ma cousine met la salade au milieu de la table.
My cousin puts the salad in the middle of the table.

---

sale [SAL] adjective **dirty**

Ma chemise est sale!
My shirt is dirty!

---

la salle [SAL] noun, fem. **room**
la salle de classe [sal-dɇ-KLAS] noun, fem. **classroom**

La salle de classe est vide.
The classroom is empty.

---

la salle à manger [sa-la-mahn̸-ZHAY] noun, fem. **dining room**

Maman entre dans la salle à manger.
Mother enters the dining room.

---

la salle de bain [sal-dɇ-BAIN̸] noun, fem. **bathroom**

La salle de bain est petite.
The bathroom is small.

---

le salon [sa-LOHN̸] noun, masc. **living room**

Qui est dans le salon?
Who is in the living room?

---

samedi [sam-DEE] noun, masc. **Saturday**

Faisons un pique-nique samedi.
Let's have a picnic Saturday.

---

le sandwich [sahn-DWEESH] noun, masc. **sandwich**

Tu veux un sandwich ou une salade?
Do you want a sandwich or a salad?

---

le sang [SAHN] noun, masc. **blood**

J'ai mal au genou. Regarde le sang!
My knee hurts. Look at the blood!

---

sans [SAHN] preposition **without**

Je vais en classes sans mon ami. Il est malade.
I'm going to class without my friend. He is sick.

---

la santé [sahn-TAY] noun, fem. **health**

Maman dit: "Les bonbons ne sont pas bons pour la santé."
Mother says, "Candy is not good for your health."

---

le saute-mouton [soht-moo-TON] noun, masc. **leapfrog**
jouer à saute-mouton **to play leapfrog**
[zhoo-ay-ah-soht-moo-TON]
idiomatic expression

Nous jouons à saute-mouton.
We play leapfrog.

---

sauter [soh-TAY] verb **to jump, to leap**

je saute	nous sautons
tu sautes	vous sautez
il, elle saute	ils, elles sautent

Le garçon saute de l'escalier.
The boy jumps from the stairs.

sauter à la corde [soh-tay-a-la-KUHRD] **jump rope**
(See **la corde**)

---

la sauterelle [soh-TREHL] noun, fem. **grasshopper**

Le garçon essaye d'attraper la sauterelle.
The boy tries to catch the grasshopper.

---

sauvage [soh-VAZH] adjective **wild**

Les animaux sauvages habitent la forêt.
Wild animals live in the forest.

---

sauver [soh-VAY] verb **to save, to rescue**

je sauve	nous sauvons
tu sauves	vous sauvez
il, elle sauve	ils, elles sauvent

Mon oncle me sauve quand je tombe dans l'eau.
My uncle saves me when I fall into the water.

---

le savant [sa-VAHN] noun, masc. **scientist**
la savante [sa-VAHNT] fem.

Je voudrais devenir savant.
I would like to become a scientist.

> Pierre and Marie Curie were famous French scientists. They discovered radium.

---

savoir [sa-VWAR] verb **to know, to know how to**

je sais	nous savons
tu sais	vous savez
il, elle sait	ils, elles savent

Je sais monter à bicyclette.
I know how to ride a bicycle.

---

le savon [sa-VOHN] noun, masc. **soap**

N'oublie pas d'employer le savon!
Don't forget to use soap!

---

la science [SYAHNS] noun, fem. **science**

J'aime aller en classe de science.
I like to go to my science class.

---

se [se] pronoun **himself, herself, themselves**

Il se lave.
He washes himself.

Elle se peigne.
She combs her hair.

Elles se lèvent à sept heures.
They get up at seven o'clock.

---

le seau [SOH] noun, masc. **pail, bucket**
les seaux pl.

Le fermier remplit le seau de lait.
The farmer fills the pail with milk.

---

sec [SEHK] adjective, masc. **dry**
sèche [SEHSH] fem.

Est-ce que le plancher est sec, Maman?
Is the floor dry, Mom?

---

le secours [SKOOR] noun, masc. **help**
Au secours! [oh-SKOOR] interjection **Help!**

Quand je tombe je crie: "Au secours!"
When I fall I cry, "Help!"

---

le secret [se-KREH] noun, masc. **secret**

Dis-moi le secret!
Tell me the secret!

---

seize [SEHZ] adjective — **sixteen**

Je dois lire seize pages ce soir!
I have to read sixteen pages this evening!

---

le sel [SEHL] noun, masc. — **salt**

Passez-moi le sel, s'il vous plaît.
Pass me the salt, please.

---

selon [SLOHN] preposition — **according to**

Selon mon frère, il va neiger demain.
According to my brother, it is going to snow tomorrow.

---

la semaine [SMEHN] noun, fem. — **week**

Le calendrier nous montre les sept jours de la semaine.
The calendar shows us the seven days of the week.

---

sensationnel [sahn-sa-syohn-NEHL] interjection — **great, sensational, marvelous, wonderful**

Tu vas au théâtre? Sensationnel!
You're going to the theater? Marvelous!

---

le sentier [sahn-TYAY] noun, masc. — **path**

Ce sentier mène au pont.
This path leads to the bridge.

---

sentir [sahn-TEER] verb — **to smell; to feel**

je sens	nous sentons
tu sens	vous sentez
il, elle sent	ils, elles sentent

Le gâteau sent bon.
The cake smells good.

---

sept [SEHT] adjective — **seven**

Voilà sept pommes.
There are seven apples.

---

septembre [sehp-TAHNBR] noun, masc. **September**

Est-ce qu'on retourne à l'école le premier septembre?
Do we go back to school on the first of September?

---

sérieux [say-RYEOH] adjective, masc. **serious**
sérieuse [say-RYEOHZ] fem.

On joue un film sérieux au cinéma.
They are playing a serious film at the movies.

---

le serpent [sehr-PAHN] noun, masc. **snake**

Est-ce qu'il y a des serpents en France?
Are there any snakes in France?

---

serrer la main à [seh-RAY] **to shake hands**
idiomatic expression

je serre la main	nous serrons la main
tu serres la main	vous serrez la main
il, elle serre la main	ils, elles serrent la main

Alain, serre la main à ton voisin.
Alan, shake hands with your neighbor.

---

la serveuse [sehr-VEOHZ] noun, fem. **server, waitress**
le serveur [sehr-VEUHR] noun, masc. **waiter, server**

La serveuse est dans le restaurant.
The waitress is in the restaurant.

---

la serviette [sehr-VYEHT] noun, fem. **napkin; towel; briefcase**

Il y a quatre serviettes sur la table.
There are four napkins on the table.

Ma serviette est dans la salle de bain.
My towel is in the bathroom.

Laurent, n'oublie pas ta serviette.
Lawrence, don't forget your briefcase.

---

servir [sehr-VEER] verb **to serve**

je sers	nous servons
tu sers	vous servez
il, elle sert	ils, elles servent

Je sers le dîner à mon chien.
I serve my dog his dinner.

---

seul [SEUHL] adjective, masc. **only; alone**
seule fem.

C'est la seule fleur dans le jardin.
It is the only flower in the garden.

Je suis seul dans le salon.
I am alone in the living room.

---

seulement [seuhl-MAHN] adverb **only**

J'ai seulement un poisson rouge.
I have only one goldfish.

---

si [SEE] adverb **so**

Le bébé mange si lentement!
The baby eats so slowly!

---

si [SEE] conjunction **if, whether**
s' (before il)

Je vais à la fenêtre pour voir s'il pleut.
I am going to the window to see if it is raining.

S'il pleut, je ne peux pas sortir.
If it is raining, I cannot go out.

---

siffler [see-FLAY] verb **to whistle**

je siffle nous sifflons
tu siffles vous sifflez
il, elle siffle ils, elles sifflent

Quand je siffle, mon ami sait que je suis à la porte.
When I whistle, my friend knows that I'm at the door.

---

silencieux [see-lahn-SYEOH] adjective, masc. **quiet, silent**
silencieuse [see-lahn-SYEOHZ] fem.

La rue dans la ville n'est jamais silencieuse.
The city street is never quiet.

---

s'il vous plaît [seel-voo-PLEH] idiomatic expression **please**
s'il te plaît (familiar)

Donnez-moi un crayon, s'il vous plaît, monsieur Duval.
Please give me a pencil, Mr. Duval.

Donne-moi un crayon, s'il te plaît, Pierrot.
Please give me a pencil, Pete.

---

le singe [SAINZH] noun, masc. **monkey**

Le singe mange une banane.
The monkey is eating a banana.

---

six [SEES, SEEZ, SEE] adjective **six**

Combien de crayons avez-vous? Six. [SEES]
How many pencils do you have? Six.

Il a six amis. [SEEZ] *(before a vowel)*
He has six friends.

Il a six clous. [SEE] *(before a consonant)*
He has six nails. (metal)

---

le soda [soh-DA] noun, masc. **soda**

Je bois du soda.
I am drinking soda.

---

la soeur [SEUHR] noun, fem. **sister**

Ma tante est la soeur de ma mère.
My aunt is my mother's sister.

---

la soif [SWAF] noun, fem. **thirst**
avoir soif [a-vwar-SWAF] idiomatic expression **to be thirsty**

Avez-vous soif? Oui, j'ai soif.
Are you thirsty? Yes, I'm thirsty. (See **avoir**)

---

le soin [SWAIN] noun, masc. **care**
avec soin [a-vehk-SWAIN] adverb **with care, carefully**

Paul verse l'eau dans le verre avec soin.
Paul pours water into the glass carefully.

---

le soir [SWAR] noun, masc. **evening, night**

Le soir je regarde la télé.
I watch television in the evening.

---

soixante [swa-SAHNT] adjective **sixty**

Il y a soixante minutes dans une heure.
There are sixty minutes in an hour.

---

soixante-dix [swa-sahnt-DEES] adjective **seventy**

La grand-mère de Nanette a soixante-dix ans.
Nancy's grandmother is seventy years old.

---

le soldat [suhl-DA] noun, masc. **soldier**

Mon cousin est soldat.
My cousin is a soldier.

---

le soleil [suh-LAY] noun, masc. **sun**

A quelle heure est-ce que le soleil se lève?
What time does the sun rise?

---

le bain de soleil [bain-de-suh-LAY] noun, masc. **sunbath**

Je prends un bain de soleil sur l'herbe.
I take a sunbath on the grass.

---

le sommeil [suh-MAY] noun, masc. **sleep**
avoir sommeil [a-vwar-suh-MAY] **to be sleepy**
idiomatic expression

Qui a sommeil?
Who is sleepy? (See **avoir**)

---

son [SOHN] adjective **his; her; its; one's**
sa [SA] fem.
ses [SEH] masc., fem., pl.

Il mène son chien dans la rue.
He is leading his dog into the street.

Regardez sa jolie robe!
Look at her pretty dress!

Ses livres sont lourds.
Her books are heavy.

---

sonner [suh-NAY] verb **to ring; to strike (clock)**

je sonne	nous sonnons
tu sonnes	vous sonnez
il, elle sonne	ils, elles sonnent

Le téléphone sonne.
The telephone is ringing.

---

la sorte [SUHRT] noun, fem. **sort, kind, type**

Quelle sorte de viande est-ce?
What kind of meat is this?

---

sortir [suhr-TEER] verb **to go out, to leave**

je sors nous sortons
tu sors vous sortez
il, elle sort ils, elles sortent

L'infirmière sort de l'hôpital.
The nurse leaves the hospital.

---

la soucoupe [soo-KOOP] noun, fem. **saucer**

La femme met la tasse sur la soucoupe.
The woman puts the cup on the saucer.

---

le souhait [soo-EH] noun, masc. **wish**

Quand je me couche je fais un souhait.
When I go to bed I make a wish.

---

le soulier [soo-LYAY] noun, masc. **shoe**

Mes souliers sont mouillés.
My shoes are wet.

---

la soupe [SOOP] noun, fem. **soup**

Ma soeur sert la soupe à mon frère.
My sister serves soup to my brother.

---

sourd [SOOR] adjective, masc. **deaf**
sourde [SOORD] fem.

Tu ne m'entends pas? Tu es sourd?
You don't hear me? You're deaf?

---

sourire [soo-REER] verb **to smile**

je souris nous sourions
tu souris vous souriez
il, elle sourit ils, elles sourient

Tu souris toujours quand je te donne un petit gâteau.
You always smile when I give you a cookie.

---

la souris [soo-REE] noun, fem. **mouse**

Il y a des souris dans ce champ.
There are mice in this field.

---

sous [soo] preposition **under**

La carotte pousse sous la terre.
The carrot grows under the ground.

---

souvent [soo-VAHN] adverb **often**

Je prends souvent l'autobus.
I often go by bus.

---

le sport [SPUHR] noun, masc. **sport**

Quel est votre sport favori?
What is your favorite sport?

---

la station-service [sta-syohn-sehr-VEES] noun, fem. **gas station**

Enfin! Violà une station-service!
Finally! There is a gas station!

---

stupide [stew-PEED] adjective **stupid, foolish**

Est-ce que l'éléphant est intelligent ou stupide?
Is the elephant intelligent or stupid?

---

le stylo [stee-LOH] noun, masc. **pen**

Je laisse toujours mon stylo à la maison.
I always leave my pen at home.

---

le stylo à bille [stee-loh-a-BEEY] noun, masc. **ballpoint pen**

J'écris avec un stylo à bille.
I am writing with a ballpoint pen.

---

la sucette [sew-SEHT] noun, fem. **lollipop**

Mmm, j'aime la sucette.
Mmm, I like the lollipop.

---

le sucre [SEWKR] noun, masc. **sugar**

Maman sert le sucre avec le thé.
Mother serves sugar with tea.

---

le sud [SEWD] noun, masc. **south**

Marseille est au sud de la France.
Marseilles is in the south of France.

---

suivre [SEW/-EEVR] verb **to follow**

je suis	nous suivons
tu suis	vous suivez
il, elle suit	ils, elles suivent

Les élèves de la classe suivent la maîtresse.
The pupils in the class follow the teacher.

---

le supermarché (See **marché**)

---

sur [SEWR] preposition **on**

La règle est sur le pupitre.
The ruler is on the desk.

---

sûr [SEWR] adjective, masc. **sure, certain**
sûre fem.

Je suis sûr que le train arrive bientôt.
I am sure that the train will come soon.

bien sûr (See **bien**)

---

la surprise [s~~ew~~r-PREEZ] noun, fem. **surprise**

Une surprise pour moi?
A surprise for me?

---

surtout [s~~ew~~r-TOO] adverb **above all, especially**

J'aime regarder la télévision, surtout le samedi matin.
I like to watch television, especially Saturday mornings.

---

surveiller [s~~ew~~r-vay-YAY] verb **to watch over, to look after**

je surveille	nous surveillons
tu surveilles	vous surveillez
il, elle surveille	ils, elles surveillent

La chatte surveille ses petits (chats).
The cat looks after her kittens.

T

ta (See **ton**)

---

la table [TABL] noun, fem. **table**

La brosse est sur la table.
The brush is on the table.

---

le tableau [ta-BLOH] noun, masc. **chalkboard, picture**
le tableau noir [ta-bloh-NWAR] noun, masc. **blackboard**

L'élève écrit au tableau noir.
The pupil writes on the blackboard.

---

le tablier [ta-BLYAY] noun, masc. **apron**

Marthe porte un tablier à l'école.
Martha wears an apron at school.

---

la tache [TASH] noun, fem. **spot, stain**

Il y a une tache sur le tapis.
There is a stain on the rug.

---

tacheté [tash-TAY] adjective, masc. **spotted**
tachetée fem.

Ma tortue est tachetée.
My turtle is spotted.

---

la taille [TAHY] noun, fem. **size; waist**

Dans un magasin on me demande:
"Quelle est votre taille?"
In a store they ask me, "What is your size?"

---

le tailleur [tah-YEUHR] noun, masc. **tailor**

Mon voisin est tailleur.
My neighbor is a tailor.

---

se taire [sé-TEHR] idiomatic expression **to be quiet**

je me tais	nous nous taisons
tu te tais	vous vous taisez
il, elle se tait	ils, elles se taisent

On me dit toujours: "Tais-toi!"
They always tell me, "Be quiet!"

---

le tambour [tahn-boor] noun, masc. **drum**

Je fais du bruit quand je joue du tambour.
I make noise when I play the drum.

---

tant [TAHN] adverb **so much, so many**

Tant de raisins!
So many grapes!

---

la tante [TAHNT] noun, fem. **aunt**

Ma tante est vendeuse.
My aunt is a salesperson.

---

le tapis [ta-PEE] noun, masc. **rug**

Le tapis est sur le plancher.
The rug is on the floor.

---

taquiner [ta-kee-NAY] verb **to tease**

je taquine	nous taquinons
tu taquines	vous taquinez
il, elle taquine	ils, elles taquinent

Mon frère me taquine toujours!
My brother always teases me!

---

tard [TAR] adverb **late**

Il est tard. Dépêchons-nous.
It is late. Let's hurry.

> "Mieux vaut tard que jamais" is a popular proverb in French. It means: "It is better late than never."

plus tard [plew-TAR] adverb **later**

Il est huit heures maintenant. Le facteur arrive plus tard.
It is eight o'clock now. The mailman comes later.

---

la tarte [TART] noun, fem. **pie**

Aimez-vous la tarte aux pommes?
Do you like apple pie?

---

la tartine [tar-TEEN] noun, fem. **bread and butter (jam) snack**

Je prends une tartine quand je rentre à la maison.
I have a snack (of bread and jam) when I come home.

---

la tasse [TAS] noun, fem. **cup**

Je mets la tasse sur la soucoupe.
I put the cup on the saucer.

---

le taxi [ta-KSEE] noun, masc. **taxi**

Mon frère conduit un taxi.
My brother drives a taxi.

---

te [tɇ] pronoun **you, to you; yourself**

Je te donne du lait.
I give you some milk.

Tu te lèves trop tard!
You get up too late!

---

le technicien (See **l'ordinateur**)

---

la télé (See **télévision**)

---

le téléphone [tay-lay-FUHN] noun, masc. **telephone**

J'aime parler au téléphone.
I like to talk on the telephone.

---

le téléviseur [tay-lay-vee-ZEUHR] noun, masc. **television set**

Le téléviseur ne marche pas.
The television set is not working.

---

la télévision [tay-lay-vee-ZYOHN] **television**
la télé [tay-LAY] noun, fem.

Mon frère et moi, nous regardons la télévision.
My brother and I watch television.

l'antenne de télévision (See **antenne**)

---

le temps [TAHN] noun, masc. **weather**

Quel temps fait-il? Il fait du soleil.
What is the weather? The sun is shining. (See **faire**)

---

la tente [TAHNT] noun, fem. **tent**

Quand je suis à la colonie de vacances je dors dans une tente.
When I am at camp I sleep in a tent.

---

le terrain de jeux [teh-rain-de-ZHEOH] noun, masc. **playground**

Nous jouons à la balle au terrain de jeux.
We play ball in the playground.

---

la terre [TEHR] noun, fem. **earth; ground**

Quand l'astronaute est sur la lune, il voit la terre.
When the astronaut is on the moon, he sees the earth.

le tremblement de terre **earthquake**
[trahm-ble-mahn-de-tehr] noun, masc.

---

terrible! [teh-REEBL] adjective **dreadful!**

J'ai une mauvaise note. Terrible!
I have a bad mark. Dreadful!

---

la tête [TEHT] noun, fem. **head**

Le soldat tourne la tête.
The soldier turns his head.

---

le thé [TAY] noun, masc. **tea**

Tu veux du thé ou du café?
Do you want tea or coffee?

---

le théâtre [tay-AHTR] noun, masc. **theater**

Qu'est-ce qu'on joue au théâtre?
What are they performing at the theater?

Tiens! [TYAIN] interjection **Say! Well!**

Tiens! Il commence à neiger.
Say! It's beginning to snow.

---

le tigre [TEEGR] noun, masc. **tiger**

Le tigre est un grand chat sauvage.
The tiger is a big, wild cat.

---

le timbre [TAINBR] noun, masc. **stamp (postage)**

Je mets un timbre sur l'enveloppe.
I put a stamp on the envelope.

---

la tirelire [teer-LEER] noun, fem. **money box, piggy bank**

Je n'ai pas beaucoup d'argent dans ma tirelire.
I do not have much money in my piggy bank.

---

tirer [tee-RAY] verb **to pull, to drag**

je tire	nous tirons
tu tires	vous tirez
il, elle tire	ils, elles tirent

Il tire le chien qui ne veut pas avancer.
He is pulling the dog that does not want to go on.

---

le tiroir [tee-RWAR] noun, masc. **drawer**

Je mets l'appareil dans un tiroir.
I put the camera in a drawer.

---

toi [TWA] pronoun **you, to you**

C'est toi, Jacques, qui as mon bâton?
Do you have my stick, Jack?

---

les toilettes [twa-LEHT] noun, fem., pl. **restroom(s)**

Les toilettes se trouvent là-bas.
The restrooms are over there.

---

le toit [TWA] noun, masc. **roof**

Je regarde la ville du toit de la maison.
I look at the city from the roof of the house.

---

la tomate [tuh-MAT] noun, fem. **tomato**

La tomate est rouge quand elle est mûre.
The tomato is red when it is ripe.

---

tomber [tohn-BAY] verb **to fall**

je tombe	nous tombons
tu tombes	vous tombez
il, elle tombe	ils, elles tombent

Le cerf-volant tombe par terre.
The kite falls to the ground.

---

ton [TOHN] adjective, masc. **your**
ta [TA] fem.
tes [TEH] masc., fem., pl.

Ton cousin est beau.
Your cousin is handsome.

Ta voisine est gentille.
Your neighbor is kind.

Tes parents sont grands.
Your parents are tall.

---

le tonnerre [tuh-NEHR] noun, masc. **thunder**

Après l'éclair on entend le tonnerre.
After the lightning you hear the thunder.

---

le tort [TUHR] noun, masc. **wrong, injustice, harm**
avoir tort [a-vwar-TUHR] **to be wrong**
idiomatic expression

Vous dites qu'il fait beau? Vous avez tort; il pleut.
You say that it is good weather? You are wrong; it is raining. (See **avoir**)

---

la tortue [tuhr-TEW] noun, fem. **turtle, tortoise**

La tortue marche lentement.
The turtle walks slowly.

---

tôt [TOH] adverb **early**

Nous nous levons tôt pour aller en ville.
We get up early to go to the city.

---

toucher [too-SHAY] verb **to touch**

je touche	nous touchons
tu touches	vous touchez
il, elle touche	ils, elles touchent

"Défense de toucher aux fleurs."
"Do not touch the flowers."

---

toujours [too-ZHOOR] adverb **always, forever**

Les feuilles tombent toujours en automne.
The leaves always fall in autumn.

---

la toupie [too-PEE] noun, fem. **top (toy)**

As-tu une toupie?
Do you have a top?

---

la tour [TOOR] noun, fem. **tower**

La Tour Eiffel est très haute.
The Eiffel Tower is very tall.

---

le tour [TOOR] noun, masc. **turn; trip**

Je voudrais faire le tour du monde.
I would like to take a trip around the world.

---

tourner [toor-NAY] verb **to turn**

je tourne	nous tournons
tu tournes	vous tournez
il, elle tourne	ils, elles tournent

Je tourne la page du dictionnaire.
I turn the page of the dictionary.

---

tousser [too-SAY] verb **to cough**

je tousse	nous toussons
tu tousses	vous toussez
il, elle tousse	ils, elles toussent

Le bébé tousse. Il a un rhume.
The baby is coughing. He has a cold.

---

tout [TOO] adjective, masc. **all, every**
tous masc., pl.
toute [TOOT] fem.

Je mets toutes mes lettres dans un tiroir.
I put all my letters in a drawer.

tout à coup [too-ta-KOO] adverb **suddenly**

Tout à coup le médecin entre.
Suddenly the doctor enters.

tout à fait [too-ta-FEH] adverb **completely**

Mon maillot n'est pas tout à fait sec.
My bathing suit is not completely dry.

tout à l'heure [too-ta-LEUHR] adverb **in a little while**

Je vais à la plage tout à l'heure.
I am going to the beach in a little while.

tous les jours **every day** (See **jour**)

tout le monde [tool-MUHND] pronoun **everybody, everyone**

Tout le monde aime le samedi soir.
Everyone likes Saturday night.

tout de suite [too-dsewEET] adverb **immediately, right away**

J'appelle le chien et il vient tout de suite.
I call the dog and he comes immediately.

---

le train [TRAIN] noun, masc. **train**

Allons jouer avec mon train électrique.
Let's play with my electric train.

---

le traîneau [treh-NOH] noun, masc. **sled**
les traîneaux pl.

Mon chien tire le traîneau.
My dog pulls the sled.

---

tranquille [trahn-KEEL] adjective **quiet, calm**

J'aime aller à la pêche quand l'eau est tranquille.
I like to go fishing when the water is calm.

---

le travail [tra-VAHY] noun, masc. **work**

Maman a beaucoup de travail à faire.
Mother has a lot of work to do.

---

travailler [tra-vah-YAY] verb **to work**

je travaille	nous travaillons
tu travailles	vous travaillez
il, elle travaille	ils, elles travaillent

Le fermier travaille dehors.
The farmer works outside.

---

traverser [tra-vehr-SAY] verb **to cross**

je traverse nous traversons
tu traverses vous traversez
il, elle traverse ils, elles traversent

On peut traverser le lac?
Can we cross the lake?

---

treize [TREHZ] adjective **thirteen**

L'escalier a treize marches.
The staircase has thirteen steps.

---

trente [TRAHNT] adjective **thirty**

Quels mois ont trente jours?
Which months have thirty days?

---

très [TREH] adverb **very**

Le château est très grand.
The castle is very big.

---

tricoter [tree-kuh-TAY] verb **to knit**

je tricote nous tricotons
tu tricotes vous tricotez
il, elle tricote ils, elles tricotent

J'apprends à tricoter.
I am learning how to knit.

---

triste [TREEST] adjective **sad**

Pourquoi es-tu triste?
Why are you sad?

C'est triste **That's too bad!**
(See **dommage**)

---

trois [TRWA] adjective **three**

Il y a trois verres sur la table.
There are three glasses on the table.

---

tromper [trohn-PAY] verb **to deceive; to cheat**

je trompe nous trompons
tu trompes vous trompez
il, elle trompe ils, elles trompent

Dans le film, le voleur trompe l'agent de police.
In the film, the robber deceives the policeman.

---

trop [TROH] adverb **too (much), too (many), too (___)**

La petite fille dit: "Cette cuiller est trop grande pour moi!"
The little girl says, "This spoon is too big for me!"

---

le trottoir [truh-TWAR] noun, masc. **sidewalk**

Le trottoir est très étroit.
The sidewalk is very narrow.

---

le trou [TROO] noun, masc. **hole**

J'ai un trou dans ma chaussette.
I have a hole in my sock.

---

trouver [troo-VAY] verb **to find; to think**

je trouve nous trouvons
tu trouves vous trouvez
il, elle trouve ils, elles trouvent

Où est mon autre gant? Je ne peux pas le trouver.
Where is my other glove? I can't find it.

Tu trouves que l'examen est difficile?
Do you think the examination is difficult?

---

il, elle se trouve [se-TROOV] **is located**
idiomatic expression
ils, elles se trouvent pl.

Le bureau de poste se trouve là-bas.
The post office is located over there.

---

tu [TEW] pronoun **you (familiar)**

Comment vas-tu?
How are you?

> "Tu" and "vous" are different ways of saying "you" in French. "Tu" is used in the family and with very close friends and relatives; "vous" is used more formally, such as when a student addresses a teacher.

---

tuer [tew-AY] verb **to kill**

je tue	nous tuons
tu tues	vous tuez
il, elle tue	ils, elles tuent

Maman tue la mouche.
Mother kills the fly.

U

un [UHN] article, masc. **a, an; one**
une [EWN] fem. **a, an; one**

Un singe est dans l'arbre.
A monkey is in the tree.

Je porte une cravate.
I am wearing a tie.

---

uni [ew-NEE] adjective, masc. **united**
unie fem.

Le garçon habite les Etats Unis.
The boy lives in the United States.

Le bâtiment des Nations Unies se trouve dans la ville de New York.
The United Nations building is located in New York City.

l'université [~~ew~~-nee-vehr-see-TAY] noun, fem. **university**

L'université se trouve dans la vallée.
The university is located in the valley.

---

l'usine [~~ew~~-ZEEN] noun, fem. **factory**

Mon père travaille à l'usine.
My father works in the factory.

---

utile [~~ew~~-TEEL] adjective **useful**

Quelques insectes sont utiles.
Some insects are useful.

V

les vacances [va-KAHNS] noun, fem., pl. **vacation**
les grandes vacances **summer vacation**
[grahnd-va-KAHNS] noun, fem., pl.

Où allez-vous pendant les grandes vacances?
Where are you going during the summer vacation?

---

vacciner [va-ksee-NAY] verb **to vaccinate**

je vaccine	nous vaccinons
tu vaccines	vous vaccinez
il, elle vaccine	ils, elles vaccinent

J'ai peur quand le médecin me vaccine.
I am afraid when the doctor vaccinates me.

---

la vache [VASH] noun, fem. **cow**

La vache est dans le champ.
The cow is in the field.

---

la vague [VAG] noun, fem. **wave**

Je vois des vagues à la plage.
I see waves at the beach.

---

la vaisselle [veh-SEHL] noun, fem. **the dishes**

Est-ce que vous lavez la vaisselle chez vous?
Do you wash the dishes at your house?

---

la valise [va-LEEZ] noun, fem. **valise, suitcase**

Je mets mes vêtements dans la valise.
I put my clothes in the valise.

---

la vallée [va-LAY] noun, fem. **valley**

Il y a beaucoup de fleurs dans la vallée.
There are many flowers in the valley.

---

la vanille [va-NEEY] noun, fem. **vanilla**

J'aime la glace à la vanille.
I like vanilla ice cream.

---

le vélo (See **bicyclette**) **bicycle**

---

le vendeur [vahn̸-DEUHR] noun, masc. **salesman, salesperson**

la vendeuse [vahn̸-DEUHZ] fem. **saleswoman, salesperson**

Le vendeur nous montre des chaussures.
The salesman shows us some shoes.

---

vendre [VAHN̸DR] verb **to sell**

je vends	nous vendons
tu vends	vous vendez
il, elle vend	ils, elles vendent

On vend des médicaments dans ce magasin.
They sell medicine in this store.

---

vendredi [vahn̸-dre̸-DEE] noun, masc. **Friday**

Qu'est-ce qu'on mange le vendredi? Du poisson!
What do we eat on Friday? Fish!

---

venir [vé-NEER] verb **to come, to arrive**

je viens	nous venons
tu viens	vous venez
il, elle vient	ils, elles viennent

Ma tante vient nous voir.
My aunt comes to see us.

---

venir de [vé-NEER-dé] idiomatic expression **to have just**

Je viens de faire un voyage en avion.
I have just taken an airplane trip.

---

le vent [VAHN] noun, masc. **wind**

Quand il fait du vent je perds mon chapeau.
When it is windy, I lose my hat. (See **faire**)

---

le ventilateur [vahn-tee-la-TEUHR] noun, masc. **fan**

Nous employons le ventilateur quand il fait chaud.
We use the fan when it is hot.

---

le ventre [VAHNTR] noun, masc. **stomach, abdomen**
avoir mal au ventre [a-vwar-ma-loh-VAHNTR] idiomatic expression **to have a stomachache**

As-tu mal au ventre?
Do you have a stomachache? (See **avoir**)

---

le ver [VEHR] noun, masc. **worm**

Il y a un ver dans la pomme.
There's a worm in the apple.

---

la vérité [vay-ree-TAY] noun, fem. **truth**

C'est la vérité!
That's the truth!

---

le verre [VEHR] noun, masc. **glass**

Je mets le verre sur la table avec soin.
I put the glass on the table carefully.

---

en verre [ahn-VEHR] **made of glass**

Mes lunettes sont en verre.
My glasses are made of glass.

---

vers [VEHR] preposition **toward**

Nous allons ver l'hôtel.
We are going toward the hotel.

---

verser [vehr-SAY] verb **to pour**

je verse	nous versons
tu verses	vous versez
il, elle verse	ils, elles versent

Marguerite verse le café dans une tasse.
Margaret pours coffee into a cup.

---

vert [VEHR] adjective, masc. **green**
verte [VEHRT] fem.

Quand la banane n'est pas mûre,
elle est verte.
When the banana is not ripe, it is green.

---

la veste [VEHST] noun, fem. **jacket**

Mon grand-père porte un pantalon
et une veste.
My grandfather wears pants and a jacket.

---

les vêtements [veht-MAHN] noun, masc., pl. **clothes, clothing**

Mes vêtements sont sur le lit.
My clothes are on the bed.

---

la viande [VYAHND] noun, fem. **meat**

La femme va à la boucherie pour acheter de la viande.
The woman goes to the butcher shop to buy meat.

---

vide [VEED] adjective **empty**

Le tiroir est vide.
The drawer is empty.

---

vieux [VYEOH] adjective, masc. **old**
vieille [VYAY] fem.
vieil [VYAY] masc., before a vowel

Le livre est vieux et la montre est vieille.
The book is old and the watch is old.

---

le village [vee-LAZH] noun, masc. **village**

Mon cousin habite un village à la campagne.
My cousin lives in a village in the country.

---

la ville [VEEL] noun, fem. **city**

La ville de New York est grande.
The city of New York is big.

---

le vin [VAIN] noun, masc. **wine**

Le garçon apporte le vin.
The waiter brings the wine.

---

vingt [VAIN] adjective **twenty**

Dix et dix font vingt.
Ten and ten are twenty.

---

violet [vyoh-LEH] adjective, masc. **violet, purple**
violette [vyoh-LEHT] fem.

Est-ce qu'il y a des fleurs violettes?
Are there any purple flowers?

---

le violon [vyoh-LOHN] noun, masc. **violin**

Le musicien joue du violon.
The musician plays the violin.

---

visiter [vee-zee-TAY] verb **to visit**

je visite	nous visitons
tu visites	vous visitez
il, elle visite	ils, elles visitent

Mes parents visitent ma colonie de vacances.
My parents visit my camp.

---

vite [VEET] adverb **fast, quickly**

Mon frère marche trop vite.
My brother walks too fast.

---

la vitrine [vee-TREEN] noun, fem. **store window**

Nous allons regarder les choses dans les vitrines.
We are going to look at the things in the store windows.

---

vivre [VEEVR] verb **to live**

je vis	nous vivons
tu vis	vous vivez
il, elle vit	ils, elles vivent

Est-ce que des animaux sauvages vivent dans cette forêt?
Do any wild animals live in this forest?

---

voici [vwa-SEE] adverb **here is, here are**

Voici ma toupie.
Here is my top. (toy)

---

voilà [vwa-LA] adverb **there is, there are**

Voilà le poisson dans l'eau.
There is the fish in the water.

---

voir [VWAR] verb **to see**

je vois	nous voyons
tu vois	vous voyez
il, elle voit	ils, elles voient

Je vois l'avion dans le ciel.
I see the airplane in the sky.

---

le voisin [vwa-ZAIN] noun, masc. **neighbor**
la voisine [vwa-ZEEN] fem.

Mon voisin Bernard demeure près de chez moi.
My neighbor Bernard lives near me.

---

la voiture [vwa-TEWR] noun, fem. **car, automobile; baby carriage**

La voiture est dans le garage.
The car is in the garage.

---

la voix [VWA] noun, fem. **voice**

La voix de ma tante est douce.
My aunt's voice is sweet.

à haute voix **in a loud voice, aloud** (See **haut**)
à voix basse **in a low voice** (See **bas**)

---

voler [vuh-LAY] verb **to fly; to steal**

je vole	nous volons
tu voles	vous volez
il, elle vole	ils, elles volent

Le pilote d'avion vole dans l'avion.
The airplane pilot flies in the airplane.

Qui vient de voler ma cuiller?
Who has just stolen my spoon?

---

le voleur [vuh-LEUHR] noun, masc. **thief, robber, burglar**

On cherche le voleur de la banque.
They are looking for the bank thief.

---

votre [VUHTR] pronoun **your**
vos [VOH] pl.

Où est votre magnétophone?
Where is your tape recorder?

Où sont vos timbres?
Where are your stamps?

---

je voudrais [VOO-DREH] — **I would like . . .**
il, elle voudrait [VOO-DREH] — **He would like, She would like . . .**
ils, elles voudraient — **They would like . . .**

Je voudrais faire une promenade.
I would like to take a walk.

Elle voudrait faire des emplettes.
She would like to go shopping.

---

vouloir [VOO-LWAR] verb — **to want, to wish**

je veux	nous voulons
tu veux	vous voulez
il, elle veut	ils, elles veulent

Le bébé pleure parce qu'il veut son jouet.
The baby is crying because he wants his toy.

vouloir dire (See **dire**) — **to mean**

---

vous [VOO] pronoun — **you, to you; yourself**

Comment allez-vous?
How are you?

Je vous donne un billet.
I am giving you a ticket.

---

le voyage [VWA-YAZH] noun, masc. — **trip**
faire un voyage [feh-ruhn-vwa-YAZH] idiomatic expression — **to take a trip**

Nous faisons un voyage au château.
We are taking a trip to the castle. (See **faire**)

---

voyager [vwa-ya-ZHAY] verb **to travel**

je voyage	nous voyageons
tu voyages	vous voyagez
il, elle voyage	ils, elles voyagent

Jacques voyage en bicyclette.
Jack travels by bicycle.

---

le voyageur [vwa-ya-ZHEUHR] noun, masc. **traveler**

Le voyageur est fatigué.
The traveler is tired.

---

vrai [VREH] adjective, masc. **true**
vraie fem.

C'est une histoire vraie!
It's a true story!

---

vraiment [vreh-MAHN] adverb **really**

Tu sais que je voudrais devenir astronaute? Vraiment!
Do you know that I would like to become an astronaut? Really!

le wagon [va-GOHN] noun, masc. **car (railroad)**

Ce train a cinq wagons.
This train has five cars.

Y

les yeux [leh-ZYEOH] masc., pl. **eyes** (See **oeil**)

Z

le zèbre [ZEHBR] noun, masc. **zebra**

Est-ce un zèbre ou un cheval?
Is it a zebra or a horse?

le zéro [zay-ROH] noun, masc. **zero**

Il y a un zéro dans le numéro dix.
There is a zero in the number ten.

le zoo [ZOH] noun, masc. **zoo**

J'aime regarder les tigres au zoo.
I like to watch the tigers at the zoo.

zoologique [zuh-uh-luh-ZHEEK] adjective

le jardin zoologique (See **jardin**) **zoo**

English-French

(Anglais-Français)

La Clef de la Prononciation Anglaise

(English Pronunciation Key)

Les Notes

1. Il y a des sons en anglais qui n'existent pas en français.

2. En général, les voyelles en anglais sont courtes.

3. Les sons des exemples en français ne sont pas exacts. Ils sont seulement approximatifs.

LES CONSONNES	
L’ortographe anglaise	Le symbole phonémique
b	b
c	k
ç	s
ch, tch	ch
d	d
f	f
g	g
j	zh
h, wh	h
dg	dj
k	k
l	l
m	m
n	n
ng	ng
p	p
qu	kw
r	r
s	s
sh, tion	sh
t	t
v	v
w	w
wh	wh, h
x	ks, gs
y	y
z, s	z
th	th
th (voiced)	th

LES VOYELLES

L'ortographe anglaise	Exemple en anglais	Symbole phonémique	Exemples en français: à peu près pareil au mot français
a e u	but	é	le rocher
a	cat	a	la balle
a o	cot	a	mal
é, a ez, ay	play	ei	le bébé
a ah	father	ah	la page
ai, ais	air	eh	l'aéroport
è, ê, e	gel	e	
ee ea	feet	i	le fils
i	hit	i	—
i uy	buy	ai	la taille
o oa ow	boat	oh	beau
oo u ou	boot	u	trouver
oy	boy	oi	—
au, ough o, augh	order	aw	le bord
ur	curtain	ur, euh	l'heure
ow, ou, ough	how	ow	—
u, oo	book	auh	le feu

A

a [ə] article — **un,** masc. **une,** fém.

A monkey is in the tree.
Un singe est dans l'arbre.

I am wearing a tie.
Je porte une cravate.

---

above all [e-bev AWL] adverbe — **surtout**

I like to watch television, Saturday mornings above all.
J'aime regarder la television, surtout le samedi matin.

---

absent [AB-sənt] adjectif — **absent,** masc. **absente,** fém.

George is absent today.
Georges est absent aujourd'hui.

---

according to [ə-KAWR-ding tə] préposition — **selon**

According to my brother, it is going to snow tomorrow.
Selon mon frère, il va neiger demain.

---

actor [AK-tər] nom — **l'acteur,** masc.
actress [AK-tres] — **l'actrice,** fém.

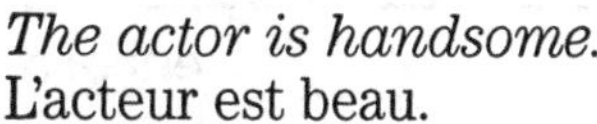

The actor is handsome.
L'acteur est beau.

---

addition (See **check**) — **l'addition**

---

address [é-DREHS] nom — **l'adresse,** fém.

What is your address?
Quelle est votre adresse?

---

adventure [ad-VEN-chər] nom **l'aventure,** fém.

I like to read the adventures of Astérix.
J'aime lire les aventures d'Astérix.

---

aerial (antenna) [EHR-yəl] nom **l'antenne de télévision,** fém.

Television antennas are on the roof of the building.
Les antennes de télévision sont sur le toit du bâtiment.

---

to be afraid of [BE-FREID] expression idiomatique **avoir peur**

Are you afraid of the lion?
As-tu peur du lion?

---

after [AF-tər] préposition **après**

September is the month after August.
Septembre est le mois après août.

---

afternoon [af-tər-NUN] nom **l'après-midi,** masc.

It is two o'clock in the afternoon.
Il est deux heures de l'après-midi.

---

again [ə-GEN] adverbe **encore**

Read the letter once again.
Lisez la lettre encore une fois.

---

against [ə-GENST] préposition **contre**

Henry puts the mirror against the wall.
Henri met le miroir contre le mur.

---

age (used in exp. with "How old...?") [EIDJ] nom **l'âge,** masc.

How old are you? I am eight (years old).
Quel âge as-tu? J'ai huit ans.

---

agreed! [é-GRID] **accord: d'accord!**
expression idiomatique

Do you want to play with me? O.K.!
Veux-tu jouer avec moi? D'accord!

---

to aid (help) [EID] verbe **aider**

j'aide	nous aidons
tu aides	vous aidez
il, elle aide	ils, elles aident

John helps his sister carry the books.
Jean aide sa soeur à porter les livres.

---

air (look) [EHR] nom **l'air,** masc.

The tiger has a ferocious look.
Le tigre a l'air féroce.

This young man is ill. He needs air.
Ce jeune homme est malade. Il a besoin de l'air.

---

airplane [EHR-plein] nom **l'avion,** fém.
by airplane **en avion**
(airplane) pilot [EHR-plein PAI-lét] nom **le pilote (d'avion)**

My cousin is an airplane pilot.
Mon cousin est pilote (d'avion).

jet airplane nom **l'avion à réaction**

airport [ehr-PAWRT] nom **l'aéroport,** masc.

My uncle works at the airport.
Mon oncle travaille à l'aéroport.

> The famous plane, the *Concorde*, flies at supersonic speed; currently, you can leave New York City on the *Concorde* and arrive in Paris, France, three and one-half hours later.

---

alarm clock [ɇ-LAHRM KLAK] nom **le réveille-matin**

The alarm clock rings too loudly.
Le réveille-matin sonne trop fort.

Alas! (What a pity!) [ɇ-LAS] interjection **Hélas!**

What a pity! You can't come with me.
Hélas! Tu ne peux pas venir avec moi.

---

alike (similar) [ɇ-LAIK] adjectif **pareil**

Our ties are similar.
Nos cravates sont pareilles.

---

all [AWL] adjectif **tout**

all over (everywhere) adverbe **partout**

I look everywhere for my watch.
Je cherche ma montre partout.

all right (okay) expression idiomatique **d'accord!**

Do you want to play with me? O.K.!
Veux-tu jouer avec moi? D'accord!

---

almost [awl-MOHST] adverbe **presque**

It is almost six o'clock.
Il est presque six heures.

---

alone [é-LOHN] adjectif **seul**

I am alone in the living room.
Je suis seul dans le salon.

---

aloud [é-LOWD] adverbe **à haute voix**

---

alphabet [AL-fa-bet] nom **l'alphabet,** masc.

There are twenty-six letters in the French alphabet?
Il y vingt-six lettres dans l'alphabet français?

---

already [awl-RE-di] adverbe **déjà**

It is already time to leave?
Il est déjà l'heure de partir?

---

also (too) [AWL-soh] adverbe **aussi**

I want some candy too!
Moi aussi, je veux des bonbons!

---

always (forever) [AWL-weiz] adverbe **toujours**

The leaves always fall in autumn.
Les feuilles tombent toujours en automne.

---

ambulance [AM-byu-lans] nom **l'ambulance,** fém.

The ambulance is going to the hospital.
L'ambulance va à l'hôpital.

American [é-MER-i-kén] nom; adjectif **américain,** masc. **américaine,** fém.

It's an American airplane.
C'est un avion américain.

---

amusing [é-MYUZ-ing] adjectif **amusant,** masc. **amusante,** fém.

The bear is amusing.
L'ours est amusant.

---

an [AN] article **un,** masc. **une,** fém.
I am wearing a tie.
Je porte une cravate.

---

and [AND] conjonction **et**
Andrew and his friend are playing together.
André et son ami jouent ensemble.

---

angry [AN-gri] adjectif **fâché,** masc. **fâchée,** fém.
When I tease my sister, Mom is angry.
Quand je taquine ma soeur, Maman est fâchée.

---

animal [AN-i-mél] nom **la bête**
The lion is a wild animal.
Le lion est une bête sauvage.

animal **l'animal,** masc. **les animaux,** pl.
The animals are in the forest.
Les animaux sont dans la forêt.

pet [pet] nom **l'animal favori,** masc.
My dog is my pet.
Mon chien est mon animal favori.

---

anniversary (birthday) [an-i-VUR-sér-i] nom **l'anniversaire,** masc.
Happy Birthday! How old are you?
Joyeux anniversaire! Quel âge as-tu?

---

annoyed [é-NOID] adjectif **ennuyé,** masc. **ennuyée,** fém.
Mother is annoyed when I make too much noise.
Maman est ennuyée quand je fais trop de bruit.

---

another [é-NÉTH-ér] adjectif **autre**
Here is another pencil.
Voici un autre crayon.

other [ÉTH-ér] adjectif **l'autre**

Here is my handkerchief. The others are on the bed.
Voici mon mouchoir. Les autres sont sur le lit.

---

answer [AN-sér] nom **la réponse**

I write the correct answer in my notebook.
J'écris la réponse correcte dans mon cahier.

to answer verbe **répondre**

je réponds	nous répondons
tu réponds	vous répondez
il, elle répond	ils, elles répondent

The little girl cannot answer the question.
La petite fille ne peut pas répondre à la question.

---

ant [ANT] nom **la fourmi**

The ant is very small.
La fourmi est très petite.

---

any [EN-i] adjectif **quelque**
any (also shows possession) **de**
du, masc. (*contraction of* de + le)
de la, fém.
des, pl. (*contraction of* de + les)

anything [EN-i-thing] pronoun **quelque chose**

Is there anything in this drawer?
Est-ce qu'il y a quelque chose dans ce tiroir?

---

apartment [é-PAHRT-ment] nom **l'appartement,** masc.

My apartment is on the third floor.
Mon appartement est au deuxième étage.

---

appearance (look) [é-PIR-éns] nom **l'air,** masc.

The tiger has a ferocious appearance (look).
Le tigre a l'air féroce.

---

appetite [AP-é-tait] nom **l'appétit,** masc.

Hearty appetite! (Enjoy your meal!)
Bon appétit!

---

apple [AP-él] nom **la pomme**

I eat an apple every day.
Je mange une pomme tous les jours.

---

appointment [é-POINT-mént] nom **le rendez-vous**

What time is your appointment with the counselor?
A quelle heure est votre rendez-vous avec le conseiller?

---

apricot [A-pri-kat] nom **l'abricot**

The apricot is delicious.
L'abricot est délicieux.

April [EI-prél] nom **avril**

It rains a lot in April.
Il pleut beaucoup en avril.

---

apron [EI-prən] nom **le tablier**

Martha wears an apron at school.
Marthe porte un tablier à l'école.

---

aquarium (fish tank) [ə-KWEHR-yəm] nom **l'aquarium,** masc.

There are some goldfish in the fish tank.
Il y a des poissons rouges dans l'aquarium.

---

arm [AHRM] nom **le bras**

The man has a sore arm.
L'homme a mal au bras.

---

armchair [AHRM-chehr] nom **le fauteuil**

I like to sit in the armchair.
J'aime m'asseoir dans le fauteuil.

---

army [AHR-mi] nom **l'armée,** fém.

Soldiers are in the army.
Les soldats sont dans l'armée.

---

around [ə-ROWND] adverbe **autour de**

I would like to take a trip around the world.
Je voudrais faire un voyage autour du monde.

---

to arrange [ə-REINDJ] verbe **arranger**

j'arrange	nous arrangeons
tu arranges	vous arrangez
il, elle arrange	ils, elles arrangent

The teacher arranges his papers.
Le professeur arrange ses papiers.

---

to arrest [ə-REST] verbe **arrêter**

j'arrête	nous arrêtons
tu arrêtes	vous arrêtez
il, elle arrête	ils, elles arrêtent

The policeman arrests the man.
L'agent arrête l'homme.

---

to arrive [é-RAIV] verbe **arriver**

j'arrive	nous arrivons
tu arrives	vous arrivez
il, elle arrive	ils, elles arrivent

The postman arrives at ten o'clock.
Le facteur arrive à dix heures.

---

artist [AHR-tist] nom **l'artiste,** masc.

My brother is an artist.
Mon frère est artiste.

---

as [AZ] préposition **comme**

As for dessert, she has chocolate ice cream.
Comme dessert elle prend une glace au chocolat.

---

to ask [ASK] verbe **demander**

je demande	nous demandons
tu demandes	vous demandez
il, elle demande	ils, elles demandent

I ask Father: "May I go to the fair?"
Je demande à Papa: "Je peux aller à la foire?"

---

astronaut [AS-tré-nawt] nom **l'astronaute,** masc., fém.

The astronaut takes a trip in a spaceship.
L'astronaute fait un voyage en fusée.

---

at [AT] préposition **à**
at night **la nuit**

At night you can see the stars.
La nuit on peut voir des étoiles.

---

to attend [ǝ-TEND] verbe **assister**

j'assiste	nous assistons
tu assistes	vous assistez
il, elle assiste	ils, elles assistent

We attend a soccer game.
Nous assistons à un jeu de football.

---

at the side of (next) [NEKST] préposition **à côté de**

At the restaurant Peter is seated next to Carolyn.
Au restaurant Pierre est assis à côté de Caroline.

August [AW-gǝst] nom **août,** masc.

In August it is hot.
En août il fait chaud.

---

aunt [ANT] nom **la tante**

My aunt is a saleslady.
Ma tante est vendeuse.

---

automobile (car) [KAHR] nom **la voiture**

The car is in the garage.
La voiture est dans le garage.

---

autumn [AW-tǝm] nom **l'automne,** masc.

In autumn it is cool.
En automne il fait frais.

---

avenue [AV-ǝ-nyu] nom **l'avenue,** fém.

The Avenue des Champs-Elysées is in Paris.
L'Avenue des Champs-Elysées est à Paris.

> L'Arc de Triomphe is located on the Avenue des Champs-Elysées.

B

baby [BEI-bi] nom **le bébé**

Mary plays with the baby.
Marie joue avec le bébé.

baby carriage [BEI-bi KAR-i̲dj] **la voiture**

---

back [BAK] nom **les dos**

Is it Robert? I don't know. I see only his back.
C'est Robert? Je ne sais pas. Je vois seulement le dos.

to give back **rendre**

---

bad [BAD] adjectif **mauvais,** masc.
mauvaise, fém.

The weather is bad today.
Il fait mauvais aujourd'hui.

that's too bad **c'est dommage!,**
expression idiomatique **c'est triste!**

---

bag [BAG] nom **le sac**

I carry a bag.
Je porte un sac.

---

baggage [BAG-i̲dj] nom **les bagages**

The baggage is ready for the trip.
Les bagages sont prêts pour le voyage.

---

baker [BEI-kɇr] nom **le boulanger**

The baker makes bread.
Le boulanger fait le pain.

---

bakery [BEI-kér-i] nom **la boulangerie**

The baker is in the bakery.
Le boulanger est dans la boulangerie.

---

ball [BAWL] nom **la balle**

The ball is round.
La balle est ronde.

to play ball [PLEI BAWL] **jouer à la balle**

---

balloon [bé-LUN] nom **le ballon**

"Oh! I'm losing my balloon," cries the little girl.
"Oh! Je perds mon ballon," crie la petite fille.

---

ballpoint pen [BAWL-point PEN] nom **le stylo à bille**

I like to write with a ballpoint pen.
J'aime écrire avec un stylo à bille.

---

banana [bé-NAN-é] nom **la banane**

The banana is ripe when it is yellow.
La banane est mûre quand elle est jaune.

---

bank [BANGK] nom **la banque**

Do you have any money in the bank?
Avez-vous de l'argent à la banque?

---

baseball [BEIS-bawl] nom **le base-ball**

My cousin plays baseball.
Mon cousin joue au base-ball.

---

basement (cellar) [BEIS-mént] nom **la cave**

There are several packages in the cellar.
Il y a plusieurs paquets dans la cave.

---

basket [BAS-kit] nom **le panier**

There are apples in the basket.
Il y a des pommes dans le panier.

---

basketball [BAS-kit-bawl] nom **le basket-ball**

My friend plays basketball.
Mon camarade joue au basket-ball.

---

bath [BATH] nom **le bain**

I take a bath at nine in the evening.
A neuf heures du soir, je prends un bain.

bathroom **la salle de bain**
sunbath **le bain de soleil**
bathing suit **le maillot**

Do you like my new bathing suit?
Tu aimes mon nouveau maillot?

---

bathroom sink **le lavabo**

The washstand is in the bathroom.
Le lavabo est dans la salle de bain.

---

to be [BI] verbe **être**

je suis	nous sommes
tu es	vous êtes
il, elle est	ils, elles sont

Dad, where are we?
Papa, où sommes-nous?

---

to be able (can) [BI EI-bl] verbe **pouvoir**

je peux	nous pouvons
tu peux	vous pouvez
il, elle peut	ils, elles peuvent

I can't do my homework. The lessons are too difficult.
Je ne peux pas faire mes devoirs. Les leçons sont trop difficiles.

---

beach [BICH] nom **la plage**

We go to the beach in summer.
Nous allons à la plage en été.

---

to be acquainted with (know) **connaître**
[BI ǝ-KWEIN-tǝd wi̱th] verbe

je connais	nous connaissons
tu connais	vous connaissez
il, elle connaît	ils, elles connaissent

Do you know my teacher?
Connais-tu mon maître?

---

to be afraid [BI ǝ-FREID] **avoir peur**
expression idiomatique

Are you afraid of the storm?
Avez-vous peur de l'orage?

---

beak [BIK] nom **le bec**

The bird has a yellow beak.
L'oiseau a un bec jaune.

---

bear [BEHR] nom **l'ours,** masc.

The bears are playing in the water.
Les ours jouent dans l'eau.

---

beard [BIRD] nom **la barbe**

My brother, who is at the university, has a beard.
Mon frère, qui est à l'université, a une barbe.

---

to be ashamed [BI ∉-SHEIMD] **avoir honte**
expression idiomatique

He is ashamed because he is naughty.
Il a honte parce qu'il est méchant.

---

beast (animal) [BIST] nom **la bête**

The lion is a wild beast.
Le lion est une bête sauvage.

---

beautiful [BYU-t∉-f∉l] adjectif **beau,** masc.

The sky is beautiful. **belle,** fém.
Le ciel est beau.

---

to be called (name) [BI KAWLD] verbe **s'appeler**

je m'appelle	nous nous appelons
tu t'appelles	vous vous appelez
il, elle s'appelle	ils, elles s'appellent

What is your name? My name is Henry.
Comment vous appelez-vous? Je m'appelle Henri.

---

be careful! [BI KEHR-f∉l] interjection **attention!**

The teacher says, "Be careful!"
Le professeur dit: "Attention!"

Pay attention! expression idiomatique **Faites attention!**

---

because [bi-KAWZ] conjonction **parce que**

I am not going to the movies because I don't have any money.
Je ne vais pas au cinéma parce que je n'ai pas d'argent.

because of **à cause de**

I have to stay home because of the snow.
Je dois rester à la maison à cause de la neige.

---

to become [bi-KŚM] verbe **devenir**

je deviens nous devenons
tu deviens vous devenez
il, elle devient ils, elles deviennent

He would like to become a doctor.
Il voudrait devenir médecin.

---

bed [BED] nom **le lit**

The cat is in my bed.
Le chat est dans mon lit.

---

to go to bed expression idiomatique **se coucher**
bedroom [bed-RUM] nom **la chambre**

This apartment has three bedrooms.
Cet appartement a trois chambres.

---

bee [BI] nom **l'abeille,** fém.

The bee is dangerous.
L'abeille est dangereuse.

---

beefsteak (steak) [BIF-steik] nom **le bifteck**

The steak is good.
Le bifteck est bon.

---

before [bi-FAWR] préposition **avant**

The teacher arrives before the students.
Le professeur arrive avant les étudiants.

---

to be frightened (afraid) [bi FRAI-tènd] **avoir peur**
expression idiomatique

Are you afraid of the storm?
Avez-vous peur de l'orage?

---

to begin [bi-GIN] verbe **commencer**

je commence	nous commençons
tu commences	vous commencez
il, elle commence	ils, elles commencent

The French class begins at nine o'clock.
La classe de français commence à 9 heures.

---

to behave [bi-HEIV] verbe **se conduire**

The children behave well at the table.
Les enfants se conduisent bien à table.

---

behind [bi-HAIND] préposition **derrière; en arrière de**

One boy is behind the other.
Un garçon est en arrière des autres.

---

behind adverbe **derrière**

Carolyn is behind the chair.
Caroline est derrière la chaise.

---

to be hungry [BI HÈN-gri] **avoir faim**
expression idiomatique

Are you hungry? Yes, I'm hungry.
Avez-vous faim? Oui, j'ai faim.

---

to believe [bi-LIV] verbe **croire**

je crois	nous croyons
tu crois	vous croyez
il, elle croit	ils, elles croient

I believe I can go to the movies.
Je crois que je peux aller au cinéma.

---

bell [BEL] nom **la cloche**

The bell rings at noon.
A midi la cloche sonne.

doorbell [DAWR-bel] nom **le bouton**

---

belt [BELT] nom **la ceinture**

Well! You're wearing a new belt!
Tiens! Tu portes une nouvelle ceinture!

---

to be quiet [BI KWAI-ət] expression idiomatique **se taire**

je me tais	nous nous taisons
tu te tais	vous vous taisez
il, elle se tait	ils, elles se taisent

They always tell me, "Be quiet!"
On me dit toujours: "Tais-toi!"

---

to be right [BI RAIT] expression idiomatique **avoir raison**

Grandmother is always right.
Grand-mère a toujours raison.

---

to be sleepy [BI SLI-pi] expression idiomatique **avoir sommeil**

Who is sleepy?
Qui a sommeil?

---

to be successful (succeed) [BI sək-SES-fəl] verbe **réussir**

je réussis	nous réussissons
tu réussis	vous réussissez
il, elle réussit	ils, elles réussissent

He succeeds in catching a fish.
Il réussit à attraper un poisson.

---

to be thirsty [BI THUR-sti] expression idiomatique **avoir soif**

Are you thirsty? Yes, I'm thirsty.
Avez-vous soif? Oui, j'ai soif.

---

better [BET-ér] adjectif — **meilleur,** masc. **meilleure,** fém.

I think that cherries are better than strawberries.
Je pense que les cerises sont meilleures que les fraises.

---

between [bi-TWIN] préposition — **entre**

What is the number between fourteen and sixteen?
Quel est le numéro entre quatorze et seize?

---

to be wrong [BI RAWNG] expression idiomatique — **avoir tort**

You say that it is good weather? You are wrong; it is raining.
Vous dites qu'il fait beau?
Vous avez tort; il pleut.

---

bicycle [BAI-sik-él] nom — **la bicyclette**

When the weather is good, Bernard rides his bicycle.
Quand il fait beau Bernard va à bicyclette.

bicycle (bike) — **le vélo**

Do you have a bike?
As-tu un vélo?

to ride a bicycle [RAID] expression idiomatique — **monter (aller) à bicyclette**

> The "Tour de France" is a famous international bicycle race around France.

---

big [BIG] adjectif — **grand,** masc.
big (obese) — **gros,** masc.
grosse, fém.

bigger — **plus grand que**
My brother is bigger than I.
Mon frère est plus grand que moi.

---

bill (money) [BIL] nom — **le billet**
I am rich! I have a ten-franc note!
Je suis riche! J'ai un billet de dix francs!

---

bird [BURD] nom — **l'oiseau,** masc.

The bird is on a branch of the tree.
L'oiseau est sur une branche de l'arbre.

---

birthday [BURTH-dei] nom — **l'anniversaire,** masc.
Happy birthday! How old are you?
Joyeux anniversaire! Quel âge as-tu?

---

to bite [BAIT] verbe — **mordre**

je mords	nous mordons
tu mords	vous mordez
il, elle mord	ils, elles mordent

Do cats bite?
Est-ce que les chats mordent?

---

to bite (insect) verbe — **piquer**

il, elle pique	ils, elles piquent

The mosquitoes like to bite me.
Les moustiques aiment me piquer.

---

black [BLAK] adjectif **noir,** masc. **niore,** fém.

I am wearing my black shoes.
Je porte mes souliers noirs.

---

blackboard [BLAK-bawrd] nom **le tableau noir**

The pupil writes on the blackboard.
L'élève écrit au tableau noir.

---

blanket [BLANG-kit] nom **la couverture**

In winter I like a warm blanket on my bed.
En hiver j'aime une couverture chaude sur le lit.

---

blind [BLAIND] adjectif **aveugle**

This man is blind.
Cet homme est aveugle

---

blonde [BLAND] adjectif **blond,** masc. **blonde,** fém.

Do you have blond hair?
Avez-vous les cheveux blonds?

---

blood [BLĖD] nom **le sang**

My knee hurts. Look at the blood!
J'ai mal au genou. Regarde le sang!

---

blow [BLOH] nom (knock) **le coup**

There are two blows on the door.
On frappe deux coups à la porte.

---

blue [BLU] adjectif **bleu,** masc. **bleue,** fém.

The sky is blue, isn't it?
Le ciel est bleu, n'est-ce pas?

---

boat [BOHT] nom **le bateau**

I see a boat in the water.
Je vois un bateau dans l'eau.

---

book [BAUHK] nom **le livre**

We are looking for some interesting books.
Nous cherchons des livres intéressants.

---

bookstore [BAUHK-stowr] nom **la librairie**

There are so many books in the bookstore!
Il y a tant de livres dans la librairie!

---

boot [BUT] nom **la botte**

When it snows I put on my boots.
Quand il neige je mets mes bottes.

---

born [BAWRN] adjectif **né,** masc. **née,** fém.

I was born on March 2nd.
Je suis né le deux mars.

---

to borrow [BAR-oh] verbe **emprunter**

j'emprunte	nous empruntons
tu empruntes	vous empruntez
il, elle emprunte	ils, elles empruntent

May I borrow the eraser?
Je peux emprunter la gomme?

---

bottle [BA-tәl] nom **la bouteille**

Be careful! The bottle is made of glass.
Attention! La bouteille est en verre.

---

boulevard [bul-VAHRD] nom **le boulevard**

Students walk on the Boulevard St. Michel in Paris.
Les étudiants se promènent sur le boulevard St-Michel à Paris.

---

bouquet [bu-KEI] nom **le bouquet**

"Here is a bouquet of flowers, Martha," says Frank.
"Voici un bouquet, Marthe," dit François.

---

box [BAKS] nom **la boîte**

There is candy in the box.
Il y a des bonbons dans la boîte.

letter box (mailbox) [LET-er baks] nom **la boîte aux lettres**

He puts the letter in the mailbox.
Il met la lettre dans la boîte aux lettres.

---

boy [BOI] nom **le garçon**

The boy is playing with his sister.
Le garçon joue avec sa soeur.

---

branch [BRANCH] nom **la branche**

The tree has many branches.
L'arbre a beaucoup de branches.

---

brave [BREIV] adjectif **courageux,** masc. **courageuse,** fém.

The prince is brave when he saves the princess.
Le prince est courageux quand il sauve la princesse.

---

bread [BRED] nom **le pain**

You see a lot of bread in the bakery.
On voit beaucoup de pain dans la boulangerie.

bread and butter (jam) snack **la tartine**
expression idiomatique

(loaf of) bread [LOHF] nom **le pain**

You see many loaves of bread in the bakery.
On voit beaucoup de pains dans la boulangerie.

roll nom **le petit pain**

A roll, please.
Un petit pain, s'il vous plaît.

toast nom **le pain grillé**

My sister prefers toast.
Ma soeur préfère le pain grillé.

---

to break [BREIK] verbe **casser**

je casse	nous cassons
tu casses	vous cassez
il, elle casse	ils, elles cassent

Be careful! Don't break the plate!
Attention! Ne casse pas l'assiette!

---

breakfast [BREK-fəst] nom **le petit déjeuner**

---

bridge [BRIDJ] nom **le pont**

Where is the bridge of Avignon?
Où est le pont d'Avignon?

---

briefcase [BRIF-keis] nom **la serviette**

Lawrence, don't forget your briefcase.
Laurent, n'oublie pas ta serviette.

---

to bring [BRING] verbe **apporter**

j'apporte	nous apportons
tu apportes	vous apportez
il, elle apporte	ils, elles apportent

They bring valises to camp.
Ils apportent des valises à la colonies de vacances.

---

to bring (people) verbe **amener**

j'amène	nous amenons
tu amènes	vous amenez
il, elle amène	ils, elles amènent

The boy brings his sister home.
Le garçon amène sa soeur à la maison.

---

broad (See **wide**) **large**

---

broadcast [BRAWD-kast] nom **l'émission,** fém.

What time is the broadcast on music from Montreal?
A quelle heure est l'émission de la musique de Montréal?

---

broom [BRUM] nom **le balai**

Mary cleans the floor with a broom.
Marie nettoie le plancher avec un balai.

---

brother [BRÉ-thér] nom **le frère**

I am little, but my brother is big.
Je suis petit, mais mon frère est grand.

---

brown (hair) [BROWN] adjectif **brun,** masc. **brune,** fém.

The boy has brown hair.
Le garçon a les cheveux bruns.

---

brown (things) adjectif **marron**

The rug is brown.
Le tapis est marron.

---

brush [BRŮSH] nom **la brosse**

The hairbrush is bigger than the toothbrush.
La brosse à cheveux est plus grande que la brosse à dents.

---

to brush (oneself) verbe **se brosser**

je me brosse	nous nous brossons
tu te brosses	vous vous brossez
il, elle se brosse	ils, elles se brossent

Laura is brushing her hair.
Laure se brosse les cheveux.

---

bucket (pail) [BŮ-kit] nom **le seau** **les seaux,** pl.

The farmer fills the bucket with milk.
Le fermier remplit le seau de lait.

---

building [BIL-ding] nom **le bâtiment**

The buildings are very tall in the city.
Les bâtiments son très hauts dans la ville.

---

bunch of flowers [BAUHNCH] nom **le bouquet**

"Here is a bunch of flowers, Martha," says Frank.
"Voici un bouquet, Marthe," dit François.

---

burglar [BUR-glėr] nom **le voleur**

They are looking for the burglar at the bank.
On cherche le voleur à la banque.

---

to burn [BURN] verbe **brûler**

je brûle	nous brûlons
tu brûles	vous brûlez
il, elle brûle	ils, elles brûlent

We burn wood in the fireplace.
On brûle du bois dans la cheminée.

---

bus [BĖS] nom **l'autobus,** masc.

The children go to school by bus.
Les enfants vont à l'école en autobus.

---

but [BĖT] conjonction **mais**

I want to go to the park but Daddy says "no."
Je veux aller au parc mais papa dit "non."

---

butcher [BAUHCH-ėr] nom **le boucher**

The butcher sells meat.
Le boucher vend de la viande.

butcher shop nom **la boucherie**

You go to the butcher shop to buy meat.
On va à la boucherie pour acheter de la viande.

---

butter [BÉT-ér] nom **le beurre**

Pass the butter, please.
Passez-moi le beurre, s'il vous plaît.

---

button [BÉT-én] nom **le bouton**

This coat has only three buttons.
Ce manteau a seulement trois boutons.

---

to buy [BAI] verbe **acheter**

j'achète	nous achetons
tu achètes	vous achetez
il, elle achète	ils, elles achètent

I would like to buy an orange.
Je voudrais acheter une orange.

---

by [BAI] préposition **par**
by air **en avion**
by car **en auto; en voiture**
by airmail **par avion**

C

cabbage [KAB-idj] nom **le chou**

Do you prefer cabbage or carrots?
Préférez-vous le chou ou les carottes?

---

café [ka-FEI] nom **le café**

There is a café on the corner.
Il y a un café au coin de la rue.

---

cake [KEIK] nom **le gâteau**

Mom makes a pretty cake for me.
Maman prépare un joli gâteau pour moi.

cookie **le petit gâteau**

---

calendar [KAL-ən-dər] nom **le calendrier**

According to the calendar, today is May 12th.
Selon le calendrier c'est aujourd'hui le 12 mai.

---

to call [KAWL] verbe **appeler**

j'appelle	nous appelons
tu appelles	vous appelez
il, elle appelle	ils, elles appellent

I call my friend.
J'appelle mon amie.

---

calm [KAHM] adjectif **tranquille**

I like to go fishing when the water is calm.
J'aime aller à la pêche quand l'eau est tranquille.

---

camera [KAM-rə] nom **l'appareil,** masc.

Look at my camera. It is new.
Regarde mon appareil. Il est nouveau.

---

camp [KAMP] nom **la colonie de vacances**

My cousin spends eight weeks at camp.
Mon cousin passe huit semaines à la colonie de vacances.

---

can [KAN] verbe **pouvoir**

je peux	nous pouvons
tu peux	vous pouvez
il, elle peut	ils, elles peuvent

I can't do my homework. The lessons are too difficult.
Je ne peux pas faire mes devoirs. Les leçons sont trop difficiles.

---

candy [KAN-di] nom **les bonbons**

Children like candy.
Les enfants aiment les bonbons.

---

capital [KAP-i-tėl] nom **la capitale**

Do you know the name of the capital of the United States?
Savez-vous le nom de la capitale des Etats-Unis?

---

car [KAHR] nom **l'auto,** fém.

The car goes along the road.
L'auto roule sur la route.

---

car (railroad) nom **le wagon**

This train has five cars.
Ce train a cinq wagons.

---

card [KAHRD] nom **la carte**

Do you know how to play cards?
Savez-vous jouer aux cartes?

---

carefully [KEHR-fė-li] adverbe **avec soin**

Paul pours water into the glass carefully.
Paul verse l'eau dans le verre avec soin.

---

carrot [KAR-ət] nom **la carotte**

Rabbits eat carrots.
Les lapins mangent des carottes.

---

to carry [KAR-i] verbe **porter**

je porte	nous portons
tu portes	vous portez
il, elle porte	ils, elles portent

The dog is carrying a newspaper in its mouth.
Le chien porte un journal dans la bouche.

---

castle [KAS-əl] nom **le château**

The king lives in a large castle.
Le roi habite un grand château.

---

cat [KAT] nom **le chat**

The cat is playing with the ball.
Le chat joue avec la balle.

---

to catch [KACH] verbe **attraper**

j'attrape nous attrapons
tu attrapes vous attrapez
il, elle attrape ils, elles attrapent

Hurray! John catches the ball.
Bravo! Jean attrape la balle.

CD [SI-DI] nom **le CD**

I love this new CD by Celine Dion!
J'adore ce nouveau CD de Céline Dion!

---

ceiling [SI-lïng] nom **le plafond**

The ceiling of the chateau is very interesting.
Le plafond du château est très intéressant.

---

celery [SEL-ri] nom **le céleri**

Mother makes a salad with celery.
Maman fait une salade avec du céleri.

---

cellar (basement) [SEL-ér] nom **la cave**

There are several packages in the cellar.
Il y a plusieures paquets dans la cave.

---

certain, sure [SUR-tén] adjectif **sûr,** masc. **sûre,** fém.

I am certain that the train will come soon.
Je suis sûr que le train arrive bientôt.

---

chair [CHEHR] nom **la chaise**

This chair is too big for me.
Cette chaise est trop grande pour moi.

---

chalk [CHAWK] nom **la craie**

The boy is writing on the blackboard with chalk.
Le garçon écrit au tableau noir avec la craie.

chalk board **le tableau noir**

---

change (money) [CHEINDJ] nom **la monnaie**

The butcher says, "Here is the change from 30 francs."
Le boucher dit: "Voici la monnaie de trente francs."

---

to change verbe **changer**

je change	nous changeons
tu changes	vous changez
il, elle change	ils, elles changent

We have to change to another train.
Il faut changer de train.

---

cheap(ly) [CHIP-(li)] adverbe **bon marché**

Bread is cheap; it is not expensive.
On vend le pain bon marché; il ne coûte pas cher.

---

to cheat (deceive) [CHIT] verbe **tromper**

je trompe	nous trompons
tu trompes	vous trompez
il, elle trompe	ils, elles trompent

In the film, the robber deceives the policeman.
Dans le film, le voleur trompe l'agent de police.

---

check (in restaurant) [CHEK] nom **l'addition**

After dinner, Dad asks for the check.
Apres le dîner, Papa demande l'addition.

(to play) checkers (See **to play**) **jouer aux dames**

---

cheerful [CHIR-fəl] adjectif **gai,** masc. **gaie,** fém.

My sister is always cheerful.
Ma soeur est toujours gaie.

---

cheese [CHIZ] nom **le fromage**

My sister has cheese for dessert.
Ma soeur prend du fromage comme dessert.

---

cherry [CHER-i] nom **la cerise**

I am going to pick cherries.
Je vais cueillir des cerises.

(to play) chess (See **to play**) **jouer aux échecs**

---

chicken [CHIK-ən] nom **le poulet**

What are we eating this evening? Chicken.
Qu'est-ce qu'on mange ce soir? Du poulet.

---

child [CHAILD] nom **l'enfant,** masc., fém.
children [CHIL-dren] pl. **les enfants,** pl.

The children are playing on the playground.
Les enfants jouent au terrain de jeux.

> An afternoon snack (usually for children) is called a "goûter."

---

chimney (fireplace) [CHIM-ni] nom **la cheminée**

The shoes are near the fireplace.
Les chaussures sont près de la cheminée.

---

chin [CHIN] nom **le menton**

Here is the doll's chin.
Voici le menton de la poupée.

---

chocolate [CHA-klit] nom **le chocolat**

What? You don't like chocolates?
Comment? Tu n'aimes pas les chocolats?

---

to choose [CHUZ] verbe **choisir**

je choisis nous choisissons
tu choisis vous choisissez
il, elle choisit ils, elles choisissent

In the examination, choose the correct answer.
Dans l'examen, choisissez la réponse correcte.

---

chop [CHAP] nom **la côtelette**

Do you prefer a veal cutlet or a lamb chop?
Préfères-tu une côtelette de veau ou de mouton?

Christmas [KRIS-MES] nom **Noël,** masc.

Christmas comes on December 25th.
Noël vient le vingt-cinq décembre.

---

church [CHURCH] nom **l'église,** fém.

There is a big church in the city.
Il y a une grande église dans la ville.

---

cigarette [sig-é-RET] nom **la cigarette**

Does your uncle smoke cigarettes?
Est-ce que ton oncle fume des cigarettes?

---

circle [SUR-kél] nom **le cercle**

The boys form a circle to play.
Les garçons forment un cercle pour jouer.

---

circus [SUR-kés] nom **le cirque**

There are many animals at the circus.
Il y a beaucoup d'animaux au cirque.

---

city [SIT-i] nom **la ville**

The city of Paris is big.
La ville de Paris est grande.

---

class [KLAS] nom **la classe**
classroom [KLAS-rum] **la salle de classe**

We are in the classroom.
Nous sommes dans la salle de classe.

---

clean [KLIN] adjectif **propre**

My hands are clean.
Mes mains sont propres.

to clean verbe **nettoyer**

je nettoie	nous nettoyons
tu nettoies	vous nettoyez
il, elle nettoie	ils, elles nettoient

Do you help your mother clean the house?
Tu aides ta mère à nettoyer la maison?

cleaning woman (maid) [KLIN-ing WÉ-mén] nom **la bonne**

The maid cleans the house.
La bonne nettoie la maison.

street cleaner **la balayeur des rues**

---

clear [KLIR] adjectif **clair,** masc. **claire,** fém.

What a beautiful, clear day!
Quelle belle journée claire!

---

clever (cunning) [KLEV-ər] adjectif **rusé,** masc. **rusée,** fém.

The cat is clever.
Le chat est rusé.

---

to climb [KLAIM] verbe **grimper**

je grimpe	nous grimpons
tu grimpes	vous grimpez
il, elle grimpe	ils, elles grimpent

The cat climbs the tree.
Le chat grimpe sur l'arbre.

---

clock [KLAK] nom **l'horloge,** fém.

The clock strikes twice. It is two o'clock.
L'horloge sonne deux fois. Il est deux heures.

---

to close [KLOHZ] verbe **fermer**

je ferme	nous fermons
tu fermes	vous fermez
il, elle ferme	ils, elles ferment

Please close the window.
Fermez la fenêtre, s'il vous plaît.

---

close friend [klohs FREND] nom **le camarade**

My friend and I are going to the park to play.
Mon camarade et moi, nous allons jouer au parc.

---

closet nom **le placard**

The closet is closed.
Le placard est fermé.

---

closet (cupboard) [KLAHZ-it] nom **l'armoire,** fém.

The cupboard is empty (bare).
L'armoire est vide.

---

close to, near préposition **près de**

Bordeaux is near the Atlantic Ocean.
Bordeaux est près de l'océan Atlantique.

---

clothes (clothing) [KLOHZ] nom **les vêtements**

My clothes are on the bed.
Mes vêtements sont sur le lit.

---

cloud [KLOWD] nom **le nuage**

The sun is behind a cloud.
Le soleil est derrière un nuage.

cloudy [KLOWD-i] adjectif **couvert**

---

clown [KLOWN] nom **le clown**

When I am at the circus I say "Hello" to the clown.
Quand je suis au cirque je dis "Bonjour" au clown.

---

coat [KOHT] nom **le manteau**

She wears a warm coat in winter.
Elle porte un manteau chaud en hiver.

---

coffee [KAF-i] nom **le café**

Do you want some coffee?
Voulez-vous du café?

---

cold [KOHLD] nom **le froid**

When it is cold in winter, I am cold.
Quand il fait froid en hiver, j'ai froid.

it is cold **il fait froid**
be cold **avoir froid**
cold (illness) **le rhume**

---

color [KƏL-ər] nom **la couleur**

What color is the banana?
De quelle couleur est la banane?

to color verbe **colorier**

je colorie	nous colorions
tu colories	vous coloriez
il, elle colorie	ils, elles colorient

We color with crayons.
Nous colorions avec les crayons de couleur.

---

comb [KOHM] nom **le peigne**

Where is my comb?
Où est mon peigne?

to comb (one's hair) verbe **se peigner**

je me peigne	nous nous peignons
tu te peignes	vous vous peignez
il, elle se peigne	ils, elles se peignent

I comb my hair before leaving the house.
Avant de sortir de la maison, je me peigne.

---

to come [KɆM] verbe **venir**

je viens	nous venons
tu viens	vous venez
il, elle vient	ils, elles viennent

My father comes from work at 6:00 o'clock.
Mon père vient du travail à six heures.

to come into verbe **entrer**

j'entre	nous entrons
tu entres	vous entrez
il, elle entre	ils, elles entrent

They come into the house.
Ils entrent dans la maison.

---

comfortable [KɆM-fɇr-tɇ-bɇl] adjectif **comfortable**

The sofa is very comfortable.
Le canapé est très comfortable.

---

to command (order) [kɇ-MAND] verbe **commander**

In the restaurant Father orders dinner.
Dans le restaurant Papa commande le dîner.

---

company [KɆM-pɇ-ni] nom **la compagnie**

The Bardot Company is located on the corner (of the street).
La Compagnie Bardot se trouve au coin de la rue.

---

to compete [kɇm-PIT] verbe **rivaliser**

We compete for a prize.
Nous rivalisons pour un prix.

---

to complain [kém-PLEIN] verbe **se plaindre**

je me plains nous nous plaignons
tu te plains vous vous plaignez
il, elle se plaint ils, elles se plaignent

My friend says that I always complain!
Mon amie dit que je me plains toujours!

---

completely [kem-PLIT-li] adverbe **tout à fait**

My bathing suit is not completely dry.
Mon maillot n'est pas tout à fait sec.

---

computer [kém-PYU-tér] nom **l'ordinateur,** masc.

My friend has a computer.
Mon amie a un ordinateur.

(computer) disk [disk] nom **le disque**
(computer) technician [TEK-ni-shén] nom **technicien,** masc. **technicienne,** fém.

---

contest [KAN-test] nom **la compétition** **le concours**

Who is going to win the contest?
Qui va gagner la compétition?

---

to continue [kén-TIN-yu] verbe **continuer**

je continue nous continuons
tu continues vous continuez
il, elle continue ils, elles continuent

I will continue to play the piano until five o'clock.
Je continue à jouer du piano jusqu'à cinq heures.

---

to cook [KAUHK] verbe **faire la cuisine**

Who's cooking?
Qui fait la cuisine?

---

cookie [KAUHK-i] nom **le petit gâteau**

---

cool [KUL] adjectif **frais,** masc. **fraîche,** fém.

It is cool
Il fait frais.

---

to copy [KAP-i] verbe **copier**

je copie	nous copions
tu copies	vous copiez
il, elle copie	ils, elles copient

We have to copy the sentences that are on the blackboard.
Il faut copier les phrases qui sont au tableau noir.

---

corn [KAWRN] nom **le maïs**

Mmm, the corn is good!
Mmm, les maïs est bon!

---

corner [KAWR-nər] nom **le coin**

You must cross the street at the corner.
Il faut traverser la rue au coin.

---

correct [kə-REKT] adjectif **correct,** masc. **correcte,** fém.

The teacher says, "Write the correct answer."
Le professeur dit: "Ecrivez la réponse correcte."

correct (fair) adjectif **juste**

But it's my turn. It isn't fair!
Mais c'est mon tour. Ce n'est pas juste!

---

to cost (See **price**) [KAST] verbe **coûter**

il, elle coûte	ils, elles coûtent

How much does this comb cost?
Combien coûte ce peigne?

---

cotton [KAT-én] nom **le coton**
made of cotton **en coton**

He is wearing a cotton shirt.
Il porte une chemise en coton.

---

to cough [KAF] verbe **tousser**

je tousse	nous toussons
tu tousses	vous toussez
il, elle tousse	ils, elles toussent

The baby is coughing. He has a cold.
Le bébé tousse. Il a un rhume.

---

counselor [KOWN-sé-lér] nom **le conseiller,** masc.
la conseillère, fém.

What is the name of the counselor?
Comment s'appelle la conseillère?

---

to count [KOWNT] verbe **compter**

je compte	nous comptons
tu comptes	vous comptez
il, elle compte	ils, elles comptent

He knows how to count from five to one: five, four, three, two, one.
Il sait compter de cinq à un: cinq, quatre, trois, deux, un.

---

country [KÉN-tri] nom **le pays**

What is the name of the country to the east of France?
Quel est le nom du pays à l'est de la France?

country (opposite of city) nom **la campagne**

It's nice weather. Let's go to the country!
Il fait beau. Allons à la compagne!

---

courageous [kə́-REI-djə́s] adjectif **courageux,** masc. **courageuse,** fém.

The prince is courageous when he saves the princess.
Le prince est courageux quand il sauve la princesse.

---

cousin [KƏZ-ə́n] nom **le cousin** **la cousine**

My cousin Paul is ten years old and my cousin Mary is eighteen.
Mon cousin Paul a dix ans et ma cousine Marie a dix-huit ans.

---

cover (blanket) [KƏV-ə́r] nom **la couverture**

In winter I like a warm blanket on my bed.
En hiver j'aime une couverture chaude sur le lit.

covered [KƏV-ə́rd] adjectif **couvert,** masc. **couverte,** fém.

The tree is covered with snow.
L'arbre est couvert de neige.

---

cow [KOW] nom **la vache**

The cow is in the field.
La vache est dans le champ.

---

cradle nom **le berceau**

---

crayon [KREI-ə́n] nom **le crayon de couleur**

I draw with a crayon.
Je dessine avec un crayon de couleur.

---

crazy (mad) [KREIZ-i] adjectif **fou,** masc. **folle,** fém.

The dog is mad.
Le chien est fou.

---

croissant nom **le croissant**

Harriet has a croissant for breakfast.
Henriette prend un croissant pour le petit déjeuner.

---

to cross [KRAS] verbe **traverser**

je traverse	nous traversons
tu traverses	vous traversez
il, elle traverse	ils, elles traversent

Can we cross the lake?
On peut traverser le lac?

---

to cry [KRAI] verbe **pleurer**

je pleure	nous pleurons
tu pleures	vous pleurez
il, elle pleure	ils, elles pleurent

I cry when somebody teases me.
Je pleure quand on me taquine.

---

cunning (clever) [KƏN-ing] adjectif **rusé,** masc. **rusée,** fém.

The thief is clever; he climbs a tree.
Le voleur est rusé; il grimpe sur un arbre.

---

cup [KƏP] nom **la tasse**

I put the cup on the saucer.
Je mets la tasse sur la soucoupe.

---

cupboard [KɆB-ɇrd] nom **le buffet**

There are plates in the cupboard.
Il y a des assiettes dans le buffet.

---

curious [KYUR-yɇs] adjectif **curieux,** masc. **curieuse,** fém.

She is curious. She would like to open the package.
Elle est curieuse. Elle voudrait ouvrir le paquet.

---

curtain [KɆR-tɇn] nom **le rideau** **les rideaux**

The curtains in my room are too long.
Les rideaux dans ma chambre sont trop longs.

---

to cut [KɆT] verbe **couper**

je coupe	nous coupons
tu coupes	vous coupez
il, elle coupe	ils, elles coupent

Dad cuts the bread with a knife.
Papa coupe le pain avec un couteau.

---

cute [KYUT] adjectif **mignon,** masc. **mignonne,** fém.

The baby is cute.
Le bébé est mignon.

---

cutlet [KɆT-lɇt] nom **la côtelette**

Do you prefer a veal cutlet or a lamb chop?
Préfères-tu une côtelette de veau ou de mouton?

D

Dad (Daddy) [DAD] nom **papa**

Daddy, I'm afraid!
Papa, j'ai peur!

---

damp [DAMP] adjectif **humide**

My bathing suit is damp.
Mon maillot est humide.

---

to dance [DANS] verbe **danser**

je danse	nous dansons
tu danses	vous dansez
il, elle danse	ils, elles dansent

My sister likes to dance.
Ma soeur aime danser.

---

dangerous [DEIN-gjér-és] adjectif **dangereux,** masc. **dangereuse,** fém.

It is dangerous to run into the street to catch a ball.
Il est dangereux de courir dans la rue pour attraper une balle.

---

to dare (to) [DEHR] verbe **oser**

j'ose	nous osons
tu oses	vous osez
il, elle ose	ils, elles osent

You dare to hit me?
Tu oses me battre?

---

dark [DAHRK] adjectif **foncé,** masc. **foncée,** fém.

She is wearing a dark blue dress.
Elle porte une robe bleu foncé.

---

date [DEIT] nom **la date**

What is the date?
Quelle est la date?

---

daughter [DA-tér] nom **la fille**

I should like to introduce my daughter, Amy.
Je vous présente ma fille, Aimée.

---

day [DEI] nom **la journée** **le jour**

I am going to spend the day at my cousin's house.
Je vais passer la journée chez ma cousine.

What day of the week is it?
Quel jour de la semaine est-ce?

---

day off nom **le jour de congé**

Thursday is a day off for French students?
Le jeudi est un jour de congé pour les élèves français?

New Year's Day nom **le Jour de l'An**

January 1st is New Year's Day.
Le premier janvier est le Jour de l'An.

every day adverbe **tous les jours**

I read every day.
Je lis tous les jours.

---

dead [DED] adjectif **mort,** masc. **morte,** fém.

You're crying? Yes, my turtle is dead.
Tu pleures? Oui, ma tortue est morte.

---

deaf [DEF] adjectif **sourd,** masc. **sourde,** fém.

You don't hear me? You're deaf?
Tu ne m'entends pas? Tu es sourd?

---

dear [DIR] adjectif — **cher,** masc. / **chère,** fém.

---

to deceive (cheat) [di-SIV] verbe — **tromper**

je trompe	nous trompons
tu trompes	vous trompez
il, elle trompe	ils, elles trompent

In the film, the robber deceives the policeman.
Dans le film, le voleur trompe l'agent de police.

December [di-SEM-bɇr] nom — **décembre,** masc.

It is cold in December.
Il fait froid en décembre.

---

to decorate [DEK-ɇ-reit] verbe — **décorer**

je décore	nous décorons
tu décores	vous décorez
il, elle décore	ils, elles décorent

He is decorating his bicycle.
Il décore sa bicyclette.

---

deep [DIP] adjectif — **profond,** masc. / **profonde,** fém.

Is the pool deep?
Est-ce que la piscine est profonde?

---

delicious [di-LISH-ɇs] adjectif — **délicieux,** masc. / **délicieuse,** fém.

The cake is delicious.
Le gâteau est délicieux.

---

delighted, happy [di-LAI-təd] adjectif **heureux,** masc. **heureuse,** fém.

Everyone is happy at a party.
A une fête tout le monde est heureux.

---

dentist [DEN-tist] nom **le dentiste**

The dentist says, "Open your mouth."
Le dentiste dit: "Ouvre la bouche."

---

desert [DEZ-ərt] nom **le désert**

The desert is very dry.
Le désert est très sec.

---

desk [DESK] nom **le bureau**

The teacher's desk is big.
Le bureau du professeur est grand.

desk (pupil's) nom **le pupitre**

---

dessert [di-ZURT] nom **le dessert**

I would like to have a strawberry tart for dessert.
Comme dessert je désire une tarte aux fraises.

---

to detest (hate) [di-TEST] verbe **détester**

je déteste	nous détestons
tu détestes	vous détestez
il, elle déteste	ils, elles détestent

He hates spinach.
Il déteste les épinards.

---

dictionary [DIK-shən-ehr-i] nom **le dictionnaire**

How many words are there in the dictionary?
Combien de mots y a-t-il dans le dictionnaire?

---

different [DIF-rent] adjectif **différent,** masc. **differente,** fém.

These loaves of bread are different.
Ces pains sont différents.

---

difficult [DIF-é-kélt] adjectif **difficile**

It is difficult to read this letter.
Il est difficile de lire cette lettre.

---

dining room (See **room**) **la salle à manger**

---

dinner [DIN-ér] nom **le dîner**

We eat dinner at eight o'clock.
Nous prenons le dîner à huit heures.

---

to direct [di-REKT] verbe **diriger**

je dirige	nous dirigeons
tu diriges	vous dirigez
il, elle dirige	ils, elles dirigent

My brother is directing the game.
Mon frère dirige le jeu.

---

dirty [DUR-ti] adjectif **sale**

My shirt is dirty!
Ma chemise est sale!

---

dishes [DISH-és] nom **la vaisselle**

Do you wash the dishes at your house?
Est-ce que vous lavez la vaisselle chez vous?

---

displeased, angry [dis-PLIZD] adjectif **fâché,** masc. **fâchée,** fém.

When I tease my sister, Mom is angry.
Quand je taquine ma soeur, Maman est fâchée.

---

distant [DIS-tént] adjectif **loin**

Robert is very distant.
Robert est très loin.

---

to do [DU] verbe **faire**

je fais	nous faisons
tu fais	vous faites
il, elle fait	ils, elles font

He does his homework.
Il fait ses devoirs.

---

doctor [DAK-tɇr] nom **le docteur, le médecin**

Mother says, "You are sick. I am going to call the doctor."
Maman dit: "Tu es malade. Je vais appeler le docteur."

---

dog [DAG] nom **le chien**

Do you have a dog?
As-tu un chien?

puppy **le petit chien**

---

doll [DAL] nom **la poupée**

My doll's name is Sylvia.
Ma poupée s'appelle Sylvie.

dollhouse **la maison de poupée**

---

dollar [DAL-ɇr] nom **le dollar**

Here is a dollar for you.
Voilà un dollar pour toi.

---

dominoes [DAM-ɇ-nohz] nom **les dominos**

My cousin plays dominoes well.
Mon cousin joue bien aux dominos.

---

donkey [DɆNG-ki] nom **l'âne,** masc.

The donkey does not want to walk!
L'âne ne veut pas marcher!

door [DAWR] nom **la porte**

Please close the door.
Fermez la porte, s'il vous plaît.

---

doorbell [DAWR-bel] nom **le bouton**

Here we are at Virginia's house.
Where is the doorbell?
Nous voici à la porte de Virginie.
Où est le bouton?

doorknob [DAWR-nob] nom **le bouton**

---

down there [DOWN -thehr] adverbe **là-bas**

Do you see your brother coming
down there?
Tu vois ton frère qui arrive, là-bas?

---

dozen [DUZ-en] adjectif **la douzaine**

She is buying a dozen pears.
Elle achète une douzaine de poires.

---

to drag (pull) [DRAG] verbe **tirer**

je tire	nous tirons
tu tires	vous tirez
il, elle tire	ils, elles tirent

He is pulling a bag of potatoes.
Il tire un sac de pommes de terre.

---

to draw [DRAW] verbe **dessiner**

je dessine	nous dessinons
tu dessines	vous dessinez
il, elle dessine	ils, elles dessinent

Go to the board and draw a house.
Va au tableau noir et dessine une maison.

---

drawer [DRAWR] nom **le tiroir**

I put the camera in a drawer.
Je mets l'appareil dans un tiroir.

---

dreadful! [DRED-fəl] interjection **terrible!**

I have a bad mark. Dreadful!
J'ai une mauvaise note. Terrible!

---

dream [DRIM] nom **le rêve**

Do you always have dreams?
Avez-vous toujours les rêves?

---

to dream verbe **rêver**

je rêve	nous rêvons
tu rêves	vous rêvez
il, elle rêve	ils, elles rêvent

I dream of going to the moon!
Je rêve d'aller à la lune!

---

dress [DRES] nom **la robe**

My doll's dress is dirty.
La robe de ma poupée est sale.

---

to dress verbe **s'habiller**

je m'habille	nous nous habillons
tu t'habilles	vous vous habillez
il, elle s'habille	ils, elles s'habillent

I get up, I get dressed, I go to school.
Je me lève, je m'habille, je vais à l'école.

---

drink [DRINGK] nom **le boisson**

Do you want to order a drink?
Tu veux commander un boisson?

---

to drink verbe **boire**

je bois	nous buvons
tu bois	vous buvez
il, elle boit	ils, elles boivent

The child is drinking milk.
L'enfant boit du lait.

---

to drive [DRAIV] verbe **conduire**

je conduis	nous conduisons
tu conduis	vous conduisez
il, elle conduit	ils, elles conduisent

Too bad! I am too young to drive the car.
Hélas! Je suis trop jeune pour conduire l'auto.

---

driver [DRAIV-ér] nom **le chauffeur**

The driver stops when the light is red.
Le chauffeur s'arrête quand le feu est rouge.

---

drum [DRÉM] nom **le tambour**

I make noise when I play the drum.
Je fais du bruit quand je joue du tambour.

---

dry [DRAI] adjectif **sec,** masc. **sèche,** fém.

Is the floor dry, Mom?
Est-ce que le plancher est sec, maman?

---

duck [DÉK] nom **le canard**

There are some ducks on the lake.
Voilà des canards sur le lac.

---

during [DUR-ing] préposition **pendant**

I sleep during the night.
Je dors pendant la nuit.

E

each [ICH] adjectif **chaque**

I put a fork at each place.
Je mets une fourchette à chaque place.

each one pronoun **chacun,** masc. **chacune,** fém.

Here are five girls; each one has a flower.
Voilà cinq jeunes filles; chacune a une fleur.

---

ear [IR] nom **l'oreille,** fém.

The wolf's ears are long.
Les oreilles du loup sont longues.

---

early [UR-li] adverbe **tôt**

The rooster gets up early.
Le coq se lève tôt.

---

to earn (win) [URN] verbe **gagner**

je gagne	nous gagnons
tu gagnes	vous gagnez
il, elle gagne	ils, elles gagnent

Our team wins!
C'est notre équipe qui gagne!

---

earth [URTH] nom **la terre**

When the astronaut is on the moon,
he sees the earth.
Quand l'astronaute est sur la lune,
il voit la terre.

---

earthquake [URTH-kweik] nom **le tremblement de terre**

I am afraid of earthquakes.
J'ai peur des tremblements de terre.

---

east [IST] nom **l'est,** masc.

When I go from Paris to Strasbourg, I go toward the east.
Quand je vais de Paris à Strasbourg, je vais vers l'est.

---

easy [I-zi] adjectif **facile**

It is easy to do my homework.
Il est facile de faire mes devoirs.

---

to eat [IT] verbe **manger**

je mange	nous mangeons
tu manges	vous mangez
il, elle mange	ils, elles mangent

On Sundays we eat turkey.
Le dimanche nous mangeons la dinde.

---

edge (See **shore**) **le bord**

---

egg [EG] nom **l'oeuf,** masc.

Do you want an egg this morning?
Tu veux un oeuf ce matin?

---

eight [EIT] adjectif **huit**

I have eight insects.
J'ai huit insectes.

---

eighteen [ei-TIN] adjectif **dix-huit**

She is eighteen years old.
Elle a dix-huit ans.

---

eighty [EI-ti] adjectif **quatre-vingts**

I have eighty marbles!
J'ai quatre-vingts billes!

---

electric [i-LEK-trik] adjectif **électrique**

Look! They sell electric typewriters!
Regarde! On vend des machines à écrire électriques!

electric stove **le fourneau électrique**

---

elephant [EL-é-fént] nom **l'éléphant,** masc.

There is a big elephant in the zoo.
Il y a un grand éléphant dans le jardin zoologique.

---

eleven [i-LEV-én] adjectif **onze**

The farmer has eleven chickens.
Le fermier a onze poulets.

---

empty [EMP-ti] adjectif **vide**

The drawer is empty.
Le tiroir est vide.

---

end [END] nom **la fin**

It is the end of the lesson.
C'est la fin de la leçon.

---

engineer [en-dji-NIR] nom **l'ingénieur,** masc.

I would like to become an engineer.
Je voudrais devenir ingénieur.

English [ING-lish] nom, adjectif **l'anglais,** masc.

They speak English in the United States.
On parle anglais aux Etats-Unis.

---

enough [i-NEF] adverbe **assez**

Do you have enough potatoes?
As-tu assez de pommes de terre?

---

to enter (go into) [EN-tər] verbe **entrer**

j'entre	nous entrons
tu entres	vous entrez
il, elle entre	ils, elles entrent

They go into the house.
Ils entrent dans la maison.

---

entrance [EN-trəns] nom **l'entrée,** fém.

We are looking for the entrance.
Nous cherchons l'entrée.

---

envelope [EN-və-lohp] nom **l'enveloppe,** fém.

The mailman gives me an envelope.
Le facteur me donne une enveloppe.

---

equal (same) [I-kwəl] adjectif **égal,** masc. **égale,** fém. **égaux,** pl.

Do you want ice cream or cake?
(Oh, it doesn't make any difference.)
(Oh, it's all the same to me.)
Tu veux la glace ou le gâteau? Oh, cela m'est égal.

---

to erase [i-REIS] verbe **effacer**

j'efface	nous effaçons
tu effaces	vous effacez
il, elle efface	ils, elles effacent

Oh, a mistake! I have to erase this word.
Oh, une faute! Je dois effacer ce mot.

eraser [i-REI-sər] nom **la brosse, la gomme**

I have to erase this sentence with the eraser.
Je dois effacer cette phrase avec la brosse.

---

error (mistake) [ER-ər] nom **la faute**

I make errors when I write in French.
Je fais des fautes quand j'écris en français.

---

especially [es-PESH-ə-li] adverbe **surtout**

I like to watch television, especially Saturday mornings.
J'aime regarder la télévision, surtout le samedi matin.

---

even [I-vən] adverbe **même**

She cries even when she is happy.
Elle pleure même quand elle est heureuse.

---

evening [IV-ning] nom **le soir**

I watch television in the evening.
Le soir je regarde la télé.

Good evening expression idiomatique **Bonsoir**

---

every [EV-ri] adjectif **tout**
tous, masc., pl.
toute, fém.

every day **tous les jours**
everybody (everyone) pronoun **tout le monde**

Everybody likes Saturday night.
Tout le monde aime le samedi soir.

everywhere [ev-ri-WHEHR] adverbe **partout**

I look everywhere for my watch.
Je cherche ma montre partout.

---

examination [eg-zam-i-NEI-shən] nom **l'examen,** masc.

Do you have a good mark on the examination?
Tu as une bonne note à l'examen?

---

excellent [EK-sə-lənt] adjectif **excellent,** masc. **excellente,** fém.

The teacher says, "This work is excellent."
Le professeur dit: "Ce travail est excellent."

---

excuse me [ek-SKYUZ MI] expression idiomatique **excusez-moi, pardon**

Excuse me. Here are your packages.
Excusez-moi. Voici vos paquets.

---

expensive [ek-SPEN-siv] adjectif **cher,** masc. **chère,** fém.

This bicycle is too expensive.
Cette bicyclette est trop chère.

---

to explain [ek-SPLEIN] verbe **expliquer**

j'explique	nous expliquons
tu expliques	vous expliquez
il, elle explique	ils, elles expliquent

Joan, can you explain this sentence to me?
Jeanne, tu peux m'expliquer cette phrase?

---

extraordinary (unusual) **extraordinaire**
[ek-STRAWR-di-ner-i] adjectif

We are going to take an extraordinary trip in a rocket ship.
Nous allons faire un voyage extraordinaire en fusée.

---

eye [AI] nom **l'oeil,** masc. **les yeux**, pl.

What color are your eyes?
De quelle couleur sont vos yeux?

F

face [FEIS] nom **la figure**

She is washing her face.
Elle se lave la figure.

---

factory [FAK-tə-ri] nom **l'usine,** fém.

My father works in the factory.
Mon père travaille à l'usine.

---

fair [FEHR] nom **la foire**

We are going to the fair to have a good time.
Nous allons à la foire pour nous amuser.

---

fair adjectif **juste**

But it's my turn. It isn't fair!
Mais c'est mon tour. Ce n'est pas juste!

---

fairy [FEHR-i] nom **la fée**
fairy tale **le conte de fées**

Read this fairy tale to me.
Lisez-moi ce conte de fées.

Cendrillon (Cinderella) is a famous fairy tale.

fall (autumn) [FAL] nom **l'automne,** masc.

In autumn it is cool.
En automne il fait frais.

to fall verbe **tomber**

je tombe	nous tombons
tu tombes	vous tombez
il, elle tombe	ils, elles tombent

The kite falls to the ground.
Le cerf-volant tombe par terre.

false [FALS] adjectif **faux,** masc. **fausse,** fém.

He is six years old, true or false?
Il a six ans, vrai ou faux?

family [FAM-é-li] nom **la famille**

How many people are there in your family?
Combien de personnes y a-t-il dans votre famille?

famous [FEI-més] adjectif **célèbre**

The president of France is famous.
Le président de la France est célèbre.

fan [FAN] nom **le ventilateur**

We use the fan when it is hot.
Nous employons le ventilateur quand il fait chaud.

far [FAHR] adverbe **loin (de)**

Is Paris far from Washington?
Est-ce que Paris est loin de Washington?

---

farm [FAHRM] nom **la ferme**

There are cows and horses on the farm.
Il y a des vaches et des chevaux à la ferme.

---

farmer [FAHR-mér] nom **le fermier**

My grandfather is a farmer.
Mon grand-père est fermier.

---

fast [FAST] adjectif **rapide**

The dog is fast when he runs after a cat.
Le chien est rapide quand il court après un chat.

---

fast adverbe **vite**

My brother walks too fast.
Mon frère marche trop vite.

---

fat [FAT] adjectif **gros,** masc. **grosse,** fém.

The elephant is fat.
L'éléphant est gros.

---

father [FAH-thér] nom **le père**

My father is a mailman.
Mon père est facteur.

Father (Daddy) nom **Papa**

Daddy, I'm afraid!
Papa, j'ai peur!

---

favorite [FEI-vér-it] adjectif **favori,** masc. **favorite,** fém.

What is your favorite toy?
Quel est ton jouet favori?

---

to fear (to be afraid of) [FIR] **avoir peur**
expression idiomatique

Are you afraid of the storm?
Avez-vous peur de l'orage?

February [FEB-ru-er-i] nom **février**

How many days are there in February?
Combien de jours y a-t-il en février?

---

to feel [FIL] verbe **sentir**

je sens	nous sentons
tu sens	vous sentez
il, elle sent	ils, elles sentent

to feel like [FIL LAIK] **avoir envie de**
expression idiomatique

I feel like taking a walk.
J'ai envie de faire une promenade.

---

feet [FIT] nom **les pieds**

---

ferocious [fer-OH-shos] adjectif **féroce**

Who is afraid of a ferocious tiger?
Qui a peur d'un tigre féroce?

---

fever [FI-vér] nom **la fièvre**

I have to stay in bed. I have a fever.
Je dois rester au lit. J'ai de la fièvre.

---

field [FILD] nom **le champ**

The sheep are in the field.
Les moutons sont dans le champ.

---

fierce (ferocious) [FIRS] adjectif **féroce**

Who is afraid of a ferocious tiger?
Qui a peur d'un tigre féroce?

---

fifteen [fif-TIN] adjectif **quinze**

Today is January 15th, the birthday of Martin Luther King, Jr.
C'est aujourd'hui le quinze janvier, l'anniversaire de Martin Luther King, Jr.

---

fifty [FIF-ti] adjectif **cinquante**

There are fifty states in the United States.
Il y a cinquante états dans les Etats-Unis.

---

to fight [FAIT] verbe **se battre**

Why are those children fighting?
Pourquoi se battent les enfants là-bas?

---

to fill [FIL] verbe **remplir**

je remplis	nous remplissons
tu remplis	vous remplissez
il, elle remplit	ils, elles remplissent

Stephen fills the box with paper.
Etienne remplit la boîte de papier.

---

film [FILM] nom **le film**

Are they playing a good film at the movies?
On joue un bon film au cinéma?

---

finally [FAI-nel-i] adverbe **enfin**

It is good weather, finally!
Il fait beau, enfin!

---

to find [FAIND] verbe **trouver**

je trouve	nous trouvons
tu trouves	vous trouvez
il, elle trouve	ils, elles trouvent

I like to find shells.
J'aime trouver des coquillages.

---

finger [FIN-gėr] nom **le doigt**

The baby has ten little fingers.
Le bébé a dix petits doigts.

---

finger nail nom **l'ongle,** masc.

I am ashamed. My fingernails are dirty.
J'ai honte. Mes ongles sont sales.

---

to finish [FIN-ish] verbe **finir**

je finis	nous finissons
tu finis	vous finissez
il, elle finit	ils, elles finisent

I am going to finish my work before going out.
Je vais finir mon travail avant de sortir.

---

fire [FAIR] nom **le feu**

The fire is hot.
Le feu est chaud.

---

fireman nom **le pompier**

The fireman is very strong.
Le pompier est très fort.

---

fireplace nom **la cheminée**

We burn wood in the fireplace.
On brûle du bois dans la cheminée.

---

fire truck **la pompe à incendie**

The fire truck makes a lot of noise.
La pompe à incendie fait beaucoup de bruit.

---

first [FURST] adjectif **premier,** masc.
Breakfast is the first meal of the day. **première,** fém.
Le petit déjeuner est le premier repas de la journée.

---

fish [FISH] nom **le poisson**

There are many fish in this lake.
Il y a beaucoup de poissons dans ce lac.

---

fishing [FISH-ing] nom **la pêche**
to go fishing expression idiomatique **aller à la pêche**

We are going fishing.
Nous allons à la pêche.

---

fish tank nom **l'aquarium,** masc.

There are some goldfish and plants in the fish tank.
Il y a des poissons rouges et des plantes dans l'aquarium.

---

five [FAIV] adjectif **cinq**

The hand has five fingers.
La main a cinq doigts.

---

to fix [FIKS] verbe **réparer**

je répare	nous réparons
tu répares	vous réparez
il, elle répare	ils, elles réparent

My brother is fixing the phonograph.
Mon frère répare le phonographe.

---

flag [FLAG] nom **le drapeau,** masc. **les drapeaux,** pl.

There are two flags in the classroom.
Il y a deux drapeaux dans la salle de classe.

---

flat [FLAT] adjectif **plat,** masc. **plate,** fém.

The field is flat.
Le champ est plat.

---

flight attendant [flait é-tendént] nom **l'hôtesse de l'air**

The flight attendant serves us a good meal.
L'hôtesse de l'air nous sert un bon repas.

---

floor [FLAWR] nom **le plancher**

The pen falls to the floor.
Le stylo tombe sur le plancher.

floor (of a building) **l'étage**
ground floor **le rez-de-chaussée**

---

flower [FLOW-ér] nom **la fleur**

We have many flowers in the garden.
Nous avons beaucoup de fleurs dans le jardin.

---

fly [FLAI] nom **la mouche**

There are flies in the kitchen!
Il y a des mouches dans la cuisine!

---

to fly verbe **voler**

je vole	nous volons
tu voles	vous volez
il, elle vole	ile, elles volent

The airplane pilot flies in the airplane.
Le pilote d'avion vole dans l'avion.

---

fog [FAG] nom **le brouillard**

It is difficult to see because of the fog.
Il est difficile de voir à cause du brouillard.

---

to follow [FAL-oh] verbe **suivre**

je suis	nous suivons
tu suis	vous suivez
il, elle suit	ils, elles siuvent

The pupils in the class follow the teacher.
Les élèves de la classe suivent la maîtresse.

---

foolish (stupid) [FU-lish] adjectif **stupide**

Is the elephant intelligent or foolish?
Est-ce que l'éléphant est intelligent ou stupide?

---

foot [FAUHT] nom **le pied,** nom.
feet [FIT] nom, pl. **les pieds,** pl.
to walk, go on foot expression idiomatique **aller à pied**

We walk to the museum.
Nous allons au musée à pied.

to have a sore foot expression idiomatique **avoir mal au pied**

---

for [fər] préposition **comme**

For dessert she has chocolate ice cream.
Comme dessert elle prend de la glace au chocolat.

---

for préposition **depuis**

She has been waiting for her aunt for an hour.
Elle attend sa tante depuis une heure.

---

for préposition **pour**

She is going to the store to buy stockings.
Elle va au magasin pour acheter des bas.

---

foreign [FAHR-ən] adjectif **étranger,** masc. **étrangère,** fém.

I would like to travel to foreign countries.
Je voudrais voyager aux pays étrangers.

---

forest [FAR-ist] nom **le bois,** masc, **la forêt,** fém.

There are a hundred trees in the forest!
Il y a cent arbres dans la forêt!

---

forever (always) [fawr-EV-ər] adverbe **toujours**

The leaves always fall in autumn.
Les feuilles tombent toujours en automne.

---

to forget [fawr-GET] verbe **oublier**

j'oublie	nous oublions
tu oublies	vous oubliez
il, elle oublie	ils, elles oublient

She always forgets her ticket.
Elle oublie toujours son billet.

---

fork [FAWRK] nom **la fourchette**

I eat meat with a fork.
Je mange la viande avec une fourchette.

---

to form (make) [FAWRM] verbe **former**

je forme	nous formons
tu formes	vous formez
il, elle forme	ils, elles forment

I make a snowball with the snow.
Je forme une balle avec la neige.

---

forty [FAWR-ti] adjectif **quarante**

Do you know the story of the forty thieves?
Savez-vous l'histoire des quarante voleurs?

---

four [FAWR] adjectif **quatre**

There are four people in my family.
Il y a quatre personnes dans ma famille.

---

fourteen [fawr-TIN] adjectif **quatorze**

July 14th is the French national holiday.
Le quatorze juillet est la fête nationale française.

---

fox [FAKS] nom **le renard**

The fox runs very fast.
Le renard court très vite.

---

franc (French monetary unit) [FRANK] nom **le franc**

Here is a five-franc note.
Voici un franc de la France.

---

free (no cost) [FRI] adjectif **gratuit,** masc. **gratuite,** fém.

It's free. It doesn't cost anything.
Il est gratuit. Ça ne coute rien.

French [FRENCH] adjectif — **français,** masc. **française,** fém.

I am reading a French book.
Je lis un livre français.

---

fresh (cool) [FRESH] adjectif — **frais,** masc. **fraîche,** fém.

It is cool at the beach.
Il fait frais à la plage.

Friday [FRAI-dei] nom — **vendredi**

What do we eat on Friday? Fish!
Qu'est-ce qu'on mange le vendredi?
Du poisson!

---

friend [FREND] nom — **l'ami,** masc. **l'amie,** fém.

I am your friend.
Je suis ton amie.

---

frightening [FRAIT-ning] adjectif — **effrayant,** masc. **effrayante,** fém.

Snakes are frightening.
Les serpents sont effrayants.

---

frog [FRAG] nom — **la grenouille**

I am trying to catch a frog.
J'essaye d'attraper une grenouille.

---

from [FROM] préposition — **de**

Greetings from your friend!
Compliments de la part de votre ami!

---

fruit [FRUT] nom **les fruits**

Here is some fruit. Do you prefer a pear or a banana?
Voici des fruits. Préférez-vous une poire ou une banane?

---

full [FAUHL] adjectif **plein,** masc. **pleine,** fém.

The valise is full of clothes.
La valise est pleine de vêtements.

---

funny [FÉN-i] adjectif **amusant,** masc. **amusante,** fém. **drôle**

The clown is funny.
Le clown est amusant.

---

future [FYU-chér] nom **l'avenir,** masc.

In the future I'm going to visit France.
Je vais visiter la France dans l'avenir.

G

game [GEIM] nom **le jeu**, masc. **les jeux**, pl.

Which game do you prefer?
Quel jeu préférez-vous?

---

garage [gé-RAHZH] nom **le garage**

The car is in the garage.
La voiture est dans le garage.

---

garden [GAHR-dən] nom **le jardin**

The garden is full of flowers in June.
Le jardin est plein de fleurs au mois de juin.

---

gas [GAS] nom **le gaz**

You have a gas stove? We have an electric stove!
Tu as un fourneau à gaz? Nous avons un fourneau électrique!

---

gasoline [gas-ə-LIN] nom **l'essence,** fém.

Daddy says, "We don't have enough gasoline."
Papa dit: "Nous n'avons pas assez d'essence."

---

gas station [GAS STEI-shən] nom **la station-service**

My mother is going to the gas station.
Ma mère va à la station-service.

---

to gather (pick) [GA-thər] verbe **cueillir**

je cueille	nous cueillons
tu cueilles	vous cueillez
il, elle cueille	ils, elles cueillent

He is going to pick some apples.
Il va cueillir des pommes.

---

gentle (soft) [DJEN-təl] adjectif **doux,** masc. **douce,** fém.

This coat is very soft.
Ce manteau est très doux.

---

gentle **gentil**
gently adverbe **doucement**

Walk gently. Mother has a headache.
Marche doucement. Maman a mal à la tête.

---

geography [dji-AG-rə-fi] nom **la géographie**

I study geography in class.
J'étudie la géographie en classe.

---

to get (receive) [GET] verbe **recevoir**

je reçois	nous recevons
tu reçois	vous recevez
il, elle reçoit	ils, elles reçoivent

I receive a postcard from my sister.
Je reçois une carte postale de ma soeur.

---

to get dressed verbe **s'habiller**

je m'habille	nous nous habillons
tu t'habilles	vous vous habillez
il, elle s'habille	ils, elles s'habillent

I get up, I get dressed, I go to school.
Je me lève, je m'habille, je vais à l'école.

---

to get up verbe **se lever**

je me lève	nous nous levons
tu te lèves	vous vous levez
il, elle se lève	ils, elles se lèvent

Get up, Edward. You're late.
Lève-toi, Edouard. Tu es en retard.

---

giant [DJAI-ént] nom **le géant**

Read me the story of "Jack and the Giant."
Lis-moi l'histoire de "Jacques et Le Géant."

---

gift [GIFT] nom **le cadeau**

A gift for me?
Un cadeau pour moi?

---

girl [GURL] nom **la fille**

The girl is wearing an apron.
La petite fille porte un tablier.

---

to give [GIV] verbe **donner**

je donne	nous donnons
tu donnes	vous donnez
il, elle donne	ils, elles donnent

Please give me the camera.
Donne-moi l'appareil, s'il te plaît.

---

to give back (return) verbe **rendre**

je rends	nous rendons
tu rends	vous rendez
il, elle rend	ils, elles rendent

He returns my roller skates.
Il me rend mes patins à roulettes.

---

glad (happy) [GLAD] adjectif **content,** masc. **contente,** fém.

The little girl is not happy.
La petite fille n'est pas contente.

glad [GLAD] adjectif **heureux,** masc.
heureuse, fém.

---

glass [GLAS] nom **le verre**

I put the glass on the table carefully.
Je mets le verre sur la table avec soin.

made of glass **en verre**

My glasses are made of glass.
Mes lunettes sont en verre.

---

glasses nom **les lunettes**

Be careful! You are going to break your glasses.
Attention! Tu vas casser tes lunettes.

---

glove [GLÉV] nom **le gant**

She is wearing white gloves.
Elle porte des gants blancs.

---

to glue [GLU] verbe **coller**

je colle	nous collons
tu colles	vous collez
il, elle colle	ils, elles collent

I glue a picture to a page of my notebook.
Je colle une image sur une page de mon cahier.

---

to go (also used with exp. of health) verbe **aller**

je vais	nous allons
tu vas	vous allez
il, elle va	ils, elles vont

Where are you going? I'm going home.
Où vas-tu? Je vais chez moi.

---

to go back (See **to return**) **retourner**

---

to go down verbe **descendre**

je descends	nous decendons
tu decends	vous decendez
il, elle decend	ils, elles descendent

The man goes down the mountain.
L'homme descend de la montagne.

---

to go into verbe **entrer**

j'entre	nous entrons
tu entres	vous entrez
il, elle entre	ils, elles entrent

They go into the house.
Ils entrent dans la maison.

---

to go out (leave) verbe **sortir**

je sors	nous sortons
tu sors	vous sortez
il, elle sort	ils, elles sortent

The nurse leaves the hospital.
L'infirmière sort de l'hôpital.

---

to go to bed verbe **coucher**

je me couche	nous nous couchons
tu te couches	vous vous couchez
il, elle se couche	ils, elles se couchent

I don't like to go to bed early.
Je n'aime pas me coucher de bonne heure.

---

to go up verbe **monter**

The kite goes up into the sky.
Le cerf-volant monte dans le ciel.

---

goat [GOHT] nom **la chèvre**

The goat eats grass on the mountain.
La chèvre mange de l'herbe à la montagne.

---

gold [GOHLD] nom **l'or,** masc.
made of gold **en or**

I would like to have a gold ring.
Je voudrais avoir une bague en or.

> A popular saying in French is: "Tout ce qui brille, n'est pas or." It is similar to the saying in English: "All that glitters is not gold."

---

goldfish **le poisson rouge**

I have five goldfish.
J'ai cinq poissons rouges.

---

good [GAUHD] adjectif **bon,** masc. **bonne,** fém.

It is an interesting book; it is a good book.
C'est un livre intéressant; c'est un bon livre.

Good afternoon [gauhd af-ter-NUN] **Bonjour (après-midi)**
expression idiomatique

"Good afternoon, children," says the teacher.
"Bonjour les enfants," dit le professeur.

Good-bye [gauhd BAY] expression idiomatique **Au revoir**

In the morning Father says "Good-bye" to his family.
Le matin papa dit: "au revoir" à sa famille.

Good evening! [gauhd IV-ning] **Bonsoir**
expression idiomatique

When father returns home at nine o'clock, he says, "Good evening!"
Quand papa retourne à la maison à neuf heures, il dit: "Bonsoir!"

Good luck! [gauhd LEK] **Bonne chance!**
expression idiomatique

Good morning [gauhd MAWR-NING] **bonjour**
expression idiomatique

---

good-looking (pretty) adjectif **joli,** masc. **jolie,** fém.

What a pretty sweater! Is it new?
Quel joli chandail! Il est neuf?

---

granddaughter [GRAND-da-ter] nom **la petite-fille**

I am the engineer's granddaughter.
Je suis la petite fille de l'ingénieur.

---

grandfather [GRAND-fah-ther] nom **le grand-père**

My grandfather likes to drive the car.
Mon grand-père aime conduire la voiture.

---

grandmother [GRAND-meth-er] nom **la grand-mère**

We are going to my grandmother's house on Sunday.
Dimanche nous allons chez ma grand-mère.

---

grandparents [GRAND-PEHR-ents] nom **les grands-parents**

I like to go to my grandparents' house.
J'aime aller chez mes grandparents.

---

grandson [GRAND-sen] nom **le petit-fils**

John is the doctor's grandson.
Jean est le petit-fils du médecin.

---

grape [GREIP] nom **le raisin**

The fox looks at the grapes.
Le renard regarde les raisins.

---

grapefruit [GREIP-frut] nom **le pamplemousse**

The grapefruit is not sweet.
Le pamplemousse n'est pas doux.

---

grass [GRAS] nom **l'herbe,** fém.

Grass is green.
L'herbe est verte.

---

grasshopper [GRAS-hap-ér] nom **la sauterelle**

The boy tries to catch the grasshopper.
Le garçon essaye d'attraper la sauterelle.

---

gray [GREI] adjectif **gris,** masc. **grise,** fém.

The mouse is gray.
La souris est grise.

Great! [GREIT] interjection **formidable**

You are going to the circus? Great!
Tu vas au cirque? Formidable!

---

great adjectif **grand,** masc. **grande,** fém.

Madame Curie is a great scientist.
Madame Curie est une grande savante.

---

green [GRIN] adjectif **vert,** masc. **verte,** fém.

When the banana is not ripe, it is green.
Quand la banane n'est pas mûre, elle est verte.

---

grocer [GROH-sér] nom **l'épicier**

The grocer sells salt and jam.
L'épicier vend du sel et de la confiture.

---

grocery store nom **l'épicerie**

You go to the grocery store to buy sugar.
On va à l'épicerie pour acheter du sucre.

---

ground (earth) [GROWND] nom **la terre**

When the astronaut is on the moon,
he sees the earth.
Quand l'astronaute est sur la lune,
il voit la terre.

---

ground floor nom **le rez-de-chaussée**

Our apartment is on the ground floor.
Notre appartement est au rez-de-chaussée.

---

to grow [GROH] verbe **pousser**

je pousse	nous poussons
tu pousses	vous poussez
il, elle pousse	ils, elles poussent

Flowers grow in the garden.
Les fleurs poussent dans le jardin.

---

to guard [GAHRD] verbe **garder**

je garde	nous gardons
tu gardes	vous gardez
il, elle garde	ils, elles gardent

---

to guess [GES] verbe **deviner**

je devine nous devinons
tu devines vous devinez
il, elle devine ils, elles devinent

Can you guess how much money I have in my hand?
Pouvez-vous deviner combien d'argent j'ai dans la main?

---

guitar [gi-TAHR] nom **la guitare**

I know how to play the guitar.
Je sais jouer de la guitare.

---

gun [GŒN] nom **le fusil**

The hunter carries a gun.
Le chasseur porte un fusil.

H

hair [HEHR] nom **le cheveu,** masc. **les cheveux,** fém.

Students at the university like long hair.
Les étudiants à l'université aiment les cheveux longs.

---

hairbrush nom **la brosse à cheveux**

---

half [HAF] adjectif **demi,** masc. **demie,** fém.

half an hour **la demi-heure**

I have been waiting for you for half an hour!
Voilà une demi-heure que je vous attends!

---

half nom **la moitié**

Give me half of the pear, please.
Donnez-moi la moitié de la poire, s'il vous plaît.

---

ham [HAM] nom **le jambon**

Will you have some ham in your sandwich?
Vous prenez du jambon dans votre sandwich?

---

hammer [HAM-ér] nom **le marteau**

Albert is working with a hammer.
Albert travaille avec un marteau.

---

hand [HAND] nom **la main**

My hands are dirty!
J'ai les mains sales!

right hand **la main droite**
left hand **la main gauche**

---

handbag [HAND-bag] nom **le sac**

I am buying a handbag for my mother.
J'achète un sac à main pour ma mère.

---

handkerchief [HANG-kér-chif] nom **le mouchoir**

I use a handkerchief when I sneeze.
J'emploie un mouchoir quand j'éternue.

---

handsome (beautiful) [HAN-sém] adjectif **beau,** masc.
beaux, masc., pl.
belle, fém.
bel, masc. (before a vowel)

The actor is handsome;
the actress is beautiful.
L'acteur est beau; l'actrice
est belle.

---

to happen [HAP-én] verbe **arriver**

j'arrive	nous arrivons
tu arrives	vous arrivez
il, elle arrive	ils, elles arrivent

What is happening?
Qu'est-ce qui arrive?

---

happy [HAP-i] adjectif **content**

The little girl is not happy.
La petite fille n'est pas contente.

happy adjectif **heureux**
Happy Birthday **Joyeux Anniversaire**

---

hard [HAHRD] adjectif **dur,** masc.
dure, fém.

This apple is too hard.
Cette pomme est trop dure.

---

hat [HAT] nom **le chapeau**

What a pretty hat!
Quel joli chapeau!

---

to hate [HEIT] verbe **détester**

je déteste	nous détestons
tu détestes	vous détestez
il, elle déteste	ils, elles détestent

He hates spinach.
Il déteste les épinards.

---

to have [HAV] verbe **avoir**

j'ai	nous avons
tu as	vous avez
il, elle a	ils, elles ont

She has a pencil.
Elle a un crayon.

to have a good time verbe **s'amuser**

je m'amuse	nous nous amusons
tu t'amuses	vous vous amusez
il, elle s'amuse	ils, elles s'amusent

I have a good time at the circus.
Je m'amuse au cirque.

---

to have a pain (ache) in the . . . **avoir mal à**
expression idiomatique

I am sick. I have a headache.
Je suis malade. J'ai mal à la tête.

---

to have a sore . . . expression idiomatique **avoir mal à**

Peter has a sore foot.
Pierre a mal au pied.

---

to have (food) verbe **prendre**

je prends	nous prenons
tu prends	vous prenez
il, elle prend	ils, elles prennent

Mom has a croissant for breakfast.
Maman prend un croissant pour le petit déjeuner.

---

to have to verbe **devoir**

je dois	nous devons
tu dois	vous devez
il, elle doit	ils, elles doivent

I have to wash my hands.
Je dois me laver les mains.

---

hay [HEI] nom **le foin**

The farmer gives hay to the horses.
Le fermier donne du foin aux chevaux.

---

he [HI] pronom **il**

---

head [HED] nom **la tête**
The soldier turns his head.
Le soldat tourne la tête.

---

health [HELTH] nom **la santé**

Mother says, "Candy is not good for your health."
Maman dit: "Les bonbons ne sont pas bons pour la santé."

---

to hear [HIR] verbe **entendre**

j'entends	nous entendons
tu entends	vous entendez
il, elle entend	ils, elles entendent

I hear the telephone ringing.
J'entends le téléphone qui sonne.

---

heart [HAHRT] nom **le coeur**

Look at all the hearts on the (playing) card!
Regardez tous les coeurs sur la carte!

---

heavy [HEV-i] adjectif **lourd,** masc. **lourde,** fém.

The valise is very heavy.
La valise est très lourde.

---

helicopter [HEL-i-kap-tər] nom **l'hélicoptère**

The helicopter goes to the airport.
L'hélicoptère va à l'aéroport.

Hello [he-LOH] interjection **bonjour**

"Hello, children," says the teacher.
"Bonjour, les enfants," dit le professeur.

---

to help [HELP] verbe **aider**

j'aide	nous aidons
tu aides	vous aidez
il, elle aide	ils, elles aident

John helps his sister carry the books.
Jean aide sa soeur à porter les livres.

Help! interjection **Au secours!**

When I fall I cry, "Help!"
Quand je tombe je crie: "Au secours!"

---

her [HUR] pronom **la**
her pronom **lui**
her adjectif **son**

---

here [HIR] adverbe **ici**

Come here, Pierrot.
Viens ici, Pierrot.

---

here (present) adverbe **présent,** masc. **présente,** fém.

My friend Joan is present; my friend Susan is absent.
Mon amie Jeanne est présente; mon amie Suzanne est absente.

---

here are adverbe **voici**

Here are my tops (toys).
Voici mes toupies.

---

here is adverbe **voici**

Here is my top (toy).
Voici ma toupie.

---

herself [HUR-SELF] pronom **se**

---

to hide [HAID] verbe **cacher**

je cache	nous cachons
tu caches	vous cachez
il, elle cache	ils, elles cachent

The boy is hiding the flowers behind him.
Le garçon cache les fleurs derrière lui.

---

to play hide-and-seek **jouer à cache-cache**
(See **to play**)

---

high [HAI] adjectif **grand,** masc.
grande, fém.

high adjectif **haut**

The Eiffel Tower is very high.
La Tour Eiffel est très haute.

---

highway (road) [HAI-wei] nom **la route**

What's the name of this road?
Quel est le nom de cette route?

---

him [HIM] pronom **le,** masc.
l' (before a vowel)
la, fém.

I like him (her) (it).
Je l'aime.
I see her (it).
Je la vois.

I see them.
Je les vois.

him pronom **lui**

She gives him a cup of coffee.
Elle lui donne un café.

---

himself [HIM-SELF] pronom **se**

He washes himself.
Il se lave.

---

his [HIZ] adjectif **son**

---

history [HIS-tə-ri] nom **l'histoire**

I like to study history.
J'aime étudier l'histoire.

---

to hit [HIT] verbe **battre**

je bats	nous battons
tu bats	vous battez
il, elle bat	ils, elles battent

He's hitting me!
Il me bat!

---

hole [HOHL] nom **le trou**

I have a hole in my sock.
J'ai un trou dans la chaussette.

---

holiday [HAL-i-dei] nom **le jour de fête**

The holiday is July 18th?
Le jour de fête est le dix-huit juillet?

---

home (house) nom **la maison**

Here is my uncle's house.
Voici la maison de mon oncle.

---

homework [HOHM-WURk] nom **le devoir**

We are going to do our homework together.
Nous allons faire nos devoirs ensemble.

---

hoop [HUP] nom **le cerceau**

The boy is rolling a big hoop.
Le garçon roule un grand cerceau.

---

to hope [HOHP] verbe **espérer**

j'espère	nous espérons
tu espères	vous espérez
il, elle espère	ils, elles espèrent

I hope to get a good mark in history.
J'espère recevoir une bonne note en historie.

---

to play hopscotch **jouer à la marelle**
(See to **play**)

---

horse [HAWRS] nom **le cheval**

The boy is riding a horse.
Le garçon monte à cheval.

---

hospital [HAS-pi-təl] nom **l'hôpital,** masc.

The nurse works at the hospital.
L'infirmière travaille à l'hôpital.

---

hot [HAT] adjectif **chaud**
It is hot **Il fait chaud**
to be hot **avoir chaud**

The boy is hot. He is going to swim.
Le garçon a chaud. Il va nager.

---

hotel [hoh-TEL] nom **l'hôtel,** masc.

What is the name of this hotel?
Quel est le nom de cet hôtel?

---

hour (time) [OWR] nom **l'heure,** fém.

What time is it?
Quelle heure est-il?

---

house [HOWS] nom **la maison**

Here is my uncle's house.
Voici la maison de mon oncle.

---

how [HOW] adverbe **comment**

How are you?
Comment allez-vous?

---

how many [hOW MEN-i] adverbe **combien**

How many toys do you have?
Combien de jouets as-tu?

how much [HOW MɆCH] **combien**

---

humid (damp) [HYU-mid] adjectif **humide**

My bathing suit is damp.
Mon maillot est humide.

---

to be hungry [HɆNG-gri] expression idiomatique **avoir faim**

Poor baby. He is hungry.
Pauvre bébé. Il a faim.

---

hunter [HɆN-tɇr] nom **le chasseur**

The hunter goes into the forest.
Le chasseur entre dans la forêt.

Hurray! [hɇ-REI] interjection **Bravo!**

---

to hurry [HɆ-ri] verbe **se dépêcher**

je me dépêche	nous nous dépêchons
tu te dépêches	vous vous dépêchez
il, elle se dépêche	ils, elles se dépêchent

They hurry because they are late.
Ils se dépêchent parce qu'ils sont en retard.

---

to hurt [HURT] expression idiomatique **avoir mal à**

My finger hurts.
J'ai mal au doigt.

---

husband [HÉZ-bénd] nom **le mari**

My aunt's husband is my uncle.
Le mari de ma tante est mon oncle.

I

I [AI] pronom **je**

I am speaking to my friends.
Je parle à mes amis.

---

ice [AIS] nom **la glace**

Let's go ice skating.
Allons patiner sur la glace.

---

ice cream [ais KRIM] nom **la glace**

Do you like vanilla ice cream?
Tu aimes la glace à la vanille?

---

ice skate [AIS SKEIT] nom **le patin à glace**
to ice-skate **patiner**

Let's go ice skating!
Allons patiner!

---

idea [ai-DI-é] nom **l'idée,** fém.

What a good idea it is to go swimming!
Quelle bonne idée d'aller nager!

---

if [IF] préposition **si**

---

immediately [i-MI-di-it-li] adverbe **tout de suite**

I call the dog and he comes immediately.
J'appelle le chien et il vient tout de suite.

---

important [im-PAWR-tənt] adjectif **important**

It is important to eat vegetables.
Il est important de manger des légumes.

---

impossible [im-PAS-i-bəl] adjectif **impossible**

It is impossible to roll this rock.
Il est impossible de rouler ce rocher.

---

in, into [IN] préposition **en; dans**

They go into the school.
Ils entrent dans l'école.

in front of [IN FRƏNT əv] préposition **devant**

There is a table in front of the sofa.
Il y a une table devant le canapé.

---

in honor of [IN AN-ər əv] expression idiomatique **en l'honneur de**

We are dining in a restaurant in honor of my daughter.
Nous dînons au restaurant en l'honneur de ma fille.

---

in order to (to) [IN AWR-dər tə] préposition **pour**

She is going to the store to buy stockings.
Elle va au magasin pour acheter des bas.

---

in the middle of [IN the MI-DƏL əv] préposition **au milieu de**

Mom puts the candy in the middle of the table.
Maman met les bonbons au milieu de la table.

(in) this way [IN this WEI] adverbe **ainsi**

The little marionettes dance this way.
Ainsi dansent les petites marionettes.

---

to indicate [IN-di-keit] verbe **indiquer**

j'indique nous indiquons
tu indiques vous indiquez
il, elle indique ils, elles indiquent

The policeman indicates that we must go by this road.
L'agent de police indique qu'il faut aller par cette route.

---

inexpensive [in-ik-SPEN-siv] adjectif **bon marché**

Bread is cheap; it is not expensive.
On vend le pain bon marché; il ne coûte pas cher.

---

insect [IN-sekt] nom **l'insecte,** masc.

I hate insects!
Je déteste les insectes!

---

intelligent [in-TEL-i-djənt] adjectif **intelligent,** masc. **intelligente,** fém.

The teacher says, "What an intelligent class!"
Le professeur dit: "Quelle classe intelligente!"

---

intentionally (on purpose) [in-TEN-shən-əl-li] adverbe **exprès**

My brother teases me on purpose. (intentionally)
Mon frère me taquine exprès.

---

interesting [IN-tər-əs-ting] adjectif **intéressant,** masc. **intéressante,** fém.

Do you think the film is interesting?
Tu trouves que le film est intéressant?

---

into [IN-tu] préposition **dans**

They go into the school.
Ils entrent dans l'école.

---

to introduce [in-tré-DUS] verbe **présenter**

je présente	nous présentons
tu présentes	vous présentez
il, elle présente	ils, elles présentent

I would like to introduce my grandson to you.
Je vous présente mon petit-fils.

---

to invite [in-VAIT] verbe **inviter**

j'invite	nous invitons
tu invites	vous invitez
il, elle invite	ils, elles invitent

My aunt invites me to her house.
Ma tante m'invite chez elle.

---

iron (appliance) [AI-érn] nom **le fer**

The iron is not working. I can't iron this dress.
Le fer ne marche pas. Je ne peux pas repasser cette robe.

iron (metal) **en fer**

The stove is made of iron.
Le fourneau est en fer.

---

to iron verbe **repasser**

je repasse	nous repassons
tu repasses	vous repassez
il, elle repasse	ils, elles repassent

He irons the shirt with an iron.
Il repasse la chemise avec un fer.

---

island [AI-lénd] nom **l'île,** fém.

Corsica is a French island.
La Corse est une île française.

Isn't that true? Isn't that so? Don't you agree? expression idiomatique **n'est-ce pas?**

The weather is bad, isn't it?
Il fait mauvais, n'est-ce pas?

My teacher is handsome, don't you agree?
Mon professeur est beau, n'est-ce pas?

---

it [IT] pronom **il,** masc.
elle, fém.

they **ils,** masc., pl.
elles, fém., pl.

Here is the pencil. It is yellow.
Voici le crayon. Il est jaune.

Where is my shoe? It's under the bed.
Où est ma chaussure? Elle est sous le lit.

It is forbidden to **défense de**
it is necessary expression idiomatique **il faut**

It is necessary to go to school.
Il faut aller à l'école.
(We have to go to school.)

It is raining. (It rains.) verbe **Il pleut.**

It rains a lot in the month of April.
Il pleut beaucoup au mois d'avril.

It is snowing. verbe **Il neige.**

Look out the window. It's snowing!
Regardez par la fenêtre. Il neige!

---

its adjectif **son**

I would like . . . verbe **je voudrais**
He would like . . . **il voudrait**
She would like . . . **elle voudrait**
They would like . . . **ils, elles voudraient**

I would like to take a walk.
Je voudrais faire une promenade.

She would like to go shopping.
Elle voudrait faire des emplettes.

J

jacket [DJAK-it] nom **la veste**

My grandfather wears pants and a jacket.
Mon grand-père porte un pantalon et une veste.

---

jackknife (pocketknife) [DJAK-NAIF] nom **le canif**

Do you have a pocketknife?
Avez-vous un canif?

---

jam [DJAM] nom **la confiture**

Please give me a piece of bread with strawberry jam.
Donnez-moi un morceau de pain avec de la confiture aux fraises, s'il vous plaît.

January [DJAN-yu-er-i] nom **janvier**

January sixth is a holiday in France.
Le six janvier est un jour de fête en France.

---

jet airplane (See **airplane**) nom **l'avion à réaction**

---

jewel [DJU-əl] nom **le bijou**
jewelry (jewels) nom **le bijou**
les bijoux, pl.

There are many jewels in the trunk.
Il y a beaucoup de bijoux dans la malle.

---

juice [DJUS] nom **le jus**
orange juice nom **le jus d'orange**
I like orange juice.
J'aime le jus d'orange.

July [dju-LAI] nom **juillet**
July 14th is the French national holiday.
Le quatorze juillet est la fête nationale française.

---

to jump [DJÉMP] verbe **sauter**

je saute	nous sautons
tu sautes	vous sautez
il, elle saute	ils, elles sautent

The boy jumps from the stairs.
Le garçon saute de l'escalier.

June [DJUN] nom **juin**
How many days are there in June?
Combien de jours y a-t-il en juin?

K

kangaroo [kang-gé-RU] nom **le kangourou**
The kangaroo is a strange animal.
Le kangourou est un animal bizarre.

---

to keep [KIP] verbe **garder**

je garde	nous gardons
tu gardes	vous gardez
il, elle garde	ils, elles gardent

I keep a dog.
Je garde un chien.

---

key [KI] nom **la clef**

Where is my key?
Où est ma clef?

---

to kick [KIK] **donner un coup de pied à**
expression idiomatique

He kicks the ball.
Il donne un coup de pied à la balle.

---

to kill [KIL] verbe **tuer**

je tue	nous tuons
tu tues	vous tuez
il, elle tue	ils, elles tuent

My mother kills the fly.
Maman tue la mouche.

---

kilometer [KIL-é-mi-tér] nom **le kilomètre**

I live five kilometers from the school.
J'habite à cinq kilomètres de l'école.

---

kind [KAIND] adjectif **gentil,** masc. **gentille,** fém.

The teacher is very kind.
La maîtresse est très gentille.

---

kind nom **la sorte**

What kind of meat is this?
Quelle sorte de viande est-ce?

---

king [KING] nom **le roi**

Is there a king in France? No, there is a president.
Est-ce qu'il y a un roi en France? Non, il y a un président.

---

kiss [KIS] nom **le baiser**

Mother is kissing the child.
Maman donne un baiser à l'enfant.

---

kitchen [KICH-én] nom **la cuisine**

Mother prepares meals in the kitchen.
Maman prépare les repas dans la cuisine.

to cook **faire la cuisine**

---

kite [KAIT] nom **le cerf-volant**
les cerfs-volants, pl.

Good, it's windy. Let's play with a kite.
Bon, il fait du vent. Allons jouer avec un cerf-volant.

---

kitten [KIT-én] nom **le petit chat, le chaton**

My kitten is black.
Mon petit chat est noir.

---

knee [NI] nom **le genou,** masc.
les genous, pl.

You have a sore knee? That's too bad!
Tu as mal au genou? C'est triste.

---

knife [NAIF] nom **le couteau; le canif**

(kitchen or table) knife **le couteau,** masc.
les couteaux, pl.

She puts a knife at each place at the table.
Elle met un couteau à chaque place à la table.

---

to knit [NIT] verbe **tricoter**

je tricote	nous tricotons
tu tricotes	vous tricotez
il, elle tricote	ils, elles tricotent

I am learning how to knit.
J'apprends à tricoter.

---

knob (See **door**) nom **le bouton**

---

knock [NAK] nom **le coup**

There a two knocks on the door. Who's there?
Il y a deux coups à la porte. Qui est là?

---

to knock verbe **frapper**

Mommy, someone is knocking at the door.
Maman, on frappe à la porte.

---

to know [NOH] verbe **connaître**

je connais	nous connaissons
tu connais	vous connaissez
il, elle connaît	ils, elles connaissent

Do you know my teacher?
Connais-tu mon maître?

---

to know verbe **savoir**

je sais	nous savons
tu sais	vous savez
il, elle sait	ils, elles savent

to know how to verbe **savoir**

je sais	nous savons
tu sais	vous savez
il, elle sait	ils, elles savent

I know how to ride a bicycle.
Je sais monter à bicyclette.

L

lady [LEI-di] nom **la dame**

Who is this lady?
Qui est cette dame?

---

lake [LEIK] nom **le lac**

There is a boat in the middle of the lake.
Il y a un bateau au milieu du lac.

---

lamp [LAMP] nom **la lampe**

The lamp is in the living-room.
La lampe est dans le salon.

---

large (See **elephant**) adjectif **grand**

---

last [LAST] adjectif **dernier,** masc. **dernière,** fém.

Paul is the last one to sit down at the table.
Paul est le dernier à s'asseoir à table.

last one nom **le dernier**

---

late [LEIT] adverbe **tard**

It is late. Let's hurry.
Il est tard. Dépêchons-nous.

---

late adverbe **retard; en retard**

Frank comes late to school.
François arrive à l'école en retard.

---

later adverbe **plus tard**

It is eight o'clock now. The mailman comes later.
Il est huit heures maintenant. Le facteur arrive plus tard.

---

to laugh [LAF] verbe **rire**

je ris	nous rions
tu ris	vous riez
il, elle rit	ils, elles rient

She laughs when she looks at the clown.
Elle rit quand il regarde les ours.

---

lawyer [LAW-yér] nom **l'avocat**

My uncle is a lawyer.
Mon oncle est avocat.

---

lazy [LEI-zi] adjectif **paresseux,** masc. **paresseuse,** fém.

My teacher says I am lazy.
Ma maîtresse dit que je suis paresseuse.

---

to lead [LID] verbe **mener**

je mène	nous menons
tu mènes	vous menez
il, elle mène	ils, elles mènent

He leads his dog outside.
Il mène son chien dehors.

---

leader [LI-dér] nom **le chef**

No! You're always playing the leader.
Mais non! Tu joues toujours le rôle du chef.

---

leaf [LIF] nom **la feuille**
leaves [LEEVZ]

There are so many leaves on the ground in autumn!
Il y a tant de feuilles sur terre en automne!

---

to leap [LIP] verbe **sauter**

je saute	nous sautons
tu sautes	vous sautez
il, elle saute	ils, elles sautent

to play leap-frog **jouer à saute-mouton**

---

to learn [LURN] verbe **apprendre**

j'apprends	nous apprenons
tu apprends	vous apprenez
il, elle apprend	ils, elles apprennent

She likes to learn French.
Elle aime apprendre le français.

---

leather [LETH-ér] nom **le cuir**
made of leather **en cuir**

My brother's jacket is made of leather.
La veste de mon frère est en cuir.

---

to leave [LIV] verbe **laisser**

je laisse	nous laissons
tu laisses	vous laissez
il, elle laisse	ils, elles laissent

I often leave my books at Michael's house.
Je laisse souvent mes livres chez Michel.

---

to leave verbe **partir**

je pars nous partons
tu pars vous partez
il, elles part ils, elles partent

My aunt is leaving at 5 o'clock.
Ma tante part à cinq heures.

---

to leave verbe **quitter**

je quitte nous quittons
tu quittes vous quittez
il, elle quitte ils, elles quittent

We leave the museum at 5 o'clock.
Nous quittons le musée à cinq heures.

---

to leave verbe **sortir**

je sors nous sortons
tu sors vous sortez
il, elle sort ils, elles sortent

The nurse leaves the hospital.
L'infirmière sort de l'hôpital.

---

left [LEFT] adjectif **gauche**
left hand nom **la main gauche**

I raise my left hand.
Je lève la main gauche.

---

to the left expression idiomatique **à gauche**

The tree is to the left of the house.
L'arbre est à gauche de la maison.

---

leg [LEG] nom **la jambe**

Birds have two legs; animals have four paws.
L'oiseau a deux jambes; l'animal a quatre pattes.

---

lemon [LEM-ən] nom **le citron**

Lemons are yellow.
Les citrons sont jaunes.

---

to lend [LEND] verbe **prêter**

je prête	nous prêtons
tu prêtes	vous prêtez
il, elle prête	ils, elles prêtent

Can you lend me your bicycle?
Peux-tu me prêter ta bicyclette?

---

leopard [LEP-ərd] nom **le léopard**

The leopard is in the forest.
Le léopard est dans la fôret.

---

less (before, to) [LES] adverbe **moins**

We are leaving at twenty minutes to two.
Nous partons à deux heures moins vingt.

---

lesson [LES-ən] nom **la leçon**

Today's lesson is difficult, isn't it?
La leçon d'aujourd'hui est difficile, n'est-ce pas?

---

to let [LET] verbe **laisser**

je laisse	nous laissons
tu laisses	vous laissez
il, elle laisse	ils, elles laissent

My brother lets me wash the car.
Mon frère me laisse laver la voiture.

---

letter [LET-ər] nom **la lettre**

I put the letter in the envelope.
Je mets la lettre dans l'enveloppe.

letter box; mailbox **la boîte aux lettres**

---

lettuce [LET-is] nom **la laitue**

Mom makes a salad with lettuce.
Maman prépare une salade avec la laitue.

---

library [LAI-brer-i] nom **la bibliothèque**

There are so many books in the library!
Il y a tant de livres dans la bibliothèque!

---

lie [LAI] nom **le mensonge**

He tells lies!
Il dit des mensonges!

---

light (See **clear**) **clair**

---

light [LAIT] nom **la lumière**

The moon does not give much light.
La lune ne donne pas beaucoup de lumière.

light (traffic) nom **le feu**

You cross the street when you see the green light.
On traverse la rue quand on voit le feu vert.

light (weight) [LAIT] adjectif **léger,** masc. **légère,** fém.

This box is light.
Cette boîte est légère.

---

lightning [LAIT-ning] nom **l'éclair,** masc.

I am afraid of lightning.
J'ai peur de l'éclair.

(light) switch **le bouton**

---

to like [LAIK] verbe **aimer**

j'aime	nous aimons
tu aimes	vous aimez
il, elle aime	ils, elles aiment

Mother likes her children.
Maman aime ses enfants.

---

lion [LAI-ən] nom **le lion**

The lion is not a gentle animal.
Le lion n'est pas un animal doux.

---

lip [LIP] nom **la lèvre**

Look! The doll is opening its lips.
Regarde! La poupée ouvre les lèvres.

---

to listen [LIS-ən] verbe **écouter**

j'écoute	nous écoutons
tu écoutes	vous écoutez
il, elle écoute	ils, elles écoutent

The boy is listening to the radio.
Le garçon écoute la radio.

---

little [LIT-əl] adjectif **petit,** masc. **petite,** fém.

The bird is small.
L'oiseau est petit.

little adverbe **un peu**

Do you want any soup? A little, please.
Voulez-vous de la soupe? Un peu, s'il vous plaît.

---

to live [LIV] verbe **demeurer**

je demeure	nous demeurons
tu demeures	vous demeurez
il, elle demeure	ils, elles demeurent

Where do you live?
Où demeurez-vous?

---

to live verbe **vivre**

je vis	nous vivons
tu vis	vous vivez
il, elle vit	ils, elles vivent

Do any wild animals live in this forest?
Est-ce que des animaux sauvages vivent dans cette forêt?

---

to live (dwell) verbe **habiter**

j'habite	nous habitons
tu habites	vous habitez
il, elle habite	ils, elles habitent

Where do you live?
Où habitez-vous?

---

living room [LIV-ing rum] nom **le salon**

Who is in the living room?
Qui est dans le salon?

---

lollipop [LAL-i-PAP] nom **la sucette**

Mmm, I like the lollipop.
Mmm, j'aime la sucette.

---

long [LAWNG] adjectif **long,** masc. **longue,** fém.

She is wearing a long dress.
Elle porte une robe longue.

---

look [LAUHK] nom **l'air**

The tiger has a ferocious look.
Le tigre a l'air féroce.

---

to look (at), watch verbe **regarder**

je regarde	nous regardons
tu regardes	vous regardez
il, elle regarde	ils, elles regardent

I like to watch television.
J'aime regarder la télévision.

---

to look after verbe **surveiller**

je surveille	nous surveillons
tu surveilles	vous surveillez
il, elle surveille	ils, elles surveillent

The cat looks after the kittens.
Le chat surveille les petits (chats).

---

to look for verbe **chercher**

je cherche	nous cherchons
tu cherches	vous cherchez
il, elle cherche	ils, elles cherchent

Father is always looking for his keys.
Papa cherche toujours ses clefs.

---

to lose [LUZ] verbe **perdre**

je perds	nous perdons
tu perds	vous perdez
il, elle perd	ils, elles perdent

Jack always loses his hat.
Jacques perd toujours son chapeau.

---

a lot (of) [LAT] adverbe **beaucoup de (d')**

Bertha has a lot of books.
Berthe a beaucoup de livres.

---

loud [LOWD] adjectif **haut,** masc. **haute,** fém.

My dog's voice is very loud.
La voix de mon chien est très haute.

in a loud voice **à haute voix**

loudly adverbe **fort**

He plays the drum too loudly.
Il joue trop fort au tambour.

---

love [LÉV] nom **l'amour,** masc.

The boy loves his dog.
Le garçon a un grand amour pour son chien.

---

to love verbe **aimer**

j'aime	nous aimons
tu aimes	vous aimez
il, elle aime	ils, elles aiment

I love my cat.
J'aime mon chat.

---

low (See **short**) adjectif **bas**

to lower (put down) [LOH-ér] verbe **baisser**

je baisse	nous baissons
tu baisses	vous baissez
il, elle baisse	ils, elles baissent

The teacher says, "Put your hands down!"
Le professeur dit: "Baissez les mains!"

---

luck [LÉK] nom **la chance**
Good luck! interjection **Bonne chance!**

Before the examination my friend says, "Good luck!"
Avant l'examen mon ami dit: "Bonne chance!"

---

to be lucky expression idiomatique **avoir de la chance**

The boy wins a prize. He is lucky.
Le garçon gagne un prix. Il a de la chance.

---

luggage (baggage) [LÉG-idj] nom **les bagages,** masc., pl.

The luggage is ready for the trip.
Les bagages sont prêts pour le voyage.

---

lunch [LÉNCH] nom **le déjeuner**

I eat lunch at noon.
Je prends le déjeuner à midi.

lunchtime **l'heure du déjeuner**

M

machine [mé-SHIN] nom **la machine**
washing machine nom **la machine à laver**

Mother wants a washing machine.
Maman désire une machine à laver.

---

mad (See **crazy**) adjectif **fou**

---

made of adjectif **en**

---

maid [MEID] nom **la bonne**

The maid cleans the house.
La bonne nettoie la maison.

---

mail a letter (See **letter**) **mettre une lettre à la poste**
mailbox (See **letter**) **la boîte aux lettres**
mail carrier nom **le facteur**

The mail carrier brings letters and packages.
Le facteur apporte des lettres et des paquets.

---

to make [MEIK] verbe **former**

je forme	nous formons
tu formes	vous formez
il, elle forme	ils, elles forment

I make a snowball with the snow.
Je forme une balle avec la neige.

---

to make (do) verbe **faire**

je fais	nous faisons
tu fais	vous faites
il, elle fait	ils, elles font

He does his homework.
Il fait ses devoirs.

Mama [MA-mə] nom **maman**

Mom, where are my socks?
Maman, où sont mes chaussettes?

---

man [MAN] nom **l'homme**
men [MEN] pl.

The man comes to fix the television set.
L'homme vient pour réparer le téléviseur.

---

many (a lot) [MEN-i] adverbe **beaucoup de (d')**

Bertha has a lot of books.
Berthe a beaucoup de livres.

---

map [MAP] nom **la carte**

Do you have a road map of France?
Avez-vous une carte des routes de la France?

---

marbles [MAHR-bəlz] nom **les billes,** fém., pl.

Boys like to play marbles.
Les garçons aiment jouer aux billes.

March [MAHRCH] nom **mars**

It is windy in March.
Il fait du vent en mars.

---

marionette [ma-ri-ə-NET] nom **la marionnette**

The marionettes are funny.
Les marionnettes sont drôles.

---

mark (in school) [MAHRK] nom **la note**

Do you have good marks?
Tu as de bonnes notes?

---

market [MAHR-kit] nom **le marché**

What do they sell at the market?
Qu'est-ce qu'on vend au marché?

---

to marry [MAR-i] verbe **épouser**

j'épouse	nous épousons
tu épouses	vous épousez
il, elle épouse	ils, elles épousent

The prince marries the princess.
Le prince épouse la princesse.

Marvelous! (Great!) [MAHR-vé-lés] interjection **formidable**

You are going to the circus? Great!
Tu vas au cirque? Formidable!

---

marvelous adjectif **sensationnel**

You're going to the theater? Marvelous!
Tu vas au théâtre? Sensationnel!

---

match [MACH] nom **l'allumette,** fém.

Matches are dangerous for children.
Les allumettes sont dangereuses pour les enfants.

May [MEI] nom **mai**

There are thirty-one days in May.
Il y a trente et un jours en mai.

---

may verbe **pouvoir**

je peux	nous pouvons
tu peux	vous pouvez
il, elle peut	ils, elles peuvent

May I go fishing?
Puis-je aller à la pêche?

---

maybe [MEI-bi] adverbe **peut-être**

Are we going horseback riding this morning? Maybe.
Nous montons à cheval ce matin? Peut-être.

---

me [MI] pronom **me**

He gives me some bread.
Il me donne du pain.

---

me pronom **moi**

Who is knocking at the door? It's me, Michael.
Qui frappe à la porte? C'est moi, Michel.

---

meal [MIL] nom **le repas**

Which meal do you prefer?
Quel repas préférez-vous?

---

to mean [MIN] verbe **vouloir dire**

What does this word mean?
Que veut dire ce mot?

---

meat [MIT] nom **la viande**

The woman goes to the butcher shop to buy meat.
La femme va à la boucherie pour acheter de la viande.

---

mechanic [mé-KAN-ik] nom **le mécanicien**

I would like to become a mechanic.
Je voudrais devenir mécanicien.

---

medicine [MED-i-sin] nom **le médicament**

I don't like this medicine.
Je n'aime pas ce médicament.

---

to meet [MIT] verbe **rencontrer**

je rencontre	nous rencontrons
tu rencontres	vous rencontrez
il, elle rencontre	ils, elles rencontrent

Who meets Little Red Riding Hood in the forest?
Qui rencontre Le Petit Chaperon Rouge dans la forêt?

---

member [MEM-bėr] nom **le membre**

He is a member of our team.
Il est membre de notre équipe.

---

menu [MEN-yu] nom **la carte**

---

merry-go-round [MER-i-goh-rownd] nom **le manège**

Look at the horses on the merry-go-round!
Regarde les chevaux du manège!

---

midnight [MID-nait] nom **minuit**

It is midnight. Why aren't you sleeping?
Il est minuit. Pourquoi ne dors-tu pas?

---

mile [MAIL] nom **le mille**

My friend lives one mile from here.
Mon ami demeure un mille d'ici.

---

milk [MILK] nom **le lait**

I drink milk and Daddy drinks coffee with milk.
Je bois du lait et Papa boit du café avec du lait.

---

million [MIL-yėn] nom **le million**

How many books do you have? A million!
Combien de livres as-tu? Un million!

---

minute [MIN-it] nom **la minute**

How many minutes are there in an hour?
Combien de minutes y a-t-il dans une heure?

---

mirror [MIR-ér] nom **le miroir**

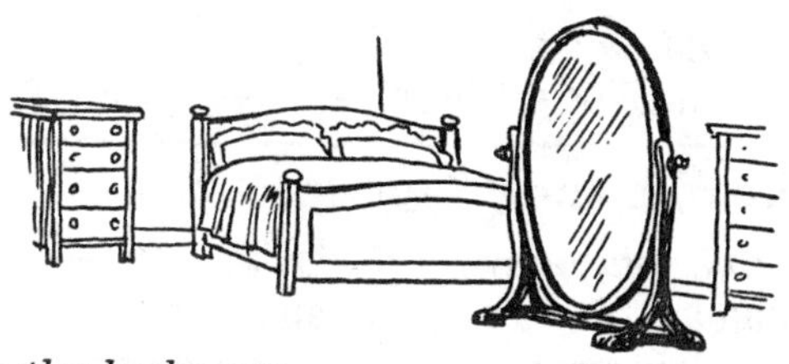

There is a mirror in the bedroom.
Il y a un miroir dans la chambre.

mirror nom **la glace**

Do you have a mirror?
Est-ce que vous avez une glace?

Miss [MIS] nom **mademoiselle**
young ladies nom **mesdemoiselles,** pl.

Miss Duval? She is a good teacher.
Mademoiselle Duval? Elle est un bon professeur.

---

mistake [mis-TEIK] nom **la faute**

I make mistakes when I write in French.
Je fais des fautes quand j'écris en français.

Mister [MIS-ter] nom **monsieur**
gentlemen **messieurs**

The man's name is Mr. Montand.
L'homme s'appelle monsieur Montand.

---

to mix [MIKS] verbe **mélanger**

je mélange	nous mélangeons
tu mélanges	vous mélangez
il, elle mélange	ils, elles mélangent

When you play dominoes, you mix the dominoes.
Quand on joue aux dominos, on mélange les dominos.

---

moist (damp) [MOIST] adjectif **humide**

My bathing suit is damp.
Mon maillot est humide.

Mom, Mommy [MAM, MA-mi] nom **Maman**

Mom, where are my socks?
Maman, où sont mes chaussettes?

---

moment [MOH-mənt] nom **le moment**

I am going into the post office for a moment.
J'entre dans la poste pour un moment.

Monday [MəN-dei] nom **lundi,** masc.

What do you do on Mondays?
Que faites-vous le lundi?

---

money [MəN-i] nom **l'argent,** masc.

He doesn't have enough money.
Il n'a pas assez d'argent.

---

money box (piggy bank) nom **la tirelire**

I do not have much money in my piggy bank.
Je n'ai pas beaucoup d'argent dans ma tirelire.

---

monkey [MəNG-ki] nom **le singe**

The monkey is eating a banana.
Le singe mange une banane.

---

month [MƏNTH] nom **le mois**

We have two months of vacation.
Nous avons deux mois de vacances.

---

moon [MUN] nom **la lune**

The astronaut walks on the moon.
L'astronaute marche sur la lune.

---

more [MAWR] adverbe **encore**

Do you want more bread?
Tu désires encore du pain?

---

more adverbe **plus**

---

morning [MAWR-ning] nom **le matin**

What do you eat in the morning?
Que mangez-vous le matin?

Good morning **Bonjour**

---

mosquito [məs-KI-toh] nom **le moustique**

Daddy, catch the mosquito! It's going to bite me.
Papa, attrapez le moustique. Il va me piquer!

---

mother [MƏTH-ər] nom **la mère**

Today is my mother's birthday.
C'est l'anniversaire de ma mère aujourd'hui.

---

mountain [MOWN-tən] nom **la montagne**

The mountains near Spain are the Pyrenees.
Les montagnes près de l'Espagne sont les Pyrénées.

---

mouse [MOWS] nom **la souris**
mice pl.

There are mice in the field.
Il y a des souris dans ce champ.

---

mouth [MOWTH] nom **la bouche**

The child opens his mouth when he cries.
L'enfant ouvre la bouche quand il pleure.

---

to move [MUV] verbe **remuer**

je remue	nous remuons
tu remues	vous remuez
il, elle remue	ils, elles remuent

She moves her fingers quickly when she plays the piano.
Elle remue vite ses doigts quand elle joue du piano.

---

movie [MU-vi] nom **le film**

Are they playing a good film at the movies?
On joue un bon film au cinéma?

---

movies nom **le cinéma**

There is a good film at the movies.
Il y a un bon film au cinéma.

Mr. [MIS-tėr] nom **M.**

Mrs. [MIS-ės] nom **Mme, madame**

Say "Good morning, Mrs. Jones" to your teacher.
Dis "Bonjour, Madame" à ta maîtresse.

---

much (See **many**) **beaucoup de (d')**

---

mud [MĖD] nom **la boue**

My hands are covered with mud!
Mes mains sont couvertes de boue!

---

museum [myu-ZI-ėm] nom **le musée**

The museum is open from 2 o'clock to 5 o'clock.
Le musée est ouvert de deux heures jusqu'à cinq heures.

---

music [MYU-zik] nom **la musique**

Do you know how to read musical notes?
Est-ce que vous savez lire les notes de musique?

musical note **la note**

---

musician [myu-ZI-shén] nom **le musicien**

The musician is handsome.
Le musicien est beau.

---

my [MAI] pronom **mon,** masc. **ma,** fém. **mes,** pl.

My brother is handsome
Mon frère est beau.

My sister is pretty.
Ma soeur est jolie.

My cousins are always cheerful.
Mes cousins sont toujours gais.

myself [mai-SELF] pronom **me; moi-même**

N

nail (finger) (See **fingernail**) **l'ongle**

---

nail (metal) [NEIL] nom **le clou**

My brother plays with nails and a hammer.
Mon frère joue avec des clous et un marteau.

---

name [NEIM] nom **le nom**

What is the name of this building?
Quel est le nom de ce bâtiment?

— name is verbe **s'appeler**

je m'appelle	nous nous appelons
tu t'appelles	vous vous appelez
il, elle s'appelle	ils, elles s'appellent

What is your name? My name is Henry.
Comment vous appelez-vous? Je m'appelle Henri.

surname [SUR-neim] nom **le nom de famille**

---

napkin [NAP-kin] nom **la serviette**

There are four napkins on the table.
Il y a quatre serviettes sur la table.

---

narrow [NAR-oh] adjectif **étroit,** masc. **étroite,** fém.

The drawer is too narrow for the papers.
Le tiroir est trop étroit pour les papiers.

---

nation [NEI-shən] nom **la nation**

There are many flags at the United Nations.
Il y a beaucoup de drapeaux aux Nations Unies.

---

national [NASH-ən-əl] adjectif **national,** masc. **nationale,** fém.

The Fourth of July is the national holiday of the United States.
Le quatre juillet est la fête nationale des États-Unis.

---

naughty [naw-ti] adjectif **méchant,** masc. **méchante,** fém.

Robert cannot go out. He is naughty.
Robert ne peut pas sortir. Il est méchant.

---

near [NIR] préposition **près de**

Bordeaux is near the Atlantic Ocean.
Bordeaux est près de l'océan Atlantique.

---

neck [NEK] nom **le cou**

My grandmother says, "My neck hurts."
Ma grand-mère dit: "J'ai mal au cou."

---

to need [NID] expression idiomatique **avoir besoin de (d')**

The fish needs water.
Le poisson a besoin d'eau.

---

needle [NID-él] nom **l'aiguille,** fém.

Here is a sewing needle.
Voici une aiguille à coudre.

---

neighbor [NEI-bér] nom **le voisin,** masc. **la voisine,** fém.

My neighbor Bernard lives near me.
Mon voisin Bernard demeure près de moi.

---

nephew [NEF-yu] nom **le neveu**

He is Mr. Duval's nephew.
Il est le neveu de monsieur Duval.

---

nest [NEST] nom **le nid**

How many eggs do you see in the nest?
Combien d'oeufs vois-tu dans le nid?

---

never [NEV-ér] adverbe **jamais**

I never want to play with you!
Je ne veux jamais jouer avec toi!

never adverbe **ne . . . jamais**

I go to school. My sister never goes to school.
Je vais à l'école. Ma soeur ne va jamais à l'école.

---

new [NU] adjectif — **neuf,** masc. **neuve,** fém.

My bicycle is new.
Ma bicyclette est neuve.

---

new adjectif — **nouveau,** masc. **nouveaux,** masc., pl. **nouvel,** masc., before a vowel **nouvelle,** fém.

Look at my new turtle!
Regarde ma nouvelle tortue!

---

newspaper [NUZ-pei-pər] nom — **le journal** **les journaux,** pl.

After dinner my uncle reads the newspaper.
Après le dîner mon oncle lit le journal.

---

next [NEKST] adjectif — **prochain,** masc. **prochaine,** fém.

The teacher says, "Next week we will have an examination."
Le professeur dit: "La semaine prochaine nous avons un examen."

---

next to préposition — **à côté de**

At the restaurant Peter is seated next to Carolyn.
Dans le restaurant Pierre est assis à côté de Caroline.

---

nice (pleasant) [NAIS] adjectif — **agréable**

Spring is a pleasant (nice) season.
Le printemps est une saison agréable.

---

nice adjectif — **gentil,** masc. **gentille,** fém.

The teacher is nice. She doesn't scold.
La maîtresse est gentille. Elle ne gronde pas.

---

niece [NIS] nom — **la nièce**

She is the lawyer's niece.
Elle est la nièce de l'avocat.

---

night [NAIT] nom **la nuit**

At night you can see the stars.
La nuit on peut voir des étoiles.

---

nine [NAIN] adjectif **neuf**

How much are nine and two?
Combien font neuf et deux?

I am nine years old.
J'ai neuf ans.

---

nineteen [nain-TIN] adjectif **dix-neuf**

Today is September 19th.
C'est aujourd'hui le dix-neuf septembre.

---

ninety [NAIN-ti] adjectif **quatre-vingt-dix**

Somebody is ninety years old?
Quelqu'un a quatre-vingt-dix ans?

---

no [NOH] adverbe **non**

Get up! No, I don't want to get up!
Lève-toi! Non, je ne veux pas me lever!

No . . . expression idiomatique **défense de**

No admittance expression idiomatique **défense d'entrer**

No admittance. We cannot enter.
Défense d'entrer. Nous ne pouvons pas entrer.

No smoking expression idiomatique **défense de fumer**

No smoking in school.
Défense de fumer à l'école.

---

noise [NOIZ] nom **le bruit**

Thunder makes a loud noise.
Le tonnerre fait un grand bruit.

---

no longer [noh-LAWNG-ér] adverbe **ne . . . plus**

I go to school.
Je vais à l'école.

My brother no longer goes to school.
Mon frère ne va plus a l'école.

No matter!—never mind **N'importe!**
expression idiomatique

You don't have a pen? No matter!
Here is a pencil.
Vous n'avez pas de stylo? N'importe.
Voici un crayon.

---

noon [NUN] nom **midi,** masc.

It is noon. It's time for lunch.
Il est midi. C'est l'heure du déjeuner.

---

north [NAWRTH] nom **le nord**

When I go from Marseilles to Paris,
I go toward the north.
Quand je vais de Marseille à Paris, je vais vers le nord.

---

nose [NOHZ] nom **le nez**

My doll's nose is cute.
Le nez de ma poupée est mignon.

---

not [NAT] adverbe **ne . . . pas**

I go to school. My grandfather does not
go to school.
Je vais à l'école. Mon grand-père ne va
pas à l'école.

---

note [NOHT] nom **le billet**

I am rich! I have a ten-franc note!
Je suis riche! J'ai un billet de dix francs!

---

note (musical) nom (See **music**) **la note**

---

notebook [NOHT-bauhk] nom **le cahier**

She writes her homework in a notebook.
Elle écrit ses devoirs dans un cahier.

---

nothing [NETH-ing] pronom **rien**

What do you have in your pocket? Nothing!
Qu'est-ce que tu as dans la poche? Rien!

November [noh-VEM-ber] nom **novembre**

November is not the last month of the year.
Novembre n'est pas le dernier mois de l'année.

---

now [NOW] adverbe **maintenant**

You have to take a bath now!
Tu dois prendre un bain maintenant!

---

number [NEM-ber] nom **le numéro**

What is your telephone number?
Quel est votre numéro de téléphone?

---

number (quantity) nom **le nombre**

You have a great number of books!
Tu as un grand nombre de livres!

---

nurse [NURS] nom **l'infirmière**

My neighbor is a nurse.
Ma voisine est infirmière.

O

to obey [oh-BEI] verbe **obéir**

j'obéis	nous obéissons
tu obéis	vous obéissez
il, elle obéit	ils, elles obéissent

When I am well-behaved, I obey my parents.
Quand je suis sage, j'obéis à mes parents.

---

occupied, busy [AK-yu-paid] adjectif **occupé,** masc. **occupée,** fém.

My brother is busy now; he is doing his homework.
Mon frère est occupé maintenant; il fait ses devoirs.

---

ocean [OH-shén] nom **l'océan**

Is the Atlantic Ocean to the west of France?
L'océan Atlantique est à l'ouest de la France?

---

ocean liner nom **le paquebot**

The ocean liner crosses the Atlantic Ocean.
Le paquebot traverse l'Océan Atlantique.

October [ak-TOH-bér] nom **octobre**

It is cool in October.
Il fait frais en octobre.

---

odd [AD] adjectif **bizarre**

Here is an odd animal.
Voici un animal bizarre!

---

odd (funny) adjectif **drôle**

The marionettes are funny.
Les marionnettes sont drôles.

---

of [év] préposition **de**

---

office [AW-fis] nom **le bureau**

Here is the office of a large company.
Voici le bureau d'une grande compagnie.

post office nom **le bureau de poste**

You go to the post office to mail a package.
On va au bureau de poste pour mettre un colis à la poste.

---

often [AW-fén] adverbe **souvent**

I often go by bus.
Je vais souvent en autobus.

---

oil [OIL] nom **l'huile,** fém.

Mother, are you putting oil in the salad?
Maman, tu mets de l'huile dans la salade?

That's funny. You put oil in the car.
C'est drôle. On met de l'huile dans l'auto.

OK (okay) [oh-KEI] expression idiomatique **accord**

Do you want to play with me? OK! **d'accord!**
Veux-tu jouer avec moi? D'accord!

---

old [OHLD] adjectif **vieux,** masc. **vieille,** fém. **vieil,** masc. before vowel

The book is old and the watch is old.
Le livre est vieux et la montre est vieille.

---

on [AHN] préposition **sur**

The ruler is on the desk.
La règle est sur le pupitre.

---

once again [wǝns ǝ-GEN] adverbe **encore une fois**

---

one (we, they, you) [WǝN] pronom **on**

Are we playing now?
On joue maintenant?

one adjectif **un**

One monkey is in the tree.
Un singe est dans l'arbre.

one (number) adjectif **une**
one hundred adjectif **cent**

There are a hundred people at the fair!
Il y a cent personnes à la foire!

one must expression idiomatique **il faut**

It is necessary (one must) to go to school.
Il faut aller à l'école.

one's son
one that (who) pronom **celui,** masc. **ceux,** masc., pl. **celle,** fém. **celles,** fém., pl.

Here is a red pen. The one that belongs to my father is yellow.
Voici un stylo rouge. Celui de mon père est jaune.

Here is a red ruler. Those which are on the table are yellow.
Voici une règle rouge. Celles qui sont sur la table sont jaunes.

---

onion [ǝN-yǝn] nom **l'oignon**

I am going to the store to buy some onions.
Je vais au marché pour acheter des oignons.

---

only [OHN-li] adjectif **seul**

---

only adverbe **seulement**

I have only one goldfish.
J'ai seulement un poisson rouge.

---

on purpose adverbe **exprès**

My brother teases me on purpose.
Mon frère me taquine exprès.

---

open [OH-pén] adjectif **ouvert,** masc.
ouverte, fém.

The window is open.
La fenêtre est ouverte.

---

to open verbe **ouvrir**

j'ouvre	nous ouvrons
tu ouvres	vous ouvrez
il, elle ouvre	ils, elles ouvrent

I open my desk to look for an eraser.
J'ouvre mon pupitre pour chercher une gomme.

---

to operate [A-pé-reit] verbe **marcher**

je marche	nous marchons
tu marches	vous marchez
il, elle marche	ils, elles marchent

This lamp is not working (operating).
Cette lampe ne marche pas.

---

or [AWR] conjonction **ou**

What would you like, peaches or apples?
Que désirez-vous, des pêches ou des pommes?

---

orange [AR-indj] nom **l'orange,** fém.

What color is the orange?
De quelle couleur est l'orange?

---

orange juice [AR-indj DJUS] nom **le jus d'orange**

---

orange adjectif **orange**

I need an orange skirt.
J'ai besoin d'une jupe orange.

---

to order [AWR-dér] verbe **commander**

je commande	nous commandons
tu commandes	vous commandez
il, elle commande	ils, elles commandent

In the restaurant Father orders dinner.
Dans le restaurant Papa commande le dîner.

in order to préposition **pour**

---

other (another) [ÉTH-ér] adjectif **autre**

Here is another pencil.
Voici un autre crayon.

---

our [OWR] adjectif **notre**
nos, pl.

Our teacher is scolding us today.
Notre maîtresse nous gronde aujourd'hui.

---

out of [OWT év] préposition **par**

My grandfather looks out of the window.
Mon grand-père regarde par la fenêtre.

---

outside [OWT-said] préposition **dehors**

My friend is waiting for me outside.
Mon ami m'attend dehors.

---

over there [oh-vér THEHR] adverbe **là-bas**

Do you see your brother coming down (over) there?
Tu vois ton frère qui arrive, là-bas?

---

to overturn [oh-vér-TURN] verbe **renverser**

je renverse	nous renversons
tu renverses	vous renversez
il, elle renverse	ils, elles renversent

The baby overturns the plate.
Le bébé renverse l'assiette.

---

owl [OWL] nom **le hibou**
hiboux, pl.

You hear the owl during the night.
On entend le hibou pendant la nuit.

---

own [OHN] adjectif **propre**

It is not my sister's book; it is my own book.
Ce n'est pas le livre de ma soeur; c'est mon propre livre.

P

package [PAK-idj] nom **le colis**
le paquet

Oh, good! A package for me!
Ah, bon! Un colis pour moi!

---

page [PEIDJ] nom **la page**

The map of France is on page ten.
La carte de la France est à la page dix.

---

pail (See **bucket**) nom **le seau**

---

to paint [PEINT] verbe **peindre**

je peins	nous peignons
tu peins	vous peignez
il, elle peint	ils, elles peignent

My sister is an artist. She likes to paint.
Ma soeur est artiste. Elle aime peindre.

---

pair [PEHR] nom **la paire**

I would like to buy a pair of gloves.
Je voudrais acheter une paire de gants.

---

pajamas [pə-DJAH-məz] nom **le pyjama**

I put on my pajamas at ten o'clock at night.
Je mets le pyjama à dix heures du soir.

---

palace [PAL-is] nom **le château**
palace nom **le palais**

The king arrives at the palace.
Le roi arrive au palais.

---

pants [PANTS] nom **le pantalon**

The boy's pants are dirty.
Le pantalon du garçon est sale.

Papa (Daddy) [PA-PA] nom **papa**

Daddy, I'm afraid!
Papa, j'ai peur!

---

paper [PEI-pər] nom **le papier**

There is some paper in my notebook.
Il y a du papier dans mon cahier.

sheet of paper **la feuille de papier**

---

parachute [PAR-ə-shut] nom **le parachute**

Is it dangerous to jump with a parachute?
Est-ce qu'il est dangereux de sauter en parachute?

---

parade [pé-REID] nom **le défilé**

We walk in the parade.
Nous marchons dans le défilé.

---

parakeet [PAR-é-kit] nom **la perruche**

We have two pretty parakeets.
Nous avons deux jolies perruches.

---

pardon me (excuse me) [PAHR-dén MI] expression idiomatique **pardon**

Excuse me! It's your pocketbook, isn't it?
Pardon! C'est votre sac, n'est-ce pas?

---

parents [PEHR-énts] nom **les parents**

My parents go to work in the morning.
Mes parents vont au travail le matin.

---

park [PAHRK] nom **le parc**

The park is near by.
Le parc est tout près d'ici.

---

parrot [PAR-ét] nom **le perroquet**

My pet is a parrot.
Un perroquet est mon animal favori.

---

part [PAHRT] nom **le rôle**

I want to play the part of the prince.
Je veux jouer le rôle du prince.

---

party [PAHR-ti] nom **la fête**

The party is July 18th?
Le jour de la fête est le dix-huit juillet?

---

to pass [PAS] verbe **dépasser**

je dépasse	nous dépassons
tu dépasses	vous dépassez
il, elle dépasse	ils, elles dépassent

The car passes the truck.
L'auto dépasse le camion.

---

to pass (spend) verbe **passer**

je passe	nous passons
tu passes	vous passez
il, elle passe	ils, elles passent

She spends two weeks in the country.
Elle passe deux semaines à la compagne.

---

passenger [PAS-e̸n-ge̸r] nom **le passager,** masc. **la passagère,** fém.

There are six passengers on the bus.
Il y a six passagers dans l'autobus.

---

to paste (glue) [PEIST] verbe **coller**

je colle	nous collons
tu colles	vous collez
il, elle colle	ils, elles collent

I glue a picture to a page of my notebook.
Je colle une image sur une page de mon cahier.

---

path [PATH] nom **le sentier**

This path leads to the bridge.
Ce sentier mène au pont.

---

paw [PAW] nom **la patte**

The dog has four paws.
Le chien a quatre pattes.

---

to pay [PEI] verbe **payer**

je paye	nous payons
tu payes	vous payez
il, elle paye	ils, elles payent

Mother pays the butcher for the meat.
Maman paye la viande au boucher.

---

peach [PICH] nom **la pêche**

People eat peaches in summer.
On mange des pêches en été.

---

peanut [PI-nət] nom **la cachuète**

The elephant likes to eat peanuts.
L'éléphant aime manger les cacahuètes.

---

pear [PEHR] nom **la poire**

Is the pear ripe?
Est-ce que la poire est mûre?

---

peas [PIZ] nom **les petits pois**

I like to eat peas.
J'aime bien manger les petits pois.

---

pen [PEN] nom **le stylo**

I always leave my pen at home.
Je laisse toujours mon stylo à la maison.

ballpoint pen nom **le stylo à bille**

I am writing with a ballpoint pen.
J'écris avec un stylo à bille.

---

pencil [PEN-sil] nom **le crayon**

Please give me a pencil.
Donnez-moi un crayon, s'il vous plaît.

---

people [PI-pəl] nom **les personnes**
les gens

There are seven people in my family.
Il y a sept personnes dans ma famille.

---

perhaps (maybe) [pur-HAPS] adverbe **peut-être**

Are we going horseback riding this morning? Maybe.
Nous montons à cheval ce matin? Peut-être.

---

permission [pur-MISH-én] nom **la permission**

Do you have permission to go to the country?
Tu as la permission d'aller à la campagne?

---

to permit [pur-MIT] verbe **laisser**

je laisse	nous laissons
tu laisses	vous laissez
il, elle laisse	ils, elles laissent

My brother lets me wash the car.
Mon frère me laisse laver la voiture.

---

person, people [PUR-SON] nom **la personne**

There are seven people in my family.
Il y a sept personnes dans ma famille.

---

pet [PET] nom **l'animal favori,** masc.

My dog is my pet.
Mon chien est mon animal favori.

---

pharmacy [FAHR-mé-si] nom **la pharmacie**

The pharmacy is located close to the park.
La pharmacie se trouve près du parc.

---

photograph (picture) [FOH-té-GRAF] nom **la photo**

Look at my picture. It's funny, isn't it?
Regarde ma photo! Elle est drôle, n'est-ce pas?

---

piano [PYA-noh] nom **le piano**
to play the piano **jouer du piano**

Who plays the piano in your family?
Qui joue du piano dans votre famille?

---

to pick [PIK] verbe **cueillir**

je cueille nous cueillons
tu cueilles vous cueillez
il, elles cueille ils, elles cueillent

He is going to pick some apples.
Il va cueillir des pommes.

---

picnic [PIK-nik] nom **le pique-nique**

We have a picnic in the country.
Nous faisons un pique-nique à la campagne.

---

picture [PIK-chér] nom **la photo**
picture **l'image,** fém.

There are many pictures in this book.
Il y a beaucoup d'images dans ce livre.

---

pie [PAI] nom **la tarte**

Do you like apple pie?
Aimez-vous la tarte aux pommes?

---

piece [PIS] nom **le morceau**

I want a piece of cheese.
Je désire un morceau de fromage.

---

pig [PIG] nom **le cochon**

The farmer has three pigs.
Le fermier a trois cochons.

---

piggy bank nom **la tirelire**

I do not have much money in my piggy bank.
Je n'ai pas beaucoup d'argent dans ma tirelire.

---

pillow [PIL-oh] nom **l'oreiller,** fém.

The pillow is comfortable.
L'oreiller est comfortable.

---

pilot (See **airplane**) [PAI-lét] nom **le pilote**

---

pin [PIN] nom **l'épingle,** fém.

What a pretty flower pin!
Quelle jolie épingle en forme de fleurs!

---

pineapple [PAI-na-pél] nom **l'ananas,** masc.

The pineapple is big.
L'ananas est grand.

---

pink [PINGK] adjectif **rose**

I like to wear my pink ribbon in my hair.
J'aime porter mon ruban rose dans les cheveux.

---

place (table setting) [PLEIS] nom **la place**

My cousin puts a knife at each setting.
Ma cousine met un couteau à chaque place.

---

planet [PLAN-it] nom **la planète**

Do you know the names of all the planets?
Savez-vous les noms de toutes les planètes?

---

plant [PLANT] nom **la plante**

There are five plants in the classroom.
Il y a cinq plantes dans la salle de classe.

---

plate [PLEIT] nom **l'assiette,** fém.

The plate is on the table.
L'assiette est sur la table.

---

to play [PLEI] verbe **jouer**

je joue	nous jouons
tu joues	vous jouez
il, elle joue	ils, elles jouent

Let's play ball.
Jouons à la balle.

Laura plays the piano.
Laure joue du piano.

to play (a game) **jouer à . . .**
to play (a musical instrument) **jouer de . . .**
to play checkers **jouer aux dames**
expression idiomatique

My friend and I play checkers.
Mon ami et moi, nous jouons aux dames.

to play chess expression idiomatique **jouer aux échecs**

My father and my uncle play chess.
Mon père et mon oncle jouent aux échecs.

to play blindman's buff **jouer à colin-maillard**
expression idiomatique

Yes, I'd like to play blindman's buff.
Oui, je voudrais jouer à colin-maillard.

to play hide-and-seek **jouer à cache-cache**
expression idiomatique

The children are playing hide-and-seek.
Les enfants jouent à cache-cache.

to play hopscotch **jouer à la marelle**
expression idiomatique

I don't know how to play hopscotch.
Je ne sais pas jouer à la marelle.

to play leapfrog **jouer à saute-mouton**
expression idiomatique

We play leapfrog.
Nous jouons à saute-mouton.

---

playground [PLEI-grownd] nom **le terrain de jeux**

We play ball in the playground.
Nous jouons à la balle au terrain de jeux.

---

playing card nom **la carte**

Do you know how to play cards?
Savez-vous jouer aux cartes?

---

pleasant [PLEZ-ənt] adjectif **agréable**

Spring is a pleasant season.
Le printemps est une saison agréable.

---

please [PLIZ] expression idiomatique **s'il vous plaît**
s'il te plaît (familiar)

Please give me a pencil, Mr. Duval.
Donnez-moi un crayon, s'il vous plaît, monsieur Duval.

Please give me a pencil, Petey.
Donne-moi un crayon, s'il te plaît, Pierrot.

---

pleasure [PLEZH-ər] nom **le plaisir**

Are you coming with us? With pleasure!
Tu viens avec nous? Avec plaisir!

---

pocket [PAK-it] nom **la poche**

I have some marbles in my pocket.
J'ai des billes dans la poche.

---

pocketbook (bag, purse) nom **le sac**
handbag **le sac à main**

I am buying a handbag for mother.
J'achete un sac à main pour maman.

---

pocketknife nom **le canif**

Do you have a pocketknife?
Avez-vous un canif?

---

to point to (out) (indicate) [POINT] verbe **indiquer**

j'indique	nous indiquons
tu indiques	vous indiquez
il, elle indique	ils, elles indiquent

The policeman indicates that we must go by this road.
L'agent de police indique qu'il faut aller par cette route.

---

police officer **l'agent (de police),** masc.
[pǝ-LIS AW-fis-er] nom

The police officer directs traffic.
L'agent de police dirige la circulation.

---

polite [pǝ-LAIT] adjectif **poli**

Mother says, "A polite child does not speak with a full mouth."
Maman dit: "L'enfant poli ne parle pas la bouche pleine."

---

poor [PUR] adjectif **pauvre**

This poor boy does not have much money.
Ce garçon pauvre n'a pas beaucoup d'argent.

---

postcard (See **postman**) nom **la carte**

---

postman (mail carrier) [POHST-mén] nom **le facteur**

The mail carrier brings letters, packages, and postcards.
Le facteur apporte des lettres, des paquets, et des cartes.

---

post office nom **la poste** **le bureau de poste**

I go to the post office to send a package.
Je vais au bureau de poste pour envoyer un paquet.

---

potato [pé-TEI-toh] nom **la pomme de terre**

Do you like potatoes?
Aimez-vous les pommes de terre?

---

to pour [PAWR] verbe **verser**

je verse	nous versons
tu verses	vous versez
il, elle verse	ils, elles versent

Margaret pours coffee into a cup.
Marguerite verse le café dans une tasse.

---

to prefer [pré-FUR] verbe **préférer**

je préfère	nous préférons
tu préfères	vous préférez
il, elle préfère	ils, elles préfèrent

Do you prefer the city or the country?
Préfères-tu la ville ou la campagne?

---

to prepare [pré-PEHR] verbe **préparer**

je prépare	nous préparons
tu prépares	vous préparez
il, elle prépare	ils, elles préparent

My brother prepares the salad.
Mon frère prépare la salade.

---

present (gift) [PREZ-ént] nom **le cadeau**
les cadeaux, pl.
Here is a birthday gift.
Voici un cadeau pour votre anniversaire.

---

present (See **here**) adjectif **présent**

---

president [PREZ-i-dént] nom **le président**
Who is the president of France?
Qui est le président de la France?

---

pretty (See **good-looking**) adjectif **joli**

---

price [PRAIS] nom **le prix**
What is the price of this suit?
Quel est le prix de ce complet?

---

prince [PRINS] nom **le prince**
princess [prin-SES] nom **la princesse**
The prince is playing in the garden.
Le prince joue dans le jardin.

---

to promise [PRAM-is] verbe **promettre**

je promets	nous promettons
tu promets	vous promettez
il, elle promete	ils, elles promettent

I promise to do my homework.
Je promets de faire mes devoirs.

---

to pull (drag) [PAUHL] verbe **tirer**

je tire	nous tirons
tu tires	vous tirez
il, elle tire	ils, elles tirent

He is pulling a bag of potatoes.
Il tire un sac de pommes de terre.

---

pumpkin [PÉM-kin] nom **la citrouille**

This is a big pumpkin.
C'est une grande citrouille.

---

to punish [PÉN-ish] verbe **punir**

je punis	nous punissons
tu punis	vous punissez
il, elle punit	ils, elles punissent

When I am naughty, Mommy punishes me.
Quand je suis méchant, Maman me punit.

---

pupil [PYU-pil] nom **l'élève**
les élèves, pl.

The pupils are in the classroom.
Les élèves sont dans la salle de classe.

---

puppy (See **dog**) nom **le petit chien**

---

purple [PUR-pél] ajdectif **violet,** masc.
violette, fém.

Are there any purple flowers?
Est-ce qu'il y a des fleurs violettes?

---

purse (See **handbag**) nom **le sac**

---

to push [PAUHSH] verbe **pousser**

je pousse	nous poussons
tu pousses	vous poussez
il, elle pousse	ils, elles poussent

He's pushing me!
Il me pousse!

---

to put down verbe **baisser**

je baisse	nous baissons
tu baisses	vous baissez
il, elle baisse	ils, elles baissent

The teacher says, "Put your hands down!"
Le professeur dit, "Baissez les mains."

to put on verbe **mettre**

je mets	nous mettons
tu mets	vous mettez
il, elle met	ils, elles mettent

My sister puts on her gloves.
Ma soeur met les gants.

Q

quarrel [KWAR-él] nom **la querelle**

My father sometimes has a quarrel with my mother.
Mon père a une querelle quelquefois avec ma mère.

---

quarter [KWAW-tér] nom **le quart**

It is a quarter after seven.
Il est sept heures et quart.

---

queen [KWIN] nom **la reine**

The queen is seated near the king.
La reine est assise près du roi.

---

question [KWES-chén] nom **la question**

The teacher asks, "Are there any questions?"
Le professeur demande: "Est-ce qu'il y a des questions?"

---

quickly (fast) [KWIK-li] adverbe **vite**

My brother walks too fast. (quickly)
Mon frère marche trop vite.

---

quiet [KWAI-ət] adjectif **silencieux**
quiet (calm) adjectif **tranquille**

I like to go fishing when the water is calm. (quiet)
J'aime aller à la pêche quand l'eau est tranquille.

R

rabbit [RAB-it] nom **le lapin**

The rabbit runs and jumps.
Le lapin court et saute.

radio [REI-di-oh] nom **la radio**

The radio is not working.
La radio ne marche pas.

railroad (See **road**) nom **le chemin de fer**

to rain [REIN] verbe **pleuvoir**

Do you think it's going to rain?
Vous pensez qu'il va pleuvoir?

It is raining **Il pleut**

rainbow [REIN-boh] nom **l'arc-en-ciel,** masc.

I like the colors of the rainbow.
J'aime les couleurs de l'arc-en-ciel.

raincoat [REIN-koht] nom **l'imperméable**

He is wearing his raincoat because it is raining.
Il porte son imperméable parce qu'il pleut.

to raise [REIZ] verbe **lever**

je lève	nous levons
tu lèves	vous levez
il, elle lève	ils, elles lèvent

The policeman raises his right hand.
L'agent de police lève la main droite.

---

rapid (See **fast**) adjectif **rapide**

---

rat [RAT] nom **le rat**

I am afraid of rats!
J'ai peur des rats!

---

to read [RID] verbe **lire**

je lis	nous lisons
tu lis	vous lisez
il, elle lit	ils, elles lisent

We are going to read in the library.
Nous allons lire dans la bibliotèque.

---

ready [RED-i] adjectif **prêt,** masc. **prête,** fém.

Are you ready? We are late.
Es-tu prêt? Nous sommes en retard.

---

really [RI-LI] adverbe **vraiment**

Do you know that I would like to become an astronaut? Really!
Vous savez que je voudrais devenir astronaute? Vraiment!

---

to receive [ri-SIV] verbe **recevoir**

je reçois	nous recevons
tu reçois	vous recevez
il, elle reçoit	ils, elles reçoivent

I receive a postcard from my sister.
Je reçois une carte postale de ma soeur.

---

red [RED] adjectif **rouge**

The cars stop when the light is red.
Les voitures s'arrêtent quand le feu est rouge.

---

refrigerator [ri-FRIDJ-é-rei-tér] nom **le réfrigérateur**

The refrigerator is in the kitchen.
Le réfrigérateur est dans la cuisine.

---

relatives [RE-lé-tivz] nom **les parents**

---

to remain (stay) [ri-MEIN] verbe **rester**

je reste	nous restons
tu restes	vous restez
il, elle reste	ils, elles se restent

---

to remember [ri-MEM-bér] verbe **se rappeler**

je me rappelle	nous nous rappelons
tu te rappelles	vous vous rappelez
il, elle se rappelle	ils, elles se rappelent

I cannot remember the name of this building.
Je ne peux pas me rappeler le nom de ce bâtiment.

---

to remove (take off) [ri-MUV] verbe **ôter**

j'ôte	nous ôtons
tu ôtes	vous ôtez
il, elle ôte	ils, elles ôtent

Take off your hat in the house.
Ôte le chapeau dans la maison.

---

to repair (fix) [ri-PEHR] verbe **réparer**

je répare	nous réparons
tu répares	vous réparez
il, elle répare	ils, elles réparent

My brother is fixing the machine.
Mon frere répare la machine.

---

to repeat [ri-PIT] verbe **répéter**

je répète	nous répétons
tu répètes	vous répétez
il, elle répète	ils, elles répètent

The teacher says, "Repeat after me."
Le maître dit: "Répétez après moi."

---

to reply (answer) [ri-PLAI] verbe **répondre**

je réponds	nous répondons
tu réponds	vous répondez
il, elles répond	ils, elles répondent

The little girl cannot answer the question.
La petite fille ne peut pas répondre à la question.

---

to rescue (save) [RES-kyu] verbe **sauver**

je sauve	nous sauvons
tu sauves	vous sauvez
il, elle sauve	ils, elles sauvent

My uncle saves me when I fall into the water.
Mon oncle me sauve quand je tombe dans l'eau.

---

to rest [REST] verbe **se reposer**

je me repose	nous nous reposons
tu te reposes	vous vous reposez
il, elle se repose	ils, elles se reposent

The child runs. He does not want to rest.
L'enfant court. Il ne veut pas se reposer.

---

restroom [REST-rum] nom **les toilettes**

Where is the restroom?
Où sont les toilettes?

---

restaurant [RES-tér-ént] nom **le restaurant**

The waiter works in this restaurant.
Le garcon travaille dans ce restaurant.

---

to return [ri-TURN] verbe **rendre**

je rends	nous rendons
tu rends	vous rendez
il, elle rend	ils, elles rendent

He returns my roller skates.
Il me rend mes patins à roulettes.

---

to return [ri-TURN] verbe **retourner**

je retourne	nous retournons
tu retournes	vous retournez
il, elle retourne	ils, elles retournent

He goes to the blackboard and then he returns to his seat.
Il va au tableau noir et puis il retourne à sa place.

---

ribbon [RIB-én] nom **le ruban**

She is wearing a pretty ribbon.
Elle porte un joli ruban.

---

rice [RAIS] nom **le riz**

The rice is delicious.
Le riz est délicieux.

---

rich [RICH] adjectif **riche**

The rich lady wears jewels.
La femme riche porte des bijoux.

---

to ride [RAID] verbe **monter**

He rides a horse.
Il monte à cheval.

---

right [RAIT] adjectif **droit,** masc.
droite, fém.

right hand nom **la main droite**

I raise my right hand.
Je lève la main droite.

---

ring [RING] nom **l'anneau,** masc.
la bague

Helen is wearing a pretty ring.
Hélène porte une jolie bague.

---

to ring verbe **sonner**

je sonne	nous sonnons
tu sonnes	vous sonnez
il, elle sonne	ils, elles sonnent

The telephone is ringing.
Le téléphone sonne.

---

ripe [RAIP] adjectif **mûr,** masc.
mûre, fém.

When the banana is yellow, it is ripe.
Quand la banane est jaune, elle est mûre.

---

river [RIV-ér] nom **la rivière**

How can we cross the river?
Comment peut-on traverser la rivière?

---

road [ROHD] nom **le chemin**

Is this the road to town?
C'est le chemin de la ville?

railroad [REIL-rohd] nom **le chemin de fer**

To go to Marseilles, I take the railroad.
Pour aller à Marseille, je prends le chemin de fer.

---

roast beef [ROHST-bif] nom **le rosbif**

I would like a roast beef sandwich, please.
Je voudrais un sandwich de rosbif, s'il vous plaît.

---

robber (thief) [RA-BÉ] nom **le voleur**

They are looking for the thief at the bank.
On cherche le voleur à la banque.

---

rock [RAK] nom **le rocher**

What a large rock over there!
Quel grand rocher là-bas!

---

role [ROHL] nom **le rôle**

I want to play the role of the prince.
Je veux jouer le rôle du prince.

---

roll [ROHL] nom **la brioche** **la petit pain**

Susan eats a roll for breakfast.
Suzanne prend une brioche pour le petit déjeuner.

---

to roll verbe **rouler**

je roule nous roulons
tu roules vous roulez
il, elle roule ils, elles roulent

The roller skate is rolling into the street.
Le patin à roulettes roule dans la rue.

---

roller skate (See **skate**) nom **le patin à roulettes**

---

roof [RUF] nom **le toit**

I look at the city from the roof of the house.
Je regarde la ville du toit de la maison.

---

room [RUM] nom **la pièce**

There are two rooms in our apartment.
Il y a deux pièces dans notre appartement.

---

room nom **la salle**
bathroom nom **la salle de bain**

The bathroom is small.
La salle de bain est petite.

classroom nom **la salle de classe**

The classroom is empty.
La salle de classe est vide.

dining room nom **la salle à manger**

Mother enters the dining room.
Maman entre dans la salle à manger.

---

rooster [RUS-tér] nom **le coq**

The rooster gets up early.
Le coq se lève de bonne heure.

---

rope [ROHP] nom **la corde**

to jump rope expression idiomatique **sauter à la corde**

Mary, Joan and I are jumping rope.
Marie, Jeanne et moi, nous sautons à la corde.

---

round [ROWND] adjectif **rond,** masc. **ronde,** fém.

The plate is round.
L'assiette est ronde.

---

route [RUT] nom **la route**

What's the name of this road? (route)
Quel est le nom de cette route?

---

row [ROH] nom **le rang**

The teacher says, "Children in the first row, stand."
La maîtresse dit: "Les enfants du premier rang, levez vous."

---

rubber [RƏB-ər] nom **le caoutchouc**

It is raining. I have to put on my rubbers.
Il pleut. Il faut mettre mes caoutchoucs.

made of rubber **en caoutchouc**

---

rug [RƏG] nom **le tapis**

The rug is on the floor.
Le tapis est sur le plancher.

---

rule [RUL] nom **la règle**

We have to obey the rules at school and at home.
Il faut obéir aux règles à l'école et à la maison.

---

ruler [RUL-ər] nom **la règle**

The ruler is long.
La règle est longue.

---

to run [RÉN] verbe **courir**

je cours	nous courons
tu cours	vous courez
il, elle court	ils, elles courent

They are running to the station because they are late.
Ils courent à la gare parce qu'ils sont en retard.

S

sack (See **bag**) nom **le sac**

---

sad [SAD] adjectif **triste**

Why are you sad?
Pourquoi es-tu triste?

---

safe and sound [SEIF-and-SOWND] expression idiomatique **sain et sauf**

I come home safe and sound.
Je retourne à la maison sain et sauf.

---

salad [SAL-éd] nom **la salade**

My cousin puts the salad in the middle of the table.
Ma cousine met la salade au milieu de la table.

---

salesperson [SEILZ-pur-sohn] nom **le vendeur** **la vendeuse**

The salesperson shows us some shoes.
Le vendeur nous montre des chaussures.

---

salt [SAWLT] nom **le sel**

Please pass me the salt.
Passez-moi le sel, s'il vous plaît.

---

same [SEIM] adjectif; adverbe **même**

My friend and I are wearing the same dress.
Mon amie et moi, nous portons la même robe.

---

sand [SAND] nom **le sable**

At the beach I sit on the sand.
A la plage, je m'assieds sur le sable.

---

sandwich [SAND-wich] nom **le sandwich**

Do you want a sandwich or a salad?
Veux-tu un sandwich ou une salade?

Saturday [SAT-ér-dei] nom **samedi**

Let's have a picnic Saturday.
Faisons un pique-nique samedi.

---

saucer [SAW-sér] nom **la soucoupe**

The woman puts the cup on the saucer.
La femme met la tasse sur la soucoupe.

---

to save [SEIV] verbe **sauver**

je sauve	nous sauvons
tu sauves	vous sauvez
il, elle sauve	ils, elles sauvent

My uncle saves me when I fall into the water.
Mon oncle me sauve quand je tombe dans l'eau.

---

to say [SEI] verbe **dire**

je dis	nous disons
tu dis	vous dites
il, elle dit	ils, elles disent

The teacher says "Good Morning" each morning.
Le professeur dit: "Bonjour" chaque matin.

Say! Well! interjection **Tiens!**

Say! It's beginning to snow.
Tiens! Il commence à neiger.

---

school [SKUL] nom **l'école,** fém.

We don't go to school on Thursdays.
Le jeudi nous n'allons pas à l'école.

---

science [SAI-ǝns] nom **la science**

I like to go to my science class.
J'aime aller à ma classe de science.

---

scientist [SAI-en-tist] nom **le savant,** masc. **la savante,** fém.

I would like to become a scientist.
Je voudrais devenir savant.

---

scissors [SIZ-ǝrz] nom **les ciseaux**

I cut the paper with scissors.
Je coupe le papier avec les ciseaux.

---

to scold [SKOHLD] verbe **gronder**

je gronde	nous grondons
tu grondes	vous grondez
il, elle gronde	ils, elles grondent

He is ashamed because his mother is scolding him.
Il a honte parce que sa mère le gronde.

---

to scream, shout [SKRIM] verbe **crier**

je crie	nous crions
tu cries	vous criez
il, elle crie	ils, elles crient

Mom shouts, "Come quickly!"
Maman crie: "Viens vite!"

---

sea [SI] nom **la mer**

Are there many fish in the sea?
Est-ce qu'il y a beaucoup de poissons dans la mer?

---

season [SI-zén] nom **la saison**

How many seasons are there?
Combien de saisons y a-t-il?

---

seat [SIT] nom **la place**

I go to the blackboard and I return to my seat.
Je vais au tableau noir et je retourne à ma place.

seated adjectif **assis,** masc. **assise,** fém.

He is seated in an armchair.
Il est assis dans un fauteuil.

---

second [SEK-énd] adjectif **deuxième**

What is the name of the second month of the year?
Quel est le nom du deuxième mois de l'année?

---

secret [SI-krit] nom **le secret**

Tell me the secret!
Dis-moi le secret!

---

secretary [SEK-ré-ter-i] nom **la dactylo,** fém. **le dactylo,** masc.

There are three secretaries in this office.
Il y a trois dactylos dans ce bureau.

---

to see [SI] verbe **voir**

je vois nous voyons
tu vois vous voyez
il, elle voit ils, elles voient

I see the airplane in the sky.
Je vois l'avion dans le ciel.

to see again verbe **revoir**

je revois nous revoyons
tu revois vous revoyez
il, elle revoit ils, elles revoient

I am going to see the film again.
Je vais revoir le film.

---

seesaw [SI-saw] nom **la balançoire**

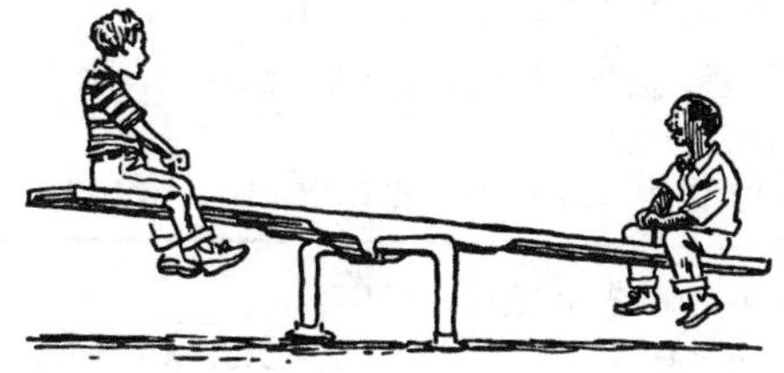

The boys are on the seesaw.
Les garçons sont sur la balançoire.

---

to sell [SEL] verbe **vendre**

je vends nous vendons
tu vends vous vendez
il, elle vend ils, elles vendent

They sell medicine in this store.
On vend des médicaments dans ce magasin.

---

to send [SEND] verbe **envoyer**

j'envoie	nous envoyons
tu envoies	vous envoyez
il, elle envoie	ils, elles envoient

My uncle is going to send me a present.
Mon oncle va m'envoyer un cadeau.

---

sentence [SEN-tẹns] nom **la phrase**

I am writing a sentence in my notebook.
J'écris une phrase dans mon cahier.

September [sep-TEM-bẹr] nom **septembre**

Do we go back to school on the first of September?
Est-ce qu'on retourne à l'école le premier septembre?

---

serious [SIR-i̱-ẹs] adjectif **sérieux,** masc. **sérieuse,** fém.

They are playing a serious film at the movies.
On joue un film sérieux au cinéma.

---

to serve [SUR̲V] verbe **servir**

je sers	nous servons
tu sers	vous servez
il, elle sert	ils, elles servent

I serve my dog his dinner.
Je sers le dîner à mon chien.

---

server (waiter, waitress) [SUR̲V-ẹr] nom **le serveur,** masc. **la serveuse,** fém.

The server brings us ice cream.
Le serveur nous apporte la glace.

---

to set [SET] verbe **mettre**

je mets	nous mettons
tu mets	vous mettez
il, elle met	ils, elles mettent

My mother sets the table.
Ma mère met le couvert.

setting (table) nom **la place**

My cousin puts a knife at each setting.
Ma cousine met un couteau à chaque place.

---

to set (sun) verbe **se coucher**

je me couche	nous nous couchons
tu te couches	vous vous couchez
il, elle se couche	ils, elles se couchent

The sun is setting.
Le soleil se couche.

---

seven [SEV-ən] adjectif **sept**

There are seven apples.
Voilà sept pommes.

---

seventeen [sev-ən-TIN] adjectif **dix-sept**

Nine and eight are seventeen.
Neuf et huit font dix-sept.

---

seventy [SEV-ən-ti] adjectif **soixante-dix**

Nancy's grandmother is seventy years old.
La grand-mère de Nanette a soixante-dix ans.

---

several [SEV-rəl] adjectif **plusieurs**

There are several cars on the road.
Il y a plusieurs autos sur la route.

---

to sew [SOH] verbe **coudre**

je couds	nous cousons
tu couds	vous cousez
il, elle coud	ils, elles cousent

Mother sews with a sewing needle.
Maman coud avec une aiguille à coudre.

---

shadow [SHAD-oh] nom **l'ombre,** fém.

Do you see the shadow?
Voyez-vous l'ombre?

---

to shake (move) [SHEIK] verbe **remuer**

je remue	nous remuons
tu remues	vous remuez
il, elle remue	ils, elles remuent

She moves her fingers quickly when she plays the piano.
Elle remue vite ses doigts quand elle joue du piano.

to shake hands verbe **serrer la main à**

je serre la main	nous serrons la main
tu serres la main	vous serrez la main
il, elle serre la main	ils, elles serrent la main

Alan, shake hands with your neighbor.
Alain, serre la main à ton voisin.

---

to share [SHEHR] verbe **partager**

je partage — nous partageons
tu partages — vous partagez
il, elle partage — ils, elles partagent

Let's share the cake!
Partageons le gâteau.

---

she [SHI] pronom **elle**

---

sheep [SHIP] nom **le mouton**

The sheep is in the field.
Le mouton est dans le champ.

---

sheet of paper [shit-əv-PEI-pər] nom **la feuille**

Give me a sheet of paper, please.
Donne-moi une feuille de papier, s'il te plaît.

---

shell [SHEL] nom **le coquillage**

I am looking for shells at the beach.
Je cherche des coquillages à la plage.

---

ship [SHIP] nom **le bateau,** masc. **les bateaux,** pl.

You cross the ocean by ship.
On traverse l'océan en bateau.

---

shirt [SHURT] nom **la chemise**

The boy is wearing a white shirt.
Le garçon porte une chemise blanche.

---

shoe [SHU] nom **la chaussure** **le soulier**

I don't like these shoes!
Je n'aime pas ces chaussures!

---

shop [SHAP] nom **la boutique**

Excuse me. Where is Mr. Le Blanc's shop?
Pardon. Où se trouve la boutique de monsieur Le Blanc?

to go shopping **faire des emplettes**

---

shore [SHAWR] nom **le bord**

I am seated on the shore of the lake.
Je suis assis au bord du lac.

---

short (length) [SHAWRT] adjectif **court,** masc. **courte,** fém.

One ruler is short; the other is long.
Une règle est courte; l'autre est longue.

---

short (height) adjectif **bas,** masc. **basse,** fém.

The tree at the left is short; the tree at the right is tall.
L'arbre à gauche est bas; l'arbre à droite est haut.

---

shoulder [SHOHL-dér] nom **l'épaule,** fém.

The ball hits Claude's shoulder.
La balle frappe l'épaule de Claude.

---

to shout [SHOWT] verbe **crier**

je crie	nous crions
tu cries	vous criez
il, elle crie	ils, elles crient

Mom shouts, "Come quickly!"
Maman crie: "Viens vite!"

---

shovel [SHÉV-él] nom **la pelle**

My brother plays with a shovel.
Mon frère joue avec une pelle.

---

to show [SHOH] verbe **montrer**

je montre nous montrons
tu montres vous montrez
il, elle montre ils, elles montrent

Show me your new pen.
Montre-moi ton nouveau stylo.

---

shower [SHOW-ér] nom **la douche**

I take a shower every morning.
Je prends une douche chaque matin.

---

sick [SIK] adjectif **malade**

What's the matter? I am sick.
Qu'as-tu? Je suis malade.

---

sideboard (cupboard, closet) [SAID-bawrd] nom **le buffet**

There are plates in the cupboard.
Il y a des assiettes dans le buffet.

---

sidewalk [SAID-wawk] nom **le trottoir**

The sidewalk is very narrow.
Le trottoir est très étroit.

---

silent [SAI-lént] adjectif **silencieux,** masc. **silencieuse,** fém.

The city street is never quiet.
La rue dans la ville n'est jamais silencieuse.

---

silly [SIL-i] adjectif **bête**

The puppy is silly.
Le petit chien est bête.

---

silver [SIL-vér] adjectif **l'argent,** masc.
made of silver **en argent**

The pin is made of silver.
L'épingle est en argent.

---

similar (See **alike**) adjectif **pareil**

---

to sing [SING] verbe **chanter**

je chante	nous chantons
tu chantes	vous chantez
il, elle chante	ils, elles chantent.

I am singing and the birds are singing.
Je chante et les oiseaux chantent.

---

sink (bathroom) (See **bathroom**) nom **le lavabo**

---

sister [SIS-tér] nom **la soeur**

My aunt is my mother's sister.
Ma tante est la soeur de ma mère.

---

to sit down [SIT DOWN] verbe **s'asseoir**

je m'assieds	nous nous asseyons
tu t'assieds	vous vous asseyez
il, elle s'assied	ils, elles s'asseyent

Grandmother sits down on a chair.
Grand-mère s'assied sur une chaise.

---

six [SIKS] adjectif **six**

How many pencils do you have? Six.
Combien de crayons avez-vous? Six.

He has six friends.
Il a six amis.

He has six nails.
Il a six clous.

---

sixteen [siks-TIN] adjectif **seize**

I have to read sixteen pages this evening!
Je dois lire seize pages ce soir!

---

sixty [SIKS-ti] adjectif **soixante**

There are sixty minutes in an hour.
Il y a soixante minutes dans une heure.

---

size [SAIZ] nom **la taille**

In a store they ask me, "What is your size?"
Dans un magasin on me demande: "Quelle est votre taille?"

---

skate [SKEIT] nom **le patin**
ice skate **le patin (à glace)**
roller skate **le patin à roulettes**

---

to skate verbe **patiner**

je patine	nous patinons
tu patines	vous patinez
il, elle patine	ils, elles patinent

Let's go skating!
Allons patiner!

---

skin [SKIN] nom **la peau**

The sun burns my skin when I take a sun bath.
Le soleil me brûle la peau quand je prends un bain de soleil.

---

skinny (thin) [SKIN-i] adjectif **maigre**

You are too thin. You must eat.
Vous êtes trop maigre. Il faut manger.

---

skirt [SKURT] nom **la jupe**

I can't choose. Which skirt do you prefer?
Je ne peux pas choisir. Quelle jupe préférez-vous?

---

sky [SKAI] nom **le ciel**

I see the moon in the sky.
Je vois la lune dans le ciel.

---

skyscraper nom **le gratte-ciel**

New York City has many skyscrapers.
La ville de New York a beaucoup de gratte-ciel.

---

sled [SLED] nom **la luge**
le traîneau

I have a good time with the sled.
Je m'amuse avec la luge.

---

to sleep [SLIP] verbe **dormir**

je dors	nous dormons
tu dors	vous dormez
il, elle dort	ils, elles dorment

Are you sleeping? I would like to talk to you.
Tu dors? Je voudrais te parler.

---

to slide (slip) [SLAID] verbe **glisser**

je glisse	nous glissons
tu glisses	vous glissez
il, elle glisse	ils, elles glissent

We slip on the ice in winter.
Nous glissons sur la glace en hiver.

to slip [SLIP] verbe **glisser**
slowly [SLOH-li] adverbe **lentement**

Grandfather walks slowly.
Grand-père marche lentement.

---

small [SMAWL] adjectif **petit,** masc.
petite, fém.

The bird is small.
L'oiseau est petit.

---

to smell [SMEL] verbe **sentir**

je sens	nous sentons
tu sens	vous sentez
il, elle sent	ils, elles sentent

The cake smells good.
Le gâteau sent bon.

---

to smile [SMAIL] verbe **sourire**

je souris	nous sourions
tu souris	vous souriez
il, elle sourit	ils, elles sourient

You always smile when I give you a cookie.
Tu souris toujours quand je te donne un petit gâteau.

---

smoke [SMOHK] nom **la fumée**

Look at the smoke!
Regarde la fumée!

---

to smoke verbe **fumer**

je fume	nous fumons
tu fumes	vous fumez
il, elle fume	ils, elles fument

Dad says that it is dangerous to smoke.
Papa dit qu'il est dangereux de fumer.

no smoking **défense de fumer**

---

snack [SNAK] nom **le goûter**

Hello, Mother. Do you have a snack for us?
Bonjour, Maman. Tu as un goûter pour nous?

---

snake [SNEIK] nom **le serpent**

Are there any snakes in France?
Est-ce qu'il y a des serpents en France?

---

to sneeze [SNIZ] verbe **éternuer**

j'éternue	nous éternouons
tu éternues	vous éternuez
il, elle éternue	ils, elles éternuent

You're sneezing. Do you have a cold?
Tu éternues. Tu as un rhume?

---

snow [SNOH] nom **la neige**

I like to play in the snow.
J'aime jouer dans la neige.

---

to snow verbe **neiger**

Is it going to snow tomorrow?
Il va neiger demain?

It is snowing **Il neige**

---

snowman [SNOH-man] nom **le bonhomme de neige**

The snowman is wearing a hat.
Le bonhomme de neige porte un chapeau.

---

so [SOH] adverbe **si**

The baby eats so slowly!
Le bébé mange si lentement!

so many adverbe **tant**

So many grapes!
Tant de raisins!

so much adverbe **tant**

So much work!
Tant de travail!

---

soap [SOHP] nom **le savon**

Don't forget to use soap!
N'oublie pas d'employer le savon!

---

soccer [SAK-ér] nom **le football**

Here is our soccer team.
Voici notre équipe de football.

---

sock [SAK] nom **la chaussette**

I would like to buy a pair of socks.
Je voudrais acheter une paire de chaussettes.

---

soda [SOH-dé] nom **le soda**

I am drinking soda.
Je bois du soda.

---

sofa [SOH-fé] nom **le canapé**

The sofa is very comfortable.
Le canapé est très confortable.

---

soft (See **gentle**) adjectif **doux**

---

softly [SAWFT-li] adverbe **doucement**

Walk softly. Mother has a headache.
Marche doucement. Maman a mal à la tête.

---

soldier [SOHL-djér] nom **le soldat**

My cousin is a soldier.
Mon cousin est soldat.

---

some [SÉM] nom **de**
some pronom **quelque**
somebody, someone pronoun **quelqu'un,** masc. **quelqu'une,** fém.

Somebody is in the restaurant.
Quelqu'un est dans le restaurant.

something pronom **quelque chose**

Is there something in this drawer?
Est-ce qu'il y a quelque chose dans ce tiroir?

sometimes adverbe **quelquefois**

Sometimes I am not well-behaved.
Quelquefois je ne suis pas sage.

---

son [SÉN] nom **le fils**

I should like to introduce my son, George.
Je vous présente mon fils, Georges.

---

song [SANG] nom **la chanson**

Which song do you prefer?
Quelle chanson préférez-vous?

---

soon [SUN] adverbe **bientôt**

The mailman will come soon.
Le facteur arrive bientôt.

See you soon! expression idiomatique **à bientôt**

I am going shopping. See you soon!
Je vais faire des emplettes. A bientôt!

---

sort (See **kind**) nom **la sorte**

---

soup [SUP] nom **la soupe**

My sister serves soup to my brother.
Ma soeur sert la soupe à mon frère.

---

south [SOWTH] nom **le sud**

Marseilles is in the south of France.
Marseille est au sud de la France.

---

space [SPEIS] nom **l'espace,** masc.

The astronauts travel in space.
Les astronautes voyagent dans l'espace.

---

spaceship [SPEIS-SHIP] nom **la fusée**

They are going to the moon in a spaceship.
On va à la lune en fusée.

---

to speak (talk) [SPIK] verbe **parler**

je parle	nous parlons
tu parles	vous parlez
il, elle parle	ils, elles parlent

We are talking about the movie on television.
Nous parlons du film à la télévision.

---

to spend (time) [SPEND] verbe **passer**

je passe	nous passons
tu passes	vous passez
il, elle passe	ils, elles passent

She spends two weeks in the country.
Elle passe deux semaines à la campagne.

---

spider [SPAI-dér] nom **l'araignée,** fém.

Who's afraid of a spider?
Qui a peur d'une araignée?

---

to spill (overturn) [SPIL] verbe **renverser**

je renverse	nous renversons
tu renverses	vous renversez
il, elle renverse	ils, elles renversent

The baby overturns the plate.
Le bébé renverse l'assiette.

---

spinach [SPIN-éch] nom **les épinards**

Spinach is green.
Les épinards sont verts.

---

spoon [SPUN] nom **la cuiller**

I don't have a spoon.
Je n'ai pas de cuiller.

---

sport [SPAWRT] nom **le sport**

What is your favorite sport?
Quel est votre sport favori?

---

spot (stain) [SPAT] nom **la tache**

There is a stain on the rug.
Il y a une tache sur le tapis.

spotted adjectif **tacheté,** masc. **tachetée,** fém.

My turtle is spotted.
Ma tortue est tachetée.

---

spring [SPRING] nom **le printemps**

You see a lot of flowers in the spring.
Au printemps on voit beaucoup de fleurs.

---

square [SKWEHR] adjectif **carré,** masc. **carrée,** fém.
The box is square.
La boîte est carrée.

---

staircase [STEHR-keis] nom **l'escalier,** masc.
I like to jump over the last step of the staircase.
J'aime sauter la dernière marche de l'escalier.

---

stamp (postage) [STAMP] nom **le timbre**
I put a stamp on the envelope.
Je mets un timbre sur l'enveloppe.

---

standing [STAN-ding] adverbe **debout**
In the classroom the teacher is standing.
Dans la salle de classe la maîtresse est debout.

---

to stand (See **to get up**) [STAND] verbe **se lever**

---

star [STAHR] nom **l'étoile,** fém.
How many stars are there in the sky?
Combien d'étoiles y a-t-il dans le ciel?

---

to start (begin) [STAHRT] verbe **commencer**

je commence	nous commençons
tu commences	vous commencez
il, elle commence	ils, elles commencent

The French class begins at nine o'clock.
La classe de français commence à neuf heures.

---

state [STEIT] nom **l'état,** masc.
From which state do you come?
De quel état venez-vous?

---

station [STEI-shén] nom **la gare**
The train is in the station.
Le train est à la gare.

---

to stay [STEI] verbe **rester**

je reste	nous restons
tu restes	vous restez
il, elle reste	ils, elles restent

I would like to stay at my grandmother's house.
Je voudrais rester chez ma grand-mère.

---

to steal [STIL] verbe **voler**

je vole	nous volons
tu voles	vous volez
il, elle vole	ils, elles volent

Who has just stolen my spoon?
Qui vient de voler ma cuiller?

---

steamship [STIM-ship] nom **le paquebot**

The steamship crosses the Atlantic Ocean.
Le paquebot traverse l'océan Atlantique.

---

step [STEP] nom **la marche**

There are many steps in front of this building.
Il y a beaucoup de marches devant ce bâtiment.

---

stick [STIK] nom **le bâton**

The policeman carries a stick.
L'agent de police porte un bâton.

---

still [STIL] adverbe **encore**

Are you still at home?
Es-tu encore à la maison?

---

to sting (bite) [STING] verbe **piquer**

il, elle pique	ils, elles piquent

The mosquitoes like to bite me.
Les moustiques aiment me piquer.

---

stocking [STAK-ing] nom **les bas**

Women wear nylon stockings.
Les femmes portent des bas de nylon.

---

stomach (See **to have a . . .**) nom **le ventre**

---

stone [STOHN] nom **la pierre**

There are many stones in the playground.
Il y a beaucoup de pierres dans le terrain de jeux.

---

to stop [STAP] verbe **arrêter**

je arrête	nous arrêtons
tu arrêtes	vous arrêtez
il, elle arrête	ils, elles arrêtent

The policeman stops the car.
L'agent arrête les autos.

---

to stop (oneself) verbe **s'arrêter**

je m'arrête	nous nous arrêtons
tu t'arrêtes	vous vous arrêtez
il, elle s'arrête	ils, elles s'arrêtent

The train stops at the station.
Le train s'arrête à la gare.

---

store [STAWR] nom **le magasin**

I'm going to the store with my friend.
Je vais au magasin avec mon amie.

---

store (market) nom **le marché**

What do they sell at the market?
Qu'est-ce qu'on vend au marché?

---

store window [STAWR WIN-doh] nom **la vitrine**

We are going to look at the things in the store windows.
Nous allons regarder les choses dans les vitrines.

---

storm [STAWRM] nom **l'orage,** masc.

It is windy during a storm.
Il fait du vent pendant l'orage.

---

story [STAWR-i] nom **le conte, l'histoire,** fém.

Read me the story of the "Three Little Kittens."
Lisez-moi le conte des "Trois petits chatons."

Charles Perrault wrote many famous stories for children.

---

stove [STOHV] nom **le fourneau**

Mother cooks on a stove.
Maman fait la cuisine sur un fourneau.

---

strange [STREINDJ] adjectif **bizarre**

Here is a strange animal!
Voici un animal bizarre!

---

stranger [STREIN-djǝr] nom **étranger,** masc. **étrangère,** fém.

Mother says, "Don't speak to strangers."
Maman dit: "Ne parlez pas aux étrangers."

---

strawberry [STRAW-ber-i] nom **la fraise**

Strawberries are red.
Les fraises sont rouges.

---

street [STRIT] nom **la rue**

It is dangerous to play ball in the street.
Il est dangereux de jouer à la balle dans la rue.

street cleaner nom **le balayeur des rues**

The street cleaner is carrying a broom.
Le balayeur des rues porte un balai.

---

string [STRING] nom **la ficelle**

I am looking for a string for my kite.
Je cherche une ficelle pour mon cerf-volant.

---

string beans [STRING-binz] nom **les haricots verts**

We have string beans for dinner.
Nous avons des haricots verts pour le dîner.

---

strong [STRAWNG] adjectif **fort,** masc. **forte,** fém.

My father is very strong.
Mon père est très fort.

---

student [STUD-ént] nom **l'étudiant,** masc. **l'étudiante,** fém.

My cousin is a student at the university.
Mon cousin est étudiant à l'université.

to study [STÉD-i] verbe **étudier**

j'étudie	nous étudions
tu étudies	vous étudiez
il, elle étudie	ils, elles étudient

I have to study this evening. I have an examination tomorrow.
Je dois étudier ce soir. J'ai un examen demain.

---

stupid [STU-pid] adjectif **stupide, bête**

Is the elephant intelligent or stupid?
Est-ce que l'éléphant est intelligent ou stupide?

---

subway [SɆB-wei] nom **le métro**

We take the subway to go to the museum.
Pour aller au musée nous prenons le métro.

---

to succeed [sɇk-SID] verbe **réussir**

je réussis	nous réussissons
tu réussis	vous réussissez
il, elle réussit	ils, elles réussissent

He succeeds in catching a fish.
Il réussit à attraper un poisson.

---

suddenly [SɆD-ɇn-li] adverbe **tout à coup**

Suddenly the doctor enters.
Tout à coup le médecin entre.

---

sugar [SHAUHG-ɇr] nom **le sucre**

He serves sugar with tea.
Il sert du sucre avec le thé.

---

suit [SUT] nom **le complet**

Father wears a suit when he goes to work.
Papa porte un complet quand il va au travail.

bathing suit **le maillot**

---

suitcase [SUT-keis] nom **la valise**

I put my clothes in the suitcase.
Je mets mes vêtements dans la valise.

---

summer [SɆM-ɇr] nom **l'été,** masc.

Do you prefer summer or winter?
Préférez-vous l'été ou l'hiver?

---

sun [SƏN] nom **le soleil**

What time does the sun rise?
A quelle heure se lève le soleil?

sunbath [SƏN-bath] nom **le bain de soleil**

I take a sunbath on the grass.
Je prends un bain de soleil sur l'herbe.

It is sunny. expression idiomatique **Il fait du soleil.**

Sunday [SƏN-dei] nom **dimanche**

We go to the park on Sundays.
Le dimanche nous allons au parc.

---

supermarket [SU-pər-MAHR-kət] nom **le supermarché**

The supermarket is a large market.
Le supermarché est un grand marché.

---

sure (See **certain**) adjectif **sur**

---

surprise [sər-PRAIZ] nom **la surprise**

A surprise for me?
Une surprise pour moi?

---

surprising adjectif **étonnant,** masc. **étonnante,** fém.

It is surprising to receive a letter from an actress.
Il est étonnant de recevoir une lettre d'une actrice.

---

sweater [SWET-ər] nom **le chandail**

I am wearing a sweater because it is cool.
Je porte un chandail parce qu'il fait frais.

---

sweet [SWIT] adjectif **doux**

This dessert is very sweet.
Ce dessert est très doux.

---

to swim [SWIM] verbe **nager**

je nage	nous nageons
tu nages	vous nagez
il, elle nage	ils, elles nagent

I go swimming in summer.
Je vais nager en été.

swimming pool (pool) nom **la piscine**

We are swimming in the pool.
Nous nageons dans la piscine.

---

swing [SWING] nom **la balançoire**

In the park the children are having a good time on the swings.
Dans le parc les enfants s'amusent sur les balançoires.

---

switch (See **to turn off**) nom **le bouton**

T

table [TEI-bəl] nom **la table**

The brush is on the table.
La brosse est sur la table.

---

tablecloth [TEI-bəl-clath] nom **la nappe**

My aunt puts the tablecloth on the table.
Ma tante met la nappe sur la table.

---

tail [TEIL] nom **la queue**

My dog wags his tail when I return home.
Mon chien remue la queue quand je retourne à la maison.

---

tailor [TEI-lər] nom **le tailleur**

My neighbor is a tailor.
Mon voisin est tailleur.

---

to take (has) [TEIK] verbe **prendre**

je prends	nous prenons
tu prends	vous prenez
il, elle prend	ils, elles prennent

Mom has a croissant for breakfast.
Maman prend un croissant pour le petit déjeuner.

to take a bath **prendre un bain**
to take a walk verbe **se promener**

je me promène	nous nous promenons
tu te promènes	vous vous promenez
il, elle se promène	ils, elles se promènent

They are walking in the park.
Elles se promènent dans le parc.

take care! interjection **attention!**

The teacher says, "Take care!"
Le professeur dit: "Attention!"

to take off verbe **ôter**

j'ôte	nous ôtons
tu ôtes	vous ôtez
il, elle ôte	ils, elles ôtent

Take off your hat in the house.
Ôte le chapeau dans la maison.

to take a trip **faire un voyage**

---

tale (See **story**) nom **le conte**
fairy tale **le conte de fées**

---

to talk [TAK] verbe **parler**

je parle	nous parlons
tu parles	vous parlez
il, elle parle	ils, elles parlent

We are talking about the movie on television.
Nous parlons du film à la télévision.

---

tall [LOWD] adjectif **haut,** masc. **haute,** fém.

The Eiffel Tower is very tall.
La Tour Eiffel est très haute.

---

tape recorder [teip ré-KAWR-dér] nom **le magnétophone**

The teacher uses a tape recorder in class.
Le professeur emploie un magnétophone dans la classe.

---

taxi [tak-SI] nom **le taxi**

My brother drives a taxi.
Mon frère conduit un taxi.

---

tea [TI] nom **le thé**

Do you want tea or coffee?
Tu veux du thé ou du café?

---

teacher [TI-cher] nom **la maîtresse,** fém. **le maître,** masc.
The teacher is kind.
La maîtresse est gentille.

teacher nom **le professeur**

The teacher is in the classroom.
Le professeur est dans la salle de classe.

---

to teach [TICH] verbe **enseigner**

j'enseigne	nous enseignons
tu enseignes	vous enseignez
il, elle enseigne	ils, elles enseignent

Who teaches music to this class?
Qui enseigne la musique dans cette classe?

---

team [TIM] nom **l'équipe,** fém.

We are all members of the same team.
Nous sommes tous membres de la même équipe.

---

tear [TIR] nom **la larme**

Grandpa says, "Enough tears!"
Grand-père dit: "Assez de larmes!"

---

to tease [TIZ] verbe **taquiner**

je taquine	nous taquinons
tu taquines	vous taquinez
il, elle taquine	ils, elles taquinent

My brother always teases me!
Mon frère me taquine toujours!

---

teeth (See **tooth**) nom, pl. **les dents**

---

telephone [TEL-é-fohn] nom **le téléphone**

I like to talk on the telephone.
J'aime parler au téléphone.

---

television [TEL-é-vizh-én] nom **la télévision**
la télé

My brother and I watch television.
Mon frère et moi, nous regardons la télévision.

television antenna nom **l'antenne de télévision**

Television antennas are on the roof of the building.
Les antennes de télévision sont sur le toit du bâtiment.

television set nom **le téléviseur**

The television set is not working.
Le téléviseur ne marche pas.

---

to tell [TEL] verbe **raconter**

Tell me a story, Mom.
Raconte-moi une histoire, Maman.

---

ten [TEN] adjectif **dix**

How many fingers do you have? Ten.
Combien de doigts avez-vous? Dix.

---

tent [TENT] nom **la tente**

When I am at camp I sleep in a tent.
Quand je suis à la colonie de vacances je dors dans une tente.

---

test (See **examination**) nom **l'examen,** masc.

---

thank you [THANGK-yu] nom **merci**

When my grandmother gives me a cookie I say, "Thank you."
Quand ma grand-mère me donne un petit gâteau je dis: "Merci."

---

that [THAT] pronom **cela**

I don't like that!
Je n'aime pas cela!

---

that pronom **que**
That's too bad! **C'est dommage!**
expression idiomatique

You don't like chocolate? That's too bad!
Vous n'aimez pas le chocolat? C'est dommage!

---

the [THE] article **le, la, les**

---

theater [THI-é-tér] nom **le théâtre**

What are they performing at the theater?
Qu'est-ce qu'on joue au théâtre?

---

their [THEHR] adjectif **leur**

---

them [THEM] pronom **eux**

I go to school with them.
Je vais à l'école avec eux.

them pronom **leur**

I give them a card.
Je leur donne une carte.

---

then [THEN] adverbe **ensuite**

I read the book; then I return the book to the library.
Je lis le livre; ensuite je rends le livre à la bibliothèque.

then adverbe **puis**

I write a letter; then I go to my friend's house.
J'écris une lettre; puis, je vais chez mon ami.

---

there [THEHR] adverbe **là-bas**
there is [THEHR iz] adverbe **il y a**

---

they [THEI] pronom **ils, elles, on**

---

thick [THIK] adjectif **épais,** masc. **épaisse,** fém.

The lemon's skin is very thick.
La peau du citron est très épaisse.

---

thief [THIF] nom **le voleur**

They are looking for the thief at the bank.
On cherche le voleur à la banque.

---

thin [THIN] adjectif **maigre**

You are too thin. You must eat.
Vous êtes trop maigre. Il faut manger.

---

thing [THING] nom **la chose**

They sell all kinds of things in this store.
On vend toutes sortes de choses dans cette boutique.

---

to think [THINGK] verbe **penser**

je pense	nous pensons
tu penses	vous pensez
il, elle pense	ils, elles pensent

I think I'll go to my friend's house. All right?
Je pense que je vais chez mon ami. D'accord?

---

thirsty (to be) (See **to drink**) verbe **avoir soif**

---

thirteen [thur-TIN] adjectif **treize**

There are thirteen steps in the staircase.
Il y a treize marches dans l'escalier.

---

thirty [THUR-ti] adjectif **trente**

Which months have thirty days?
Quels mois ont trente jours?

---

this [THIS] adjectif **ce**

This little girl is well-behaved. **cette,** fém.
Cette petite fille est sage. **ces,** pl.
cet, masc. form before a vowel

---

this pronom **ceci**

Mmm, this is good!
Mmm, ceci est bon!

---

thousand [THOW-zénd] adjectif **mille**

How much does a car cost? A thousand francs?
Combien coûte une auto? Mille francs?

---

three [THRI] adjectif **trois**

There are three glasses on the table.
Il y a trois verres sur la table.

---

throat [THROHT] nom **la gorge**

The teacher says softly, "I have a sore throat."
La maîtresse dit doucement: "J'ai mal à la gorge."

---

to throw [THROH] verbe **lancer**

je lance	nous lançons
tu lances	vous lancez
il, elle lance	ils, elles lancent

He's throwing a pillow at me!
Il me lance un oreiller!

---

thunder [THÉN-dér] nom **le tonnerre**

After the lightning you hear the thunder.
Après l'éclair on entend le tonnerre.

Thursday [THURZ-dei] nom **jeudi**

My birthday is Thursday.
Jeudi est mon anniversaire.

---

ticket [TIK-it] nom **le billet**

Here is my ticket, sir.
Voici mon billet, monsieur.

---

tie [TAI] nom **la cravate**

Daddy's tie is too big for me.
La cravate de Papa est trop grande pour moi.

---

time (hour) [TAIM] nom **l'heure**

What time is it?
Quelle heure est-il?

It is dinner time. It is seven thirty. (It is half past seven.)
C'est l'heure du dîner. Il est sept heures et demie.

---

time (repeated action) [TAIM] nom **la fois**

They knock three times at the door.
On frappe trois fois à la porte.

---

tip [TIP] nom **le pourboire**

The man leaves a tip for the waiter.
L'homme laisse un pourboire pour le garçon.

---

tired [TAIRD] **fatigué,** masc. **fatiguée,** fém.

After two hours of work in the garden, I am tired.
Après deux heures de travail dans le jardin, je suis fatigué.

---

to [TÉ] préposition **à**

They are going to Paris.
Ils vont à Paris.

---

toast [TOHST] nom **le pain grillé**

My sister prefers toast.
Ma soeur préfère le pain grillé.

---

today [té-DEI] adverbe **aujourd'hui**

Today is January 12th.
Aujourd'hui c'est le douze janvier.

---

toe [TOH] nom **l'orteil,** masc.

The baby looks at his toes.
Le bébé regarde ses orteils.

---

together [té-GETH-ér] adverbe **ensemble**

We are going to the grocery store together.
Nous allons à l'épicerie ensemble.

---

tomato [té-MEI-toh] nom **la tomate**

The tomato is red when it is ripe.
La tomate est rouge quand elle est mûre.

---

tomorrow [té-MAR-oh] adverbe **demain**

Tomorrow I am going to camp.
Demain je vais à la colonie de vacances.

---

tongue [TÉNG] nom **la langue**

I burn my tongue with hot soup.
Je me brûle la langue avec la soupe chaude.

---

too [TU] adverbe **aussi**

I want some candy too!
Moi aussi, je veux des bonbons!

---

too (many) (much) adverb **trop**

The little girl says, "This is too much for me!"
La petite fille dit: "C'est trop pour moi!"

---

tooth [TUTH] nom **la dent**

I have a toothache.
J'ai mal aux dents.

toothache nom **mal aux dents**
toothbrush nom **la brosse aux dents**
toothpaste nom **le dentifrice**

Mom, I don't like this toothpaste.
Maman, je n'aime pas ce dentifrice.

---

top (toy) [TAP] nom **la toupie**

Do you have a top?
As-tu une toupie?

---

tortoise (turtle) [TAWR-tis] nom **la tortue**

The turtle walks slowly.
La tortue marche lentement.

---

to touch [TECH] verbe **toucher**

je touche	nous touchons
tu touches	vous touchez
il, elle touche	ils, elles touchent

"Do not touch the flowers."
"Défense de toucher les fleurs."

---

toward [TAWRD] préposition **vers**

We are going toward the hotel.
Nous allons vers l'hôtel.

---

towel [TOW-el] nom **la serviette**

My towel is in the bathroom.
Ma serviette est dans la salle de bain.

---

tower [TOW-er] nom **la tour**

The Eiffel Tower is very tall.
La Tour Eiffel est très haute.

---

toy [TOI] nom **le jouet**

What kind of toys do you have?
Quelle sorte de jouets as-tu?

---

traffic [TRAF-ik] nom **la circulation**

The traffic stops for the red light.
La circulation s'arrête au feu rouge.

---

train [TREIN] nom **le train**

Let's play with my electric trains.
Allons jouer avec mon train électrique.

---

to travel [TRAV-el] verbe **voyager**

je voyage	nous voyageons
tu voyages	vous voyagez
il, elle voyage	ils, elles voyagent

Are you traveling by car or by airplane?
Vous voyagez en auto ou en avion?

traveler nom **le voyageur**

The traveler is tired.
Le voyageur est fatigué.

---

tree [TRI] nom **l'arbre,** masc.

We are sitting under a tree.
Nous sommes assis sous l'arbre.

---

trip [TRIP] nom **le voyage, le tour**
to take a trip expression idiomatique **faire un voyage**

We are taking a trip to the castle.
Nous faisons un voyage au château.

---

trousers (pants) [TROW-zérs] nom **le pantalon**

The boy's pants are dirty.
Le pantalon du garçon est sale.

---

truck [TRÉK] nom **le camion**

The truck is carrying vegetables.
Le camion porte des légumes.

---

true [TRU] adjectif **vrai,** masc.
vraie, fém.

It's a true story!
C'est une histoire vraie!

---

trunk [TRÉNGK] nom **la malle**

It is difficult to carry this trunk.
Il est difficile de porter cette malle.

---

truth [TRUTH] nom **la vérité**

It's true. I only tell the truth.
C'est vrai. Je ne dis que la vérité.

---

to try [TRAI] verbe **essayer**

j'essaye	nous essayons
tu essayes	vous essayez
il, elle essaye	ils, elles essayent

She tries to carry the heavy package.
Elle essaye de porter le paquet lourd.

Tuesday [TUZ-dei] nom **mardi**

Is Tuesday a day off?
Est-ce que mardi est un jour de congé?

---

turkey [TUR-ki] nom **la dinde**

Do you like to eat turkey?
Tu aimes manger la dinde?

---

turn [TURN] nom **le tour**
to turn verbe **tourner**

je tourne	nous tournons
tu tournes	vous tournez
il, elle tourne	ils, elles tournent

I turn the page of the dictionary.
Je tourne la page du dictionnaire.

to turn off verbe **éteindre**

j'éteins	nous éteignons
tu éteins	vous éteignez
il, elle éteint	ils, elles éteignent

I turn off the light.
J'éteins la lumière.

---

turtle [TUR-təl] nom **la tortue**

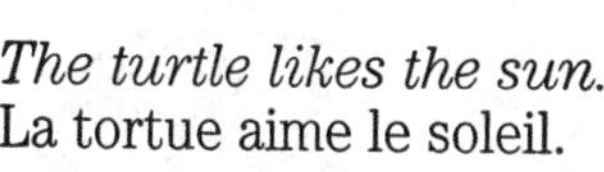

The turtle likes the sun.
La tortue aime le soleil.

---

twelve [TWELV] adjectif **douze**

There are twelve bananas in a dozen.
Il y a douze bananes dans une douzaine.

---

twenty [TWEN-ti] adjectif **vingt**

Ten and ten are twenty.
Dix et dix font vingt.

---

twice [TWHAIS] adverbe **deux fois**

---

two [TU] adjectif **deux**

I see two cats.
Je vois deux chats.

---

typewriter [TAIP-rai-tør] nom **la machine à écrire**

She wants a typewriter for her birthday.
Elle désire une machine à écrire pour son anniversaire.

---

typist [TAIP-ist] nom **la dactylo**

There are three typists in this office.
Il y a trois dactylos dans ce bureau.

U

ugly [ØG-li] adjectif **laid,** masc. **laide,** fém.

I don't like this hat; it's ugly.
Je n'aime pas ce chapeau; il est laid.

---

umbrella [øm-BREL-ø] nom **le parapluie**

That's a pretty umbrella.
C'est un joli parapluie.

---

uncle [ÉNG-kél] nom **l'oncle**

My uncle is my mother's brother.
Mon oncle est le frère de ma mère.

---

under [ÉN-dér] préposition **sous**

The carrot grows under the ground.
La carotte pousse sous la terre.

---

to understand [én-dér-STAND] verbe **comprendre**

je comprends	nous comprenons
tu comprends	vous comprenez
il, elle comprend	ils, elles comprennent

Do you understand today's lesson?
Tu comprends la leçon d'aujourd'hui?

---

unhappy [én-HAP-i] adjectif **malheureux,** masc. **malheureuse,** fém.

He is unhappy because he can't play ball.
Il est malheureux parce qu'il ne peut pas jouer à la balle.

---

united [u-NAIT-éd] **uni,** masc. **unie,** fém.

The boy lives in the United States.
Le garçon habite les Etats-Unis.

The United Nations building is located in New York City.
Le bâtiment des Nations Unies se trouve dans la ville de New York.

United Nations [u-NAIT-éd NEI-shénz] **Les Nations Unies**
United States [u-NAIT-éd STEITS] **Les Etats-Unis**

---

university (See **student**) nom **l'université,** fém.

---

until [én-TIL] préposition **jusqu'à**

We are in school until three o'clock.
Nous sommes à l'école jusqu'à trois heures.

---

unusual (See **extraordinary**) adjectif **extraordinaire**

---

upstairs **en haut**

Where are you? Upstairs.
Où es-tu? En haut.

---

us [ǝs] pronom **nous**

---

to use [YUZ] verbe **employer**

j'emploie	nous employons
tu emploies	vous employez
il, elle emploie	ils, elles emploient

She uses scissors to cut the ribbon.
Elle emploie les ciseaux pour couper le ruban.

---

useful adjectif **utile**

Some insects are useful.
Quelques insectes sont utiles.

V

vacation [vei-KEI-shǝn] nom **les vacances**
summer vacation **les grandes vacances**

Where are you going during the summer vacation?
Où allez-vous pendant les grandes vacances?

---

to vaccinate [VAK-sin-eit] verbe **vacciner**

je vaccine	nous vaccinons
tu vaccines	vous vaccinez
il, elle vaccine	ils, elles vaccinent

I am afraid when the doctor vaccinates me.
J'ai peur quand le médecin me vaccine.

---

vacuum cleaner **l'aspirateur,** masc.
[VAK-yu-ém-kli-nér] nom
Mother uses the vacuum cleaner to clean the house.
Pour nettoyer la maison, Maman emploie l'aspirateur.

---

valise [vé-LIS] nom **la valise**
I put my clothes in the valise.
Je mets mes vêtements dans la valise.

---

valley [VAL-i] nom **la vallée**
There are many flowers in the valley.
Il y a beaucoup de fleurs dans la vallée.

---

vanilla [vé-NIL-é] nom **la vanille**
I like vanilla ice cream.
J'aime la glace à la vanille.

---

vegetable [VEDJ-té-bél] nom **le légume**
Vegetables are delicious with meat.
Les légumes sont délicieux avec la viande.

---

very [VER-i] adverbe **très**
The castle is very big.
Le château est très grand.

---

village [VIL-idj] nom **le village**
My cousin lives in a village in the country.
Mon cousin habite un village à la campagne.

---

violet (See **purple**) nom **violet**

---

violin [VAI-oh-lin] nom **le violon**
The musician plays the violin.
Le musicien joue du violon.

---

to visit [VIZ-it] verbe **visiter**

je visite nous visitons
tu visites vous visitez
il, elle visite ils, elles visitent

My parents visit my camp.
Mes parents visitent ma colonie de vacances.

---

voice [VOIS] nom **la voix**

My aunt's voice is sweet.
La voix de ma tante est douce.

in a loud voice **à haute voix**
aloud **à haute voix**
in a low voice **à voix basse**

W

to wag [WAG] verbe **remuer**

je remue nous remuons
tu remues vous remuez
il, elle remue ils, elles remuent

The dog wags the tail.
Le chien remue la queue.

---

waist (size) [WEIST] nom **la taille**

In a store they ask me,
"What is your size?"
Dans un magasin on me demande:
"Quelle est votre taille?"

---

waiter [WEI-tér] nom **le garçon**

The waiter brings the dessert.
Le garçon apporte le dessert.

---

to wait for [WEIT fe̸r] verbe **attendre**

j'attends	nous attendons
tu attends	vous attendez
il, elle attend	ils, elles attendent

She is waiting for her friend.
Elle attend son amie.

---

waitress [WEI-tre̸s] nom **la serveuse**

The waitress is in the restaurant.
La serveuse est dans le restaurant.

---

to wake up [WEIK e̸p] verbe **se réveiller**

je me réveille	nous nous réveillons
tu te réveilles	vous vous réveillez
il, elle se réveille	ils, elles se réveillent

We wake up early.
Nous nous réveillons de bonne heure.

---

to walk (energetically) [WAWK] verbe **marcher**

je marche	nous marchons
tu marches	vous marchez
il, elle marche	ils, elles marchent

We walk in the parade.
Nous marchons dans le défilé.

to walk (to stroll) verbe **se promener**

je me promène	nous nous promenons
tu te promènes	vous vous promenez
il, elle se promène	ils, elles promènent

They are walking in the park.
Elles se promènent dans le parc.

---

wall [WAL] nom **le mur**

There is a picture of a rocket ship on my bedroom wall.
Il y a une image d'une fusée au mur de ma chambre.

---

to want, wish [WAHNT] verbe **désirer**

je désire	nous désirons
tu désires	vous désirez
il, elle désire	ils, elles désirent

What do you wish, sir?
Monsieur désire?

to want verbe **vouloir**

je veux	nous voulons
tu veux	vous voulez
il, elle veut	ils, elles veulent

The baby is crying because he wants his toy.
Le bébé pleure parce qu'il veut son jouet.

---

war [WAWR] nom **la guerre**

My uncle is a soldier in the war.
Mon oncle est soldat à la guerre.

---

warm (See **hot**) adjectif **chaud**

---

to wash (something or someone) [WAHSH] verbe **laver**

je lave	nous lavons
tu laves	vous lavez
il, elle lave	ils, elles lavent

She is washing the car.
Elle lave la voiture.

to wash (oneself) verbe **se laver**

je me lave	nous nous lavons
tu te laves	vous vous lavez
il, elle se lave	ils, elles se lavent

I wash my hands before eating.
Je me lave les mains avant de manger.

washing machine **la machine à laver**

washstand nom **le lavabo**

The washstand is in the bathroom.
Le lavabo est dans la salle de bain.

---

watch [WACH] nom **la montre**

What a shame, my watch doesn't work.
Hélas, ma montre ne marche pas.

---

to watch verbe **regarder**

je regarde	nous regardons
tu regardes	vous regardez
il, elle regarde	ils, elles regardent

I like to watch television.
J'aime regarder la télévision.

to watch over (looks after) **surveiller**
[WACH-oh-vér] verbe

je surveille	nous surveillons
tu surveilles	vous surveillez
il, elle surveille	ils, elles surveillent

The cat looks after the kittens.
Le chat surveille les petits (chats).

---

water [WA-tér] nom **l'eau,** fém. **les eaux,** pl.

There is water in the swimming pool.
Il y a de l'eau dans la piscine.

---

watermelon [WA-tér-mel-én] nom **la pastèque**

Watermelon is a delicious fruit.
La pastèque est un fruit délicieux.

---

wave [WEIV] nom **la vague**

I see waves at the beach.
Je vois des vagues à la plage.

---

we [WI] pronom **nous**

We are going to the beach.
Nous allons à la plage.

---

we pronom **on**

Are we playing now?
On joue maintenant?

---

weak [WIK] adjectif **faible**

The poor boy is weak because he is sick.
Le pauvre garçon est faible parce qu'il est malade.

---

wealthy (rich) [WEL-thi] adjectif **riche**

The rich lady wears jewels.
La femme riche porte des bijoux.

---

to wear [WEHR] verbe **porter**

je porte	nous portons
tu portes	vous portez
il, elle porte	ils, elles portent

She is wearing a hat.
Elle porte un chapeau.

---

weather [WETH-ér] nom **le temps**

What is the weather? The sun is shining.
Quel temps fait-il? Il fait du soleil.

Wednesday [WENZ-dei] nom **mercredi**

Today is Wednesday—they are serving chicken.
C'est aujourd'hui mercredi—on sert du poulet.

---

week [WIK] nom **la semaine**

The calendar shows us the seven days of the week.
Le calendrier nous montre les sept jours de la semaine.

---

to weep (cry) [WIP] verbe **pleurer**

je pleure	nous pleurons
tu pleures	vous pleurez
il, elle pleure	ils, elles pleurent

I cry when somebody teases me.
Je pleure quand on me taquine.

You're welcome. [YUR-WEL-kém] expression idiomatique **il n'y a pas de quoi, Je vous en prie.**

---

well [WEL] adverbe **bien**

I'm feeling very well, thank you.
Je vais très bien, merci.

---

well-behaved [WEL-bi-HEIVD] adjectif **sage**

Little girls are better behaved than little boys.
Les petites filles sont plus sages que les petits garçons.

Well done! Hurray! [wel-DÉN] interjection **bravo**

Arnold answers the question well. "Well done!" says the teacher.
Arnaud répond bien à la question. Le professeur dit: "Bravo!"

---

west [WEST] nom **l'ouest,** masc.

When I go from Lyons to Bordeaux, I go toward the west.
Quand je vais de Lyon à Bordeaux, je vais vers l'ouest.

---

wet [WET] adjectif **mouille,** masc. **mouillée,** fém.

My notebook is falling into the water. Oh, it is wet!
Mon cahier tombe dans l'eau. Oh, il est mouillé!

---

what? [WHAT] adverbe **comment?**

What?
Comment?

---

what adverbe **quoi**

What? You don't have the change for the bus?
Quoi? Tu n'as pas la monnaie pour l'autobus?

what **que**
what **quel**
what a . . . ! **quel,** masc.
quelle, fém.

What a beautiful dress!
Quelle belle robe!

---

wheat [WHIT] nom **le blé**

I see wheat in the fields.
Je vois le blé dans les champs.

---

wheel [WHIL] nom **la roue**

My uncle fixes the wheel of my bicycle.
Mon oncle répare la roue de ma bicyclette.

---

when [WHEN] adverbe **quand**

I read a book when it rains.
Je lis un livre quand il pleut.

---

where [WHEHR] adverbe **où**

Where are my glasses?
Où sont mes lunettes?

---

whether (if) [WHETH-ér] adverbe **si**
s' (before il)

I am going to the window to see if it is raining.
Je vais à la fenêtre pour voir s'il pleut.

---

which [WHICH] adjectif, pronom **que**
which adjectif **quel,** masc.
which pronoun **quelle,** fém.
qui

I am looking for my pen, which is on the rug.
Je cherche mon stylo qui est sur le tapis.

---

to whistle [WHIS-él] verbe **siffler**

je siffle nous sifflons
tu siffles vous sifflez
il, elle siffle ils, elles sifflent

When I whistle, my friend knows that I'm at the door.
Quand je siffle, mon ami sait que je suis à la porte.

---

white [WHAIT] adjectif **blanc,** masc. **blanche,** fém.

My shoes are white.
Mes souliers sont blancs.

---

who [HU] pronom **qui**

Who is coming to visit us?
Qui vient chez nous?

---

whole [HOHL] adjectif **entier,** masc. **entière,** fém.

Of course I would like to eat the whole cake!
Bien sûr je voudrais manger le gâteau entier!

---

whom [HUM] pronom **que**, **qu'** (before a vowel)

The woman whom I see is my aunt.
La femme que je vois est ma tante.

---

why? [WHAI] adverbe **pourquoi**

Why are you late?
Pourquoi êtes-vous en retard?

---

wide [WAID] adjectif **large**

The boulevard is a wide street.
Le boulevard est une large rue.

---

wide street [WAID-STRIT] nom **le boulevard**

Students walk on the Boulevard St. Michel in Paris.
Les étudiants se promènent sur le boulevard St-Michel à Paris.

---

wife [WAIF] nom **la femme**

Mother is my father's wife.
Maman est la femme de mon père.

---

wild [WAILD] adjectif **féroce, sauvage**

Who is afraid of a wild tiger?
Qui a peur d'un tigre féroce?

---

to win [WIN] verbe **gagner**

je gagne	nous gagnons
tu gagnes	vous gagnez
il, elle gagne	ils, elles gagnent

Our team wins!
C'est notre équipe qui gagne!

---

wind [WIND] nom **le vent**

It is windy and I lose my hat.
Il fait du vent et je perds mon chapeau.

---

window [WIN-doh] nom **la fenêtre**

The dog likes to look out the window.
Le chien aime regarder par la fenêtre.

store window **la vitrine**

---

wine [WAIN] nom **le vin**

The waiter brings the wine.
Le garçon apporte le vin.

---

wing [WING] nom **l'aile,** fém.

The airplane has two wings.
L'avion a deux ailes.

---

winner [WIN-ér] nom **le gagnant,** masc. **la gagnante,** fém.

I like to be the winner!
J'aime être la gagnante!

---

winter [WIN-tér] nom **l'hiver,** masc.

It is cold in winter.
En hiver il fait froid.

---

wise [WAIZ] adjectif **sage**

Grandfather is wise.
Grand-père est sage.

---

wish [WISH] nom **le souhait**

When I go to bed I make a wish.
Quand je me couche je fais un souhait.

---

to wish verbe **désirer**

je désire	nous désirons
tu désires	vous désirez
il, elle désire	ils, elles désirent

What do you wish, sir?
Monsieur désire?

---

to wish (want) nom **vouloir**

je veux	nous voulons
tu vuex	vous voulez
il, elle veut	ils, elles veulent

The baby is crying because he wants his toy.
Le bébé pleure parce qu'il veut son jouet.

---

with [WITH] préposition **avec**

Mary is at the beach with her friends.
Marie est à la plage avec ses amies.

with care **avec soin**

Paul pours water into the glass carefully.
Paul verse l'eau dans le verre avec soin.

---

without [with-OWT] préposition **sans**

I'm going to class without my friend. He is sick.
Je vais à mes classes sans mon ami. Il est malade.

---

wolf [WAUHLF] nom **le loup**

Who's afraid of the bad wolf?
Qui a peur du méchant loup?

> In French they say: "Quand on parle du loup, on en voit la queue." In English this is very roughly translated as: "When we speak of the wolf, we see its tail," or, making a little more sense, "Speak of the devil, and he's here."

---

woman [WAUHM-en] nom **la femme**

These two women are going shopping.
Ces deux femmes vont faire des emplettes.

---

wonderful [WƏN-dər-fəl] adjectif **extraordinaire**

We are going to take a wonderful trip in a spaceship.
Nous allons faire un voyage extraordinaire en fusée.

Wonderful! (Great!) interjection **formidable**

You are going to the circus? Great!
Tu vas au cirque? Formidable!

---

woods [WAUHDZ] nom **la forêt, le bois**

I am going into the woods.
Je vais dans le bois.

---

wool [WAUHL] nom **la laine**
made of wool, woolen **en laine**

My coat is made of wool.
Mon manteau est en laine.

---

word [WURD] nom **le mot**

I'm thinking of a word that begins with the letter "a."
Je pense à un mot qui commence avec la lettre "a."

---

work [WURK] nom **le travail**

My mother has a lot of work to do.
Ma mère a beaucoup de travail.

---

to work verbe **travailler**

je travaille	nous travaillons
tu travailles	vous travaillez
il elle travaille	ils, elles travaillent

The farmer works outside.
Le fermier travaille dehors.

---

to work (things) [WURK] verbe **marcher**

je marche	nous marchons
tu marches	vous marchez
il, elle marche	ils, elles marchent

This lamp is not working.
Cette lampe ne marche pas.

---

world [WURLD] nom **le monde**

How many nations are there in the world?
Combien de nations y a-t-il dans le monde?

---

worm [WURM] nom **le ver**

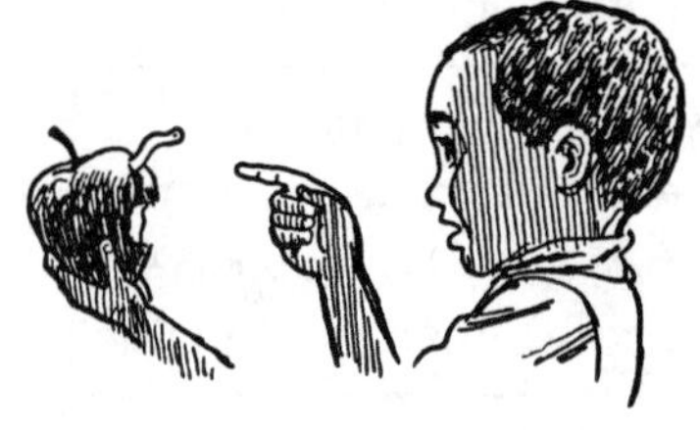

There's a worm in the apple.
Il y a un ver dans la pomme.

---

to write [RAIT] verbe **écrire**

j'écris	nous écrivons
tu écris	vous écrivez
il, elle écrit	ils, elles écrivent

The teacher says, "Write the date on the blackboard."
La maîtresse dit: "Écrivez la date au tableau noir."

(to be) wrong [RONG] expression **avoir tort**

Y

year [YIR] nom **l'année,** fém.

There are twelve months in a year.
Il y a douze mois dans une année.

year nom **l'an,** masc.

I'm nine years old.
J'ai neuf ans.

---

yellow [YEL-oh] adjectif **jaune**

Corn is yellow.
Le maïs est jaune.

---

yes [YES] adverbe **oui**

Do you want some candy? Yes, of course!
Veux-tu des bonbons? Oui, bien sûr!

---

yesterday [YES-tér-dei] adverbe **hier**

Today is May 10; yesterday (was) May 9.
C'est aujourd'hui le dix mai; hier, le neuf mai.

---

you [YU] pronom **on**

When you look out of the window, you see the Eiffel Tower.
Quand on regarde par la fenêtre, on voit la Tour Eiffel.

you pronom (familiar) **te**

I give you some milk.
Je te donne du lait.

you pronom (familiar) **toi**

Do you have my stick, Jack?
C'est toi, Jacques, qui as mon bâton?

you pronom **vous**

How are you?
Comment allez-vous?

I am giving you a ticket.
Je vous donne un billet.

you (familiar) pronom **tu**

How are you?
Comment vas-tu?

you have to expression idiomatique **il faut**

It is necessary to go to school.
(We have to go to school.)
Il faut aller à l'école.

---

young [YƏNG] adjectif **jeune**

The puppy is young. It is six weeks old.
Le petit chien est jeune. Il a six semaines.

---

your [YAWR] adjectif **ton,** masc. **ta,** fém. **tes,** pl. **votre** **vos,** pl.

Your cousin is handsome.
Ton cousin est beau.

Your neighbor is kind.
Ta voisine est gentille.

Your parents are tall.
Tes parents sont grands.

Where is your tape recorder?
Où est votre magnétophone?

Where are your stamps?
Où sont vos timbres?

---

you're welcome [YUR-WEL-kəm] **de rein; je vous en prie; il n'y a pas de quoi; pas de quoi**

Z

zebra [ZI-brə] nom **le zèbre**

Is it a zebra or a horse?
Est-ce un zèbre ou un cheval?

---

zero [ZIR-oh] nom **le zéro**

There is a zero in the number ten.
Il y a un zéro dans le numéro dix.

---

zoo [ZU] nom **le zoo**

I like to watch the tigers at the zoo.
J'aime regarder les tigres au zoo.

DAYS OF THE WEEK
Les Jours de la Semaine

English/Anglais	Français/French
Monday	lundi
Tuesday	mardi
Wednesday	mercredi
Thursday	jeudi
Friday	vendredi
Saturday	samedi
Sunday	dimanche

MONTHS OF THE YEAR
Les Mois de L'Année

English/Anglais	Français/French
January	janvier
February	février
March	mars
April	avril
May	mai
June	juin
July	juillet
August	août
September	septembre
October	octobre
November	novembre
December	décembre

PERSONAL NAMES
Prenoms

Boys/*Les Garçons*

English/Anglais	Français/French
Allen	Alain [a-LAIN]
Albert	Albert [al-BEHR]
Andrew	André [ahn-DRAY]
Anthony	Antoine [ahn-TWAN]
Arnold	Arnaud [ar-NOH]
Arthur	Arthur [ar-TEWR]
Charles	Charles [SHARL]
Claud	Chaude [KLOHD]
David	David [da-VEED]
Edward	Edouard [eh-DWAR]
Eugene	Eugène [euh-ZHEHN]
Frank	Francois [frahn-SWA]
Frederick	Frédéric [fray-day-REEK]
George	Georges [ZHUHRZH]
Henry	Henri [ahn-REE]
James, Jack	Jacques [ZHAK]
Jerome	Jérôme [zhay-ROHM]
John	Jean [ZHAHN]
Lawrence	Laurent [luh-RAHN]
Leo	Léon [lay-OHN]
Mark	Marc [MARK]
Michael	Michel [mee-SHEHL]
Paul	Paul [PUHL]
Peter	Pierre [PYEHR]
Philip	Philippe [fee-LEEP]
Ralph	Raoul [ra-OOL]
Robert	Robert [ruh-BEHR]
William	Guillaume [gee-OHM]

Girls/*Les Jeunes Filles*	
English/Anglais	Français/French
Amy	Aimée [ay-MAY]
Ann	Anne [AN]
Beatrice	Béatrice [bay-a-TREES]
Bertha	Berthe [BEHRT]
Carolyn	Caroline [ca-ruh-LEEN]
Claire	Claire [KLEHR]
Colette	Colette [kuh-LEHT]
Denise	Denise [dé-NEEZ]
Dorothy	Dorothée [duh-ruh-TAY]
Elizabeth	Elisabeth [ay-lee-za-BEHT]
Elsie	Elise [ay-LEEZ]
Emily	Emilie [ay-mee-LEE]
Frances	Françoise [frahn-SWAZ]
Harriet	Henriette [ahn-ree-EHT]
Helen	Hélène [ay-LEHN]
Jacquelyn	Jacqueline [zha-KLEEN]
Jane, Jean, Joan	Jeanne [ZHAN]
Laura	Laure [LUHR]
Louise	Louise [LWEEZ]
Margaret	Marguerite [mar-guh-REET]
Martha	Marthe [MART]
Mary	Marie [ma-REE]
Nancy	Nanette [na-NEHT]
Susan	Suzanne [sew-zan]
Sylvia	Sylvie [seel-VEE]
Theresa	Thérèse [tay-REHZ]
Virginia	Virginie [veer-zhee-NEE]
Yvonne	Yvonne [EE-VUHN]

CLASSROOM EXPRESSIONS *Expressions de Classe*	
English/Anglais	Français/French
again	encore une fois
aloud	à haute voix
Answer the question.	Répondez à la question. (Réponds)
Begin.	Commencez. (Commence.)
Bring me the book.	Apportez-moi le livre. (Apporte-moi)
Close the door.	Fermez la porte. (Ferme)
Count from one to five.	Comptez de un à cinq. (Compte)
Excellent!	Excellent! Bravo!
Draw a flower.	Dessinez une fleur. (Dessine)
Give me a pencil.	Donnez-moi un crayon. (Donne-moi)
Go to the window.	Allez à la fenêtre. (Va)
Go back to your seat.	Retournez à votre place. (Retourne à ta place.)
Good-bye.	Au revoir.
Hello.	Bonjour.
Let us sing.	Chantons.
Listen.	Ecoutez. (Ecoute)
Look at the blackboard.	Regardez le tableau noir. (Regarde)
Open the door.	Ouvrez la porte. (Ouvre)
Pay attention!	Faites attention! (Fais)
Please	S'il vous plaît (S'il te plaît)

CLASSROOM EXPRESSIONS (continued) *Expressions de Classe*	
English/Anglais	Français/French
Repeat!	Répétez! (Répète!)
See you tomorrow.	A demain.
Sit down.	Asseyez-vous. (Assieds-toi.)
Stand up.	Levez-vous. (Lève-toi.)
Thank you.	Merci.
You're welcome.	De rien. Je vous en prie. (Je t'en prie.)

NUMBERS
Nombres

English Anglais	Français French
one	un
two	deux
three	trois
four	quatre
five	cinq
six	six
seven	sept
eight	huit
nine	neuf
ten	dix
eleven	onze
twelve	douze
thirteen	treize
fourteen	quatorze
fifteen	quinze
sixteen	seize
seventeen	dix-sept
eighteen	dix-huit
nineteen	dix-neuf
twenty	vingt
twenty-one	vingt et un
twenty-two	vingt-deux
twenty-three	vingt-trois
twenty-four	vingt-quatre
twenty-five	vingt-cinq
twenty-six	vingt-six

twenty-seven	vingt-sept
twenty-eight	vingt-huit
twenty-nine	vingt-neuf
thirty	trente
thirty-one	trente et un
thirty-two	trente-deux
thirty-three	trente-trois
thirty-four	trente-quatre
thirty-five	trente-cinq
thirty-six	trente-six
thirty-seven	trente-sept
thirty-eight	trente-huit
thirty-nine	trente-neuf
forty	quarante
forty-one	quarante et un
forty-two	quarante-deux
forty-three	quarante-trois
forty-four	quarante-quatre
forty-five	quarante-cinq
forty-six	quarante-six
forty-seven	quarante-sept
forty-eight	quarante-huit
forty-nine	quarante-neuf
fifty	cinquante
fifty-one	cinquante et un
fifty-two	cinquante-deux
fifty-three	cinquante-trois
fifty-four	cinquante-quatre
fifty-five	cinquante-cinq
fifty-six	cinquante-six
fifty-seven	cinquante-sept

fifty-eight	cinquante-huit
fifty-nine	cinquante-neuf
sixty	soixante
sixty-one	soixante et un
sixty-two	soixante-deux
sixty-three	soixante-trois
sixty-four	soixante-quatre
sixty-five	soixante-cinq
sixty-six	soixante-six
sixty-seven	soixante-sept
sixty-eight	soixante-huit
sixty-nine	soixante-neuf
seventy	soixante-dix
seventy-one	soixante et onze
seventy-two	soixante-douze
seventy-three	soixante-treize
seventy-four	soixante-quatorze
seventy-five	soixante-quinze
seventy-six	soixante-seize
seventy-seven	soixante-dix-sept
seventy-eight	soixante-dix-huit
seventy-nine	soixante-dix-neuf
eighty	quatre-vingts
eighty-one	quatre-vingts-un
eighty-two	quatre-vingts-deux
eighty-three	quatre-vingts-trois
eighty-four	quatre-vingts-quatre
eighty-five	quatre-vingts-cinq
eighty-six	quatre-vingts-six
eighty-seven	quatre-vingts-sept
eighty-eight	quatre-vingts-huit

eighty-nine	quatre-vingts-neuf
ninety	quatre-vingts-dix
ninety-one	quatre-vingts-onze
ninety-two	quatre-vingts-douze
ninety-three	quatre-vingts-treize
ninety-four	quatre-vingts-quatorze
ninety-five	quatre-vingts-quinze
ninety-six	quatre-vingts-seize
ninety-seven	quatre-vingts-dix-sept
ninety-eight	quatre-vingts-dix-huit
ninety-nine	quatre-vingts-dix-neuf
one hundred	cent
two hundred	deux cents
three hundred	trois cents
four hundred	quatre cents
five hundred	cinq cents
six hundred	six cents
seven hundred	sept cents
eight hundred	huit cents
nine hundred	neuf cents
one thousand	mille
one million	un million

FRENCH-AMERICAN CONVERSION TABLES

CURRENCY, WEIGHTS, AND MEASURES

Monnaies, Poids, Mesures

Français French	English Anglais
1 franc	$0.20 (20 cents)*
5 francs	$1.00*
10 francs	$2.00*
1 centimeter	0.39 inches**
1 kilometer	0.62 miles**
10 kilometers	6.21 miles**
1 gram	0.035 ounces**
1 kilogram	2.20 pounds**

English Anglais	Français French
1 dollar	5 francs*
5 dollars	25 francs*
10 dollars	50 francs*
1 inch	2.54 centimeters**
1 foot	30.5 centimeters**
1 yard	91.4 centimeters**
1 mile	1.61 kilometers**
1 ounce	28.3 grams**
1 pound	453.6 grams**

* Because of fluctuations in exchange rates, it is necessary to consult the finance section of your daily newspaper or the foreign currency exchange section of your local bank.

** Approximately

PARTS OF SPEECH
Mots Grammaticaux

English Anglais	Français French
adjective (adj.)	l'adjectif
article	l'article
adverb (adv.)	l'adverbe
conjunction	la conjonction
idiomatic expression	l'expression idiomatique
interjection	l'interjection
noun, feminine (fem.)	le nom (féminin)
noun, masculine (masc.)	le nom (masculin)
preposition	la préposition
pronoun (pron.)	le pronom
verb	le verbe
verb form	la forme du verbe

French Verb Supplement

Les Verbes

Regular Verbs

PRESENT TENSE	PAST TENSES		FUTURE
	IMPERFECT	PASSÉ COMPOSÉ	
CHANTER (to sing)			
Je chante	chantais	j'ai chanté	chanterai
tu chantes	chantais	tu as chanté	chanteras
il, elle chante	chantait	il, elle a chanté	chantera
nous chantons	chantions	nous avons chanté	chanterons
vous chantez	chantiez	vous avez chanté	chanterez
ils, elles chantent	chantaient	ils, elles ont chanté	chanteront
FINIR (to finish, to end)			
Je finis	finissais	j'ai fini	finirai
tu finis	finissais	tu as fini	finiras
il, elle finit	finissait	il, elle a fini	finira
nous finissons	finissions	nous avons fini	finirons
vous finissez	finissiez	vous avez fini	finirez
ils, elles finissent	finissaient	ils, elles ont fini	finiront
RENDRE (to give back, to return)			
Je rends	rendais	j'ai rendu	rendrai
tu rends	rendais	tu as rendu	rendras
il, elle rend	rendait	il, elle a rendu	rendra
nous rendons	rendions	nous avons rendu	rendrons
vous rendez	rendiez	vous avez rendu	rendrez
ils, elles rendent	rendaient	ils, elles ont rendu	rendront

Irregular Verbs

ALLER (to go)

Je vais	allais	je suis allé(e)	irai
tu vas	allais	tu es allé(e)	iras
il, elle va	allait	il, elle est allé(e)	ira
nous allons	allions	nous sommes allé(e)s	irons
vous allez	alliez	vous êtes allé(e)s	irez
il, elles vont	allaient	ils, elles sont allé(e)s	iront

AVOIR (to have)

J'ai	avais	j'ai eu	aurai
tu as	avais	tu as eu	auras
il, elle a	avait	il, elle a eu	aura
nous avons	avions	nous avons eu	aurons
vous avez	aviez	vous avez eu	aurez
ils, elles ont	avaient	ils, elles ont eu	auront

DIRE (to say, to tell)

Je dis	disais	j'ai dit	dirai
tu dis	disais	tu as dit	diras
il, elle dit	disait	il, elle a dit	dira
nous disons	disions	nous avons dit	dirons
vous dites	disiez	vous avez dit	direz
ils, elles disent	disaient	ils, elles ont dit	diront

ETRE (to be)

Je suis	étais	j'ai été	serai
tu es	étais	tu as été	seras
il, elle est	était	il, elle a été	sera
nous sommes	étions	nous avons été	serons
vous êtes	étiez	vous avez été	serez
ils, elles sont	étaient	ils, elles ont été	seront

FAIRE (to do, to make)

Je fais	faisais	j'ai fait	ferai
tu fais	faisais	tu as fait	feras
il, elle fait	faisait	il, elle a fait	fera
nous faisons	faisions	nous avons fait	ferons
vous faites	faisiez	vous avez fait	ferez
ils, elles font	faisaient	ils, elles ont fait	feront

METTRE (to put, to place)

Je mets	mettais	j'ai mis	mettrai
tu mets	mettais	tu as mis	mettras
il, elle met	mettait	il, elle a mis	mettra
nous mettons	mettions	nous avons mis	mettrons
vous mettez	mettiez	vous avez mis	mettrez
ils, elles mettent	mettaient	ils, elles ont mis	mettront

POUVOIR (to be able, can)

Je peux *or* puis	pouvais	j'ai pu	pourrai
tu peux	pouvais	tu as pu	pourras
il, elle peut	pouvait	il, elle a pu	pourra
nous pouvons	pouvions	nous avons pu	pourrons
vous pouvez	pouviez	vous avez pu	pourrez
ils, elles peuvent	pouvaient	ils, elles ont pu	pourront

PRENDRE (to take)

Je prends	prenais	j'ai pris	prendrai
tu prends	prenais	tu as pris	prendras
il, elle prend	prenait	il, elle a pris	prendra
nous prenons	prenions	nous avons pris	prendrons
vous prenez	preniez	vous avez pris	prendrez
ils, elles prennent	prenaient	ils, elles ont pris	prendront

SAVOIR (to know)

Je sais	savais	j'ai su	saurai
tu sais	savais	tu as su	sauras
il, elle sait	savait	il, elle a su	saura
nous savons	savions	nous avons su	saurons
vous savez	saviez	vous avez su	saurez
ils, elles savent	savaient	ils, elles ont su	sauront

VENIR (to come)

Je viens	venais	je suis venu(e)	viendrai
tu viens	venais	tu es venu(e)	viendras
il, elle vient	venait	il, elle est venu(e)	viendra
nous venons	venions	nous sommes venu(e)s	viendrons
vous venez	veniez	vous êtes venu(e)s	viendrez
ils, elles viennent	venaient	ils, elles sont venu(e)s	viendront

VOIR (to see)

Je vois	voyais	j'ai vu	verrai
tu vois	voyais	tu as vu	verras
il, elle voit	voyait	il, elle a vu	verra
nous voyons	voyions	nous avons vu	verrons
vous voyez	voyiez	vous avez vu	verrez
ils, elles voient	voyaient	ils, elles ont vu	verront

VOULOIR (to want)

Je veux	voulais	j'ai voulu	voudrai
tu veux	voulais	tu as voulu	voudras
il, elle veut	voulait	il, elle a voulu	voudra
nous voulons	voulions	nous avons voulu	voudrons
vous voulez	vouliez	vous avez voulu	voudrez
ils, elles veulent	voulaient	ils, elles ont voulu	voudront

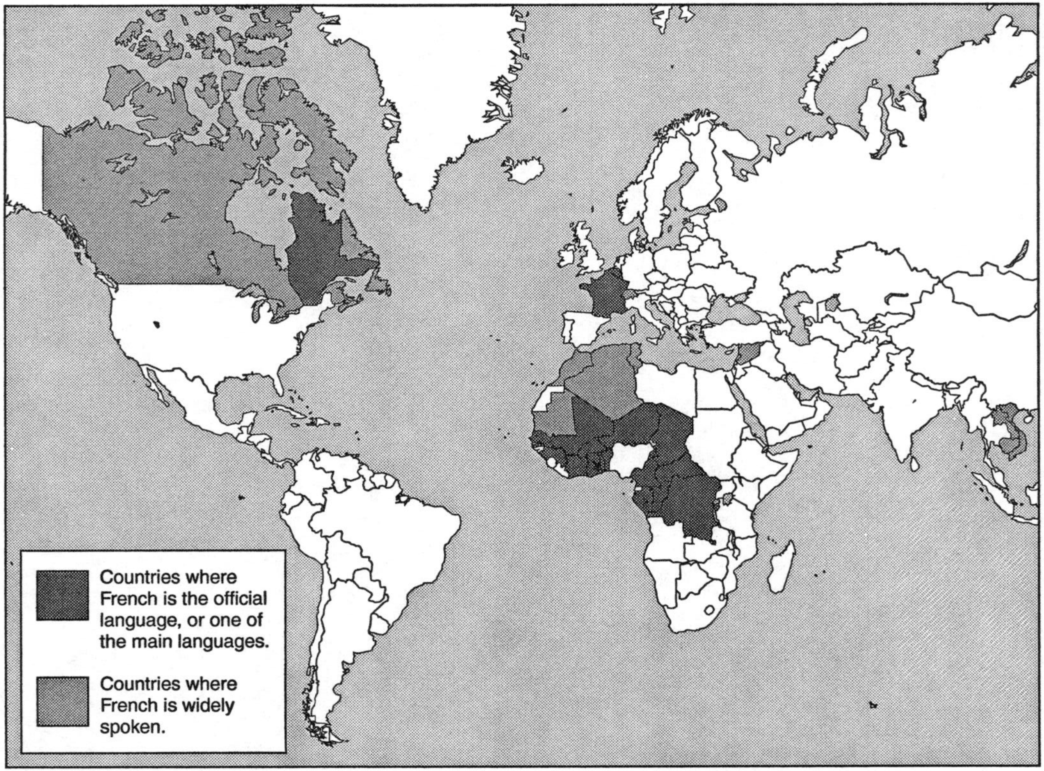

Belgium
Benin
Burkina Faso
Cameroon
Canada
Central African Republic
Chad
Congo
Côte D'Ivoire
France
French Guiana
Guadelupe
Martinique
Réunion
St.Pierre & Miquelon
French Polynesia
Gabon
Guinea
Mali
Monaco
Niger
Senegal
Seychelles
Togo
Zaire

Algeria
Andorra
Cambodia
Dijibouti
Haiti
Laos
Lebanon
Luxembourg
Mauritania
Mauritus
Morrocco
Rwanda
Switzerland
Syria
Tunisia
Vanuatu
Vietnam